Stephen E. Ambrose

Rise to Globalism

American Foreign Policy
Since 1938

Fourth Revised Edition

PENGUIN BOOKS

PENGUIN BOOKS
Viking Penguin Inc., 40 West 23rd Street,
New York, New York 10010, U.S.A.
Penguin Books Ltd, Harmondsworth, Middlesex, England
Penguin Books Australia Ltd, Ringwood, Victoria, Australia
Penguin Books Canada Limited, 2801 John Street,
Markham, Ontario, Canada L3R 1B4
Penguin Books (N.Z.) Ltd, 182–190 Wairau Road,
Auckland 10, New Zealand

First published, with subtitle *American Foreign Policy, 1938–1970*, 1971
Reprinted 1972, 1973, 1975
Revised edition, with subtitle *American Foreign Policy, 1938–1976*,
published 1976
Reprinted 1977, 1978, 1979
Second revised edition, with subtitle *American Foreign Policy, 1938–1980*,
published 1980
Reprinted 1980, 1981 (twice), 1982
Third revised edition, with subtitle *American Foreign Policy Since 1938*,
published 1983
Reprinted 1984
Fourth revised edition, with subtitle *American Foreign Policy Since 1938*,
published 1985
Reprinted 1986 (twice)

Published simultaneously in Canada

LIBRARY OF CONGRESS CATALOGING IN PUBLICATION DATA
Ambrose, Stephen E.
  Rise to globalism.
  Bibliography: p.
  Includes index.
  1. United States—Foreign relations—1945–
2. United States—Foreign relations—1933–1945.
I. Title.
E744.A477 1985   327.73   84-26557
ISBN 0 14 02.2622 2

Printed in the United States of America by
R. R. Donnelley & Sons Company, Harrisonburg, Virginia
Set in Baskerville

To Barry and Andy
May their backpacks always be full enough

Acknowledgments

I should like to thank, first of all, the many students who have found the time and taken the trouble to write me about their reactions to this book. Their criticisms, suggestions, disagreements, and praise were gratefully received, then considered and digested, and finally incorporated into this revision. It is an equal pleasure to acknowledge the aid I have received from my own students at the University of New Orleans, who constantly force me, through their questions, to rethink—and sometimes change—my interpretations.

Two friends require special mention. Dr. Gordon Mueller of the University of New Orleans, over hundreds of cocktails through the years, has given me the benefit of his deep knowledge of and insights into European diplomacy, meanwhile providing me with a basic introduction to the world energy situation. Dr. Julian Pleasants of the University of Florida originally suggested this revision to me. He is a good source for refreshing ideas on international relations, or for detailed information on all aspects of modern American diplomacy.

Contents

List of Maps

Maps by David Roberts, University of New Orleans

Introduction

In 1939, on the eve of World War II, the United States had an Army of 185,000 men with an annual budget of less than $500 million. America had no military alliances and no American troops were stationed in any foreign country. The dominant political mood was isolationism. America's physical security, the *sine qua non* of foreign policy, seemed assured, not because of American alliances or military strength but because of the distance between America and any potential enemy.

Forty-five years later the United States had a huge standing Army, Air Force and Navy. The budget of the Department of Defense was over $300 billion. The United States had military alliances with fifty nations, 1.5 million soldiers, airmen, and sailors stationed in 117 countries, and an offensive capability sufficient to destroy the world may times over. It had used military force to intervene in Indochina, Lebanon, the Dominican Republic, Grenada, and Central America, supported an invasion of Cuba, distributed enormous quantities of arms to friendly governments around the world, and fought a costly war in Korea. But despite all the money spent on armaments and no matter how far outward America extended her power, the technological revolution had overcome distance, and with the loss of her protective insulation, America's national security was constantly in jeopardy.

The debacle in Vietnam, combined with the weakening of the office of the Presidency brought about by Richard Nixon's disgrace, started the pendulum swinging back again, away from intervention and toward a new isolationism. By the mid-seventies people were not so keen anymore about standing up to every Communist everywhere. They recognized that there were limits to American power. Although the military did not shrink in size, its rate of growth slowed and temptations to enter local conflicts in Africa and the Middle East were spurned. Relations with Russia and China had dominated the foreign policy of the forties, fifties, and sixties, but in the seventies the focus shifted to the Middle East and the Third World.

In the eighties, the pendulum swung again, as Ronald Reagan escalated both the arms race and America's anticommunism. Enormous sums were spent on both conventional and strategic weapons, while aggressive action was taken in Grenada, Central America, and Lebanon, and an economic embargo was attempted against the Soviet Union.

Shifts in attitudes preceded these bewildering changes in policy. Before World War II most Americans believed in a natural harmony of interests between nations, assumed that there was a common commitment to peace, and argued that no nation or people could profit from a war. These beliefs implied that peace was the normal condition between states and that war, if it came, was an aberration resulting from the irrational acts of evil or psychotic men. It was odd that a nation that had come into existence through a victorious war, gained large portions of its territory through war, established its industrial revolution and national unity through a bloody civil war, and won a colonial empire through war, could believe that war profited no one. Yet most Americans did so believe.

The American analysis of the basis of international relations made it difficult for the United States to react effectively to the world crisis of the late thirties. America, England, and France wished to maintain the status quo without having to fight for it—thus they wished for peace. Germany, Italy, and Japan wished to change the status quo without having to fight in order to do so—thus they too wished for peace. But there was a basic difference in the wishing, and the American assumption that there was a world interest in peace was utopian.

During and after World War II Americans changed their attitudes. They did not come to relish war, but they did learn to accept it. They also became aware of their own vulnerability, which supported the belief, so popular after Pearl Harbor, that "if we don't fight them there, we'll have to fight them in San Francisco." Threats had to be met early and overseas. Certainly not all Americans accepted this analysis, but enough did to give the Cold War Presidents widespread support for adventures overseas, at almost any cost.

Technological change, especially in military weapons, gave added impetus to the new expansionism. For the first time in its history the United States could be threatened from abroad. High-speed ships, long-range bombers, jet aircraft, atomic weapons, and eventually intercontinental missiles all combined to endanger the physical security of the United States.

Simultaneously, America became vulnerable to foreign economic threats. Before World War II the United States was about as self-sufficient as any great nation is ever likely to be, especially in such basic items as energy resources, steel production, and agriculture. But an increasingly complex economy, coupled with the tremendous economic boom of the postwar years maintained by cheap energy, made America increasingly dependent on foreign sources.

And so, the irony. America had far more military power in the eighties than she had had in the late thirties, but she was less secure. America was far richer in the eighties than she had been during the Depression, but also more vulnerable to economic blackmail.

It was an unexpected outcome. At the conclusion of World War II America was at the top of the mountain. In all the world only the United States had a healthy economy, an intact physical plant capable of mass production of goods, and excess capital. American troops occupied Japan, the only important industrial power in the Pacific, while American influence was dominant in France, Britain, and western Germany, the industrial heart of Europe. The Pacific and the Mediterranean had become American lakes. Above all, the United States had a monopoly on the atomic bomb.

Yet despite the nation's preeminent position in the world,

America's leaders in the summer of 1945 feared the future for three reasons. The first was political: The possibility of the emergence of another Hitler, a role Stalin seemed already to have assumed. The second was technological: The atomic secret could not be kept forever, and the German development of rocket weapons indicated that in the next war American cities would be targets. The third fear was economic: With the coming of peace there would be a return to depression. One way to avoid depression was through increased foreign trade, but if the rest of the world nationalized its basic industries and/or closed its markets, America would be unable to compete abroad.

To meet this threat the Americans hoped to shape the postwar world so that free enterprise, with an open door for trading, would become the rule rather than the exception. President Harry S Truman and other officials took it for granted that free, private enterprise was essential to a free, open, democratic society, and they were willing to save democracy at home by imposing it abroad. The program had some spectacular successes, primarily in Western Europe and Japan. Meanwhile the continuation of a war economy within the United States, an almost wholly unexpected development, helped ward off a return to depression. Indeed, the economy boomed in the postwar years, in part thanks to the arms race.

The arms race came about because the United States and the U.S.S.R. were deeply suspicious of each other, and with good reason. Economic rivalry and ideological differences helped fuel the race, but another important factor was the pace of scientific and technological change in the postwar period. Nuclear weapons and the missiles to deliver them became the pivot around which much of the Cold War revolved. The fear that its opponents would move ahead on this or that weapons system drove each nation to make an all-out effort in the arms race. In the United States the resulting growth of the armed services and their suppliers—the military-industrial complex—gave generals, admirals, and industrialists new sources of power, leading to a situation in which Americans tended to find military solutions to political problems. The President was frequently tempted to accept advice to use military power, precisely because it was so easily available. No people or nation, it seemed, could stand against the American military. Not until the late sixties did large numbers of Americans learn the costly lesson that the power to destroy is not the power to control.

The United States of the Cold War period, like ancient Rome, was concerned with all political problems in the world. The loss of even one country to Communism, therefore, while not in itself a threat to American physical security, carried implications that officials in Washington found highly disturbing. They became greatly concerned with the appearance as well as the reality of events, and there was much talk of dominoes. Who ruled the Dominican Republic, for example, was of concern to one or two American corporations only, and clearly nothing that happened on that tiny island posed the slightest threat to American military or economic security. But the State Department, the White House, and the C.I.A. were certain that if the Communists won in the Dominican Republic, they would soon win elsewhere. In the early sixties, few important officials argued that South Vietnam was essential to the defense of the United States, but the attitude that "we have to prove that wars of national liberation don't work" (a curious attitude for the children of the American Revolution to hold) did carry the day, aided in no small measure by the argument that if Vietnam went Communist, all Southeast Asia would soon follow. The Pacific islands would come next, and eventually the fight would be on America's West Coast.

The attitude that what happened anywhere in the world was important to the United States differed radically from the American outlook of 1939. One reason for the change was the astonishing growth of America's overseas military bases. The American armed forces flowed into many vacuums at the end of the war, and once American troops were stationed on foreign soil, that soil was included in the list of America's "vital interests."

But America's rise to globalism was by no means mindless, just as it was not exclusively a reaction to the Communist challenge or a response to economic needs. A frequently heard expression during World War II was that "America has come of age." Americans had a sense of power, of bigness, of destiny. They had saved the world from Hitler; now they would save the world from Stalin. In the process, American influence and control would expand. During World War II Henry Luce of *Life* magazine spoke for most political leaders as well as American businessmen, soldiers, and the public generally when he said that the twentieth century would be the American century. Politicians looked for areas in which American influence could dominate. Businessmen looked for profitable markets and new sources of cheap raw materials; the military looked for overseas bases. All found what they wanted as America inaugurated a program of expansion that had no inherent limits.

Americans who wanted to bring the blessings of democracy, capitalism, and stability to everyone meant just what they said—the whole world, in their view, should be a reflection of the United States. Americans launched a crusade for freedom that would be complete only when freedom reigned everywhere. Conservatives like Senator Robert Taft doubted that such a goal was obtainable, and old New Dealers like Henry Wallace argued that it could only be achieved at the cost of domestic reform. But most politicians and nearly all businessmen and soldiers signed on as crusaders.

While America's businessmen, soldiers, and politicians moved into South and Central America, Europe, and Southeast Asia, her leaders rarely paused to wonder if there were limits to American power. The disorderly expansion and the astronomical growth of areas defined as constituting a vital American interest, seemed to Washington, Wall Street, and the Pentagon to be entirely normal and natural. Almost no important public figure argued that the nation was overextended, just as no one could suggest any attitude toward Communism other than unrelieved hostility.

But ultimately, military reality, combined with the obvious truth that American empire builders were never as ruthless as they might have been without the restraints of their own moral heritage and culture, did put limits on American expansion. At no time after 1945 was the United States capable of destroying Russia or her allies without taking on totally unacceptable risks herself; at no time was the United States able to establish an imperial dominion free from her own moral constraints. The crusade against Communism, therefore, took the form of containment rather than attack. As a policy, containment, with its implication of an acceptance of a permanently divided world, led to widely felt frustration. These frustrations were deepened by self-imposed constraints on the use of force in Korea, Vietnam, and elsewhere. But scarcely anyone seriously considered an alternative to containment until that policy broke down so totally in Vietnam and Cambodia.

The failure of containment in Indochina led to another basic shift in attitude toward America's role in the world. It was not a return to isolationism, 1939 style—the pendulum did not swing that far. It was a general realization that, given the twin restraints of fear of provoking a Russian nuclear strike and America's reluctance to use her full military power, there was relatively little the United States could accomplish by force of arms. Even Reagan has shown an awareness of these limits, in Poland, Afghanistan, and even Central America, and in withdrawing from Lebanon.

After Vietnam there was also a shift in the focus of American foreign policy, especially after 1973, when the Arab oil boycott made Americans suddenly aware that the Middle East was so important to them. Nixon's 1972 trip to China, the emergence of black Africa, and the discovery of abundant raw materials in both Africa and South America, helped turn American eyes from the northern to the southern half of the globe. This shift emphasized the fundamentally changed nature of the American economy, from self-sufficiency to increasing dependency on others for basic supplies. America in the 1980s was richer and more powerful—and more vulnerable—than at any time in her history.

I returned and saw under the sun that the race is not to the swift, nor the battle to the strong, neither yet bread to the wise nor riches to men of understanding, but time and chance happeneth to them all.

ECCLESIASTES

We are willing to help people who believe the way we do, to continue to live the way they want to live.

DEAN ACHESON

[1]

The Twisting Path to War

> I hate war.
> FRANKLIN DELANO ROOSEVELT

The United States was fairly well satisfied with the world of 1938. Germany was a threat, especially after Adolf Hitler's victory at the Munich Conference of that year, but it seemed possible that Hitler would now be satisfied to consolidate his gains in Austria and Czechoslovakia. Certainly as long as Britain and France continued to stand against Hitler, the United States had nothing to fear militarily from Germany. Elsewhere, anti-Communism was triumphing in Spain, while in central and eastern Europe governments hostile to the Soviet Union continued to contain Communism.

On the other side of the world the United States, in combination with the British, French, and Dutch, still held the upper hand. American control of Hawaii and the Philippines, Dutch control of the Netherlands East Indies (N.E.I., today's Indonesia), French control of Indochina (today's Laos, Cambodia, and Vietnam), and British control of India, Burma, Hong Kong and Malaya, gave the Western powers a dominant position in Asia. Japan, ruled by her military, was aggressive, determined to end white man's rule in Asia, and thus a threat to the status quo. But Japan lacked crucial natural resources, most notably oil, and was tied down by her war in China.

On the great landmass connecting Europe and Asia, Russia was relatively weak and nonexpansive. In the Middle East and Africa, European colonialism dominated. In Latin America, American economic imperialism, although tempered politically by F.D.R.'s Good Neighbor policy, guaranteed cheap raw materials for American industries, and a dependable market.

The United States in 1938 saw no pressing need for any great change in the world. Isolationism reigned in the Congress, reflecting a national mood. The Nye Committee, conducting a Senate investigation, had "proved" that Wall Street had dragged the United States into World War I in order to protect bankers' loans to the Allies, and had shown that corporations had enjoyed exorbitant wartime profits while evading taxation. The explanation that World War I had been fought for the benefit of big business was easily accepted by a Depression generation that blamed its current economic ills on the same businessmen.

The attitude of the President himself reinforced isolationism. Unlike Winston Churchill, Hitler, or the Japanese leaders, and unlike his cousin Theodore Roosevelt, Franklin D. Roosevelt saw neither glory nor romance in war, nor did he feel that it strengthened the national fiber. If not a pacifist, F.D.R. was certainly no militarist. On a number of occasions he declared, with deep emotion, "I hate war."

American foreign policy in 1938, then, was to support the status quo, but only through vaguely worded statements. Roosevelt, Secretary of State Cordell Hull, and a majority of the American people did not want a German domination of Europe or a Japanese domination of Asia, but neither were they ready to do much to stop it. Least of all were they willing to improve the armed forces so that the United States could threaten to punish aggression.

In mid-March of 1939 Hitler's armies overran Czechoslovakia. Roosevelt failed to support a Senate resolution that would have repealed the arms embargo (required in case of war by the neutrality acts of the mid-thirties) and allowed American industries to sell war goods to France and Britain on a cash-and-carry basis. Although F.D.R. and a majority of the people had declared that their sympathies lay with the democracies, they had also demonstrated to Hitler that in the immediate future he had nothing to fear from the United States. On August 23, 1939, Hitler announced the Nazi-Soviet Pact, which provided for the division of Poland between Russia and Germany and relieved Germany of the nightmare of a two-front war. On September 1, 1939, the Nazis struck Poland; two days later Britain and France declared war on Germany, and World War II was under way.

The outbreak of war had widespread repercussions on the American domestic scene. Americans split sharply over the question of how to react, what to do about it. Although most wished to stay out, the isolationists resisted any steps that might lead to aid for the democracies, fearing that the United States would thereby become so committed to an Allied victory that, as in 1917, she would be drawn into war against her will. Interventionists, meanwhile, wanted to abandon neutrality and give material aid to Britain and France. Roosevelt took a middle ground. In a speech to a special session of Congress F.D.R. declared four times that his policy was designed to keep the United States out of war. He then asked for repeal of the embargo on arms and approval of a cash-and-carry system. Congress agreed in November 1939.

Cash-and-carry symbolized much that was to follow. It did align the United States with the democracies, reiterate American concern and friendship for Western Europe, and make it clear that the country would resist any attempt to upset the balance of power in Europe. But it also indicated that the United States was unwilling to pay a high price to stop Hitler. America would sell arms to the democracies as long as the democracies picked them up and carried them off. Later, when the threat from Germany loomed larger, Roosevelt went farther, but never, even after Pearl Harbor, was he willing to cut deeply into the civilian economy, or to pay a high cost in lives or goods to defeat Hitler. The theme of America's participation in World War II was victory at the lowest possible cost.

The irony was that the United States, after paying the least of all the Allies in lives or (in relative terms) in material expended for the war, gained the most from victory. F.D.R.'s policy of limited mobilization, which continued throughout the war, left the United States at the war's conclusion in by far the most powerful position of all the nations in the world.

There was another ironic outcome: Millions of Americans came to believe that their country had been tricked by the Soviet Union during the wartime conferences, that the United States had made enormous sacrifices for no purpose, and that the only real winner was Russia—which had lost nearly half its productive capacity and twenty million people. The important point, nevertheless, was that the United States had taken Britain's place and played her nineteenth-century role of avoiding huge battles on the Continent, paying others to do the fighting, and thereby being the only nation at the conclusion strong enough to assume a predominant position. Whether this was a brilliant application of a policy of following national self-interest, or just geographical luck, or a combination of both, did not really matter. America did as much as was necessary, although during the early stages of the war it appeared that she was taking uncommonly large risks by not doing more.

Just how great those risks were, Roosevelt knew as did few others in the world. On October 11, 1939, world-renowned physicist Albert Einstein, a Jewish refugee from the Nazis, warned F.D.R. that the Germans were working on the problem of harnessing atomic energy into a bomb. If Hitler had an atomic bomb, he would surely conquer the world. Roosevelt was impressed by Einstein's message. He conferred privately with key Congressional leaders and together they started the Manhattan Project. This secret project was designed to build an atomic bomb capable of being dropped from an airplane, and to get it built before Hitler could complete his own plans.

The Manhattan Project was the beginning of the marriage between science and government in the United States, and thus one of the most important legacies of World War II. It was also the first use of extreme secrecy about government activities, justified on the grounds of national security. In the case of the Manhattan Project, most members of Congress did not even know where the funds they had appropriated were going.

But although Roosevelt was willing to act decisively in the race for an atomic bomb, there was otherwise a distinct limit on the American contribution to stopping Hitler. After German armies overran Poland, a period of stagnation set in on the western front. Americans called it a "phony war" and saw no pressing reason to strain themselves to build up their strength. F.D.R. increased the regular army from 210,000 to 217,000 and asked for an army budget of $853 million, which the Congress cut by nearly 10 percent. These paltry figures constituted an announcement to the world that the United States did not intend to fight in Europe in the near future.

The German spring offensive of 1940 brought forth a tough verbal but limited practical response from the United States. Although isolationists were supposedly strongest in Congress, Congress proved more willing than F.D.R. to begin preparing America for war. The President asked for a supplemental appropriation to raise troop strength to 255,000; Congress, after hearing Chief of Staff George C. Marshall's desperate appeals, raised the force to 375,000. The Nazis, meanwhile, rolled on. On May 15 the new British Prime Minister, Winston Churchill, urgently requested forty or fifty American destroyers to protect Britain's Atlantic supply line. Churchill called it a matter of "life or death." Roosevelt was reluctant to act. On June 5, with the fall of France imminent and Britain about to be left standing alone, he told a Cabinet official that it would require an act of Congress to transfer the destroyers to England and implied that he was not ready to ask for such a bill.

He was ready to speak out. On June 10, 1940, the President told the graduating class of the University of Virginia that the United States would follow "two obvious and simultaneous courses," extending to France and Britain "the material resources of this nation" and speeding up the development of these resources so that the American armed forces could be strengthened. The speech was hailed by interventionists in the United States as setting a new course, but the French quickly discovered its limits. On June 14 French Premier Paul Reynaud appealed to Roosevelt to send American troops to Europe in France's hour of need. Roosevelt refused. Even had he wanted to act, he had no troops available to send overseas. Within the week the French signed an armistice with Germany.

The fall of France was a shattering blow. No one, not even the Germans and least of all the American army experts, had forecast it. The United States now faced an entirely new situation. No longer could the nation comfortably expect that the British and French would stop the Germans. The British, standing alone, might survive, although even that was questionable, but would never be able to roll back the Nazis by themselves. The best-disciplined and most highly educated and productive nation in Europe now dominated the Continent. The balance of power was gone. Hitler posed no immediate military threat to the New World, but if he could conquer England and get control of the British fleet, then overrun Russia—suddenly real possibilities—he would command the greatest military might the world had ever known. What could happen then was anyone's guess, but it was becoming increasingly apparent that it behooved Americans to do something more than sit by and watch. Hitler could be stopped and some kind of balance could be restored in Europe only if others came to Britain's aid.

Isolationism was obviously an obstacle to forthright Presidential action, but F.D.R. had an inner conflict that reflected the public confusion. He was very much of his time and place, sharing general attitudes on the mistake of entering World War I. In a famous election speech in Boston on October 30, 1940, F.D.R. declared: "And while I am talking to you mothers and fathers, I give you one more assurance. I have said this before, but I shall say it again and again and again: Your boys are not going to be sent into any foreign wars."

Neither, it seemed, was a great deal of American equipment. The British still obtained supplies only on a cash-and-carry basis and they lacked the destroyers necessary to protect the convoys transporting those goods they could afford to purchase. On July 21, 1940, Churchill made another eloquent plea for destroyers: "Mr. President, with great respect I must tell you that in the long history of the world this is a thing to do NOW." The British were losing merchant shipping in appalling numbers, the Battle of Britain was reaching its peak, and the German General Staff was preparing plans for an invasion of the British Isles.

The President allowed private groups to work out the details of a destroyers-for-bases deal, which eventually (September 2) gave the British fifty overage destroyers in return for rent-free bases on British possessions from Bermuda to British Guiana. "What is most striking about the . . . deal," Robert Divine has noted, "is the caution and reluctance with which the President acted," a reflection of Roosevelt's own doubts about a proper policy. Divine concludes, "What may have appeared on the surface to be a bold and courageous act by the President was in reality a carefully calculated and virtually foolproof maneuver."

There was, meanwhile, a growing tension between the War Department and the White House. General Marshall took it as established policy that the United States looked forward to Hitler's defeat and wanted to make a contribution to it. He reasoned that the only way to do so was to meet and defeat the German Army on the plains of northwestern Europe. To take on the Wehrmacht, Marshall needed a mass army; to get that he needed conscription. But given the tenor of Roosevelt's third-term campaign, there was no possibility that the President could give public support to a conscription bill.

Once again Congress proved more willing to act than the President. Private groups, led by Republicans Henry L. Stimson and Elihu Root, Jr., persuaded Congressmen favoring intervention to introduce a selective-service bill in both houses of Congress. Roosevelt remained aloof, but he did give General Marshall permission to support the bill; the President also helped by appointing Stimson, an interventionist, Secretary of War. In late August of 1940 Congress authorized the President to call the National Guard

and other reserves to active duty for one year, and on
September 16 it provided for selective service for one year.
Both measures limited the employment of troops to the
Western Hemisphere.

In November 1940 Roosevelt won the election. Churchill,
among others, thought that the reelected President would
be willing to assume a more active role in the struggle
against Hitler. The Prime Minister sent F.D.R. a lengthy
and bleak description of the British situation, emphasizing
that his nation was running out of money. Cash-and-carry
would no longer suffice, for "the moment approaches when
we shall no longer be able to pay cash for shipping and
other supplies."

Roosevelt responded sympathetically. On December 7,
1940, he called in the press, outlined the British dilemma,
and said he believed that "the best defense of Great Britain
is the best defense of the United States." Seeking to avoid
the mistakes of Woodrow Wilson and the long controversy
over World War I war debts, Roosevelt said he wanted to
simply lend or lease to England the supplies she needed.
He compared his scheme to the idea of lending a garden
hose to a neighbor whose house was on fire.

In a radio address to the nation a few days later Roosevelt
justified lend-lease as essential to national security. If England fell, "all of us in the Americas would be living at the
point of a gun." He said the best way to keep the United
States out of the war was to "do all we can now to support
the nations defending themselves against attack by the Axis."
He declared again that he had no intention of sending
American boys to Europe; his sole purpose was to "keep
war away from our country and our people." He would do
this by making America the "great arsenal of democracy."

The isolationists were furious. They charged that lend-
lease was a most unneutral act, placing the United States
squarely on the British side. Senator Taft found the idea
of loaning military equipment absurd. He said it was rather
like loaning chewing gum: "Once it had been used you
didn't want it back."

By early March, 1941, however, the administration had

overcome the opposition, and the lend-lease bill went through Congress with an initial appropriation of $7 billion. Secretary Stimson correctly called it "a declaration of economic war." Bold as lend-lease was in its conception, however, the practice was something less. American officials used the new system as a wedge to get American firms into the British Commonwealth market and to force the British to sell their holdings on the American continents, and the Army resisted sending arms needed in the United States to Britain, so that the total amount of goods shipped, in comparison with the need, was small. Lend-lease may have been the most unsordid act in human history, as a grateful Churchill called it, but by itself it was hardly sufficient to do the job.

What was needed was a more extensive American involvement. Realizing this, Roosevelt declared an Atlantic neutrality zone that extended almost to Iceland, ordering the Navy to patrol the area and report the location of German submarines to the British. In April 1941 American troops moved into Greenland. In July, following Hitler's invasion of Russia, F.D.R. increased American involvement. American troops occupied Iceland, which released British troops for the Middle East, and the U.S. Navy began escorting convoys as far as Iceland. By September the U.S. Navy was fully at war with Germany in the Atlantic, the first in a series of "Presidential wars" entered into by the chief executive without the Constitutionally required Congressional declaration of war. Not only was it undeclared, it was also an unknown war, at least to the American public. When a German submarine fired a torpedo at the American destroyer stalking it, F.D.R. brazenly denounced the "rattlesnakes of the Atlantic" for the supposedly unprovoked act and ordered the Navy to shoot on sight at all German submarines they encountered. In October F.D.R. persuaded Congress to remove nearly all restrictions on American commerce; henceforth, American merchant vessels could carry goods to British ports.

Roosevelt's tone, in public and private, was by November of 1941 one of unrestrained belligerency. German advances to the gates of Moscow made it impossible to underestimate the threat. Roosevelt seems to have reasoned that Hitler could not long permit American ships to transport goods to Britain. The Germans would have to order their submarine captains to sink the American vessels. F.D.R. could then overcome isolationist opposition in Congress and obtain a declaration of war.

Whether he was right or not will never be known. It is clear that by December 1941 American foreign policy in Europe had failed to make any significant contribution to stopping, much less overcoming, Hitler. In retrospect, the steps the President and the Congress took to protect American interests in Europe were halting and limited. Everything hinged on Russia and Britain. If they kept going, America could—eventually—supply them with the tools and men to do the job. The United States in the meantime was taking great risks.

The American ship of state was drifting, without a rudder or power, in a storm. The world's greatest industrial democracy could not stem the tide of Fascism. Roosevelt's caution was so great that in September 1941, when the original selective-service bill ran out and had to be repassed if the soldiers already partly trained were to be retained in the Army, he refused to pressure Congress, either privately or publicly. Working behind the scenes, General Marshall was able to get the draft bill passed—by one vote. Even this left the U.S. Army ridiculously small (1.6 million men) if the nation ever intended to play a role in the conflict raging in Europe.

Fortunately for the United States, the British and Russians held out, making it possible for America to later exert her power to help win the war. Fortunately, too, the Japanese solved Roosevelt's problem of how to get fully involved in the war.

Japan was the aggressor in the Pacific, as Mussolini was in the Mediterranean and Hitler was in Europe. Since the mid-thirties, Japan had been involved in a war of conquest in China. From the beginning the United States had insisted that Japan must pull back and respect the Open Door in China, but because F.D.R. had not supported his demands with action, the Japanese ignored him.

The overall Japanese program called for Asia for the Asians, although under the new setup some Asians were going to be more equal than others. The Japanese proposed to substitute themselves for the white rulers in China, Indochina, Malaya, Burma, the Philippines, and the N.E.I. It was essential to the Japanese that they control these areas if Japan were to be a great power, for despite her human resources Japan was almost devoid of critical raw materials, especially oil, which was available in Southeast Asia.

The American colony of the Philippines lay directly athwart the Japanese proposed line of advance. Whether correctly or not, the Japanese were convinced that the United States would never allow them to advance into Malaya or the N.E.I. without striking against their lines of communications. More fundamentally, they believed that the United States would never willingly allow them to become a great power and would consistently oppose their advance southward. Thus, although the Japanese realized that they were doomed if they goaded the United States into war and the United States chose to fight it to a finish, they felt they were also doomed without war. "Japan entered the war," a prince of the Japanese imperial family later wrote, "with a tragic determination and in desperate self-abandonment."

The fall of France in 1940 and Britain's preoccupation with Germany opened the door to Southeast Asia for Japan. Bogged down in her war with China, Japan decided to overcome her crippling shortage of oil through a program of southward expansion. Only the Soviet Union and the United States were potentially strong enough in the Pacific to interfere; Japan moved politically to minimize these threats. In the late summer of 1940 she signed a five-year nonaggression pact with the Soviets, an agreement that Stalin, fearing Hitler, was happy to sign.

Rise to Globalism

Japan also entered into the Tripartite Pact with the Germans and Italians, a defensive alliance that pledged mutual support if any one of the three signatories were attacked. The German invasion of Russia in June 1941 opened new possibilities for Japan, and a great debate within Japan ensued. Should Japan take advantage of Russia's desperate position vis-à-vis Germany and attack the Soviet through Siberia? Some military leaders thought so. Others argued that because of Hitler's involvement in the east, Germany no longer posed a serious threat to England; this strengthened the Anglo-American position in the Pacific because Churchill was now free to send part of the fleet from the home isles to Britain's Asian colonies (as he in fact did do in 1941). Japan, therefore, should seek to reach an agreement with the United States, making such concessions as were necessary to stave off war. Still others held out for the long-planned conquest of Southeast Asia.

Roosevelt listened in on the debate through the medium of MAGIC,* the code name applied to intercepted and decoded Japanese messages, and characterized it as "a real drag-down and knock-out fight . . . to decide which way they were going to jump—attack Russia, attack the South Seas [or] sit on the fence and be more friendly with us." The decision was to reject war with Russia and instead move south immediately, meanwhile trying to avoid war with the United States by carrying on negotiations as long as possible. The first step was the unresisted occupation of French Indochina, which gave Japan possession of air and naval bases stretching from Hanoi to Saigon, from which she could launch attacks on Singapore, the Philippines, and the N.E.I.

---

* While the Americans were listening in on the Japanese, the British had broken the German code (they called their system ULTRA) and the Germans had broken the British code. And while the Japanese were decoding American messages, the Russians were reading Japanese radio traffic. On balance the Americans got more useful information from MAGIC and the British from ULTRA than the Axis got from their monitoring systems.

American strategy in the summer of 1941 was embodied in a paper entitled "RAINBOW 5." Never specific on implementation, it called for a holding action in the Pacific with an all-out offensive in Europe, assuming that the Japanese would be relatively easy to deal with once Hitler was eliminated. Moreover, if the United States put its major effort into defeating Japan, it might win in the Pacific and still lose in Europe. American military weakness supported the conclusion, for although the American fleet had been stationed in Pearl Harbor in 1940 by F.D.R. (against naval advice) as a deterrent to the Japanese, it was by no means strong enough to deal an effective blow against them.

Given this situation, the U.S. Navy did not wish to provoke the Japanese. It wanted time, not only to bring about Hitler's defeat but also to build a first-class striking force. The Chief of Naval Operations, Admiral Harold R. Stark, advised the President to do nothing when the Japanese moved into French Indochina. But whatever the military realities, F.D.R. also had political realities to deal with. The polls indicated that nearly 70 percent of the people were willing to risk war in the Pacific rather than let Japan continue her expansion. F.D.R. froze all Japanese assets in the United States. The British and Dutch supported his move. The effect of the freeze was to create an economic blockade of Japan. She could not buy oil, steel, or other necessities.

The embargo made it clear to the Japanese that they either had to pull back from Indochina and even China itself, thereby reaching an agreement with the United States that would have provided them with access to oil, or go to war. The one slim hope remaining was that America's fear of a two-ocean war would impel Roosevelt to compromise. From August until November, 1941, the Japanese sought some form of acceptable political compromise, all the while sharpening their military plans and preparations. If the diplomatic offensive worked, the military offensive could be called off, including the planned attack on the U.S. fleet at Pearl Harbor.

In essence, the Japanese demanded from the United States

a free hand in Asia. There were variations through a series of proposals, but the central points always included an end to American support for China, an Anglo-American promise not to "meddle in nor interrupt" a settlement between Japan and China, a Western recognition of Japan's "special position" in French Indochina, an Anglo-American agreement not to reinforce their bases in the Far East, and a resumption of commercial relations with Japan, which included selling oil.

Although the Americans were willing to go part way to compromise, they would not consider giving the Japanese a free hand in China. Since it was precisely on this point that the Japanese were most adamant, conflict was inevitable. Neither side wanted war, in the sense that each would have preferred to gain its objectives without having to fight for them, but both were willing to move on to a showdown. In Japan it was the military who pressed for action, over the protests of the civilians, while in America the situation was reversed. Prime Minister Fumimaro Konoye of Japan resigned in October when he was unable to secure military approval of a partial withdrawal from China in order to "save ourselves from the crisis of a Japanese-American war." His successor, General Hideki Tojo, was willing to continue negotiations with the United States, but only until late November. If no progress was made by then, Japan would strike.

In the United States Roosevelt stood firm, even though his military advisers strongly urged him to avoid a crisis with Japan until he had dealt with Germany. Secretary Hull made one last effort for peace, suggesting on November 21 that the United States should offer a three months' truce. Japan might have accepted, but Chiang Kai-shek, the Chinese leader, protested vehemently, and Roosevelt would not allow Hull to make the offer. "I have washed my hands of the Japanese situation," Hull told Stimson on November 27, "and it is now in the hands of . . . the Army and Navy."

A little over a week later, on Sunday, December 7, 1941, the Japanese launched their attack, hitting Pearl Harbor, the Philippines, Malaya, and Thailand.* They soon added the N.E.I. to the list. On December 8 the Anglo-Americans declared war on Japan, but the United States still had no more excuse to go to war with Germany than it had had on December 6, so even in the excitement over Pearl Harbor, F.D.R. did not dare ask Congress for a declaration of war on Germany. All earlier war plans had assumed that the United States and the United Kingdom would concentrate their efforts against Germany; suddenly it seemed that the war would take an entirely unexpected course, with the Americans fighting only the Japanese. On December 11 Hitler ended the uncertainty by declaring war on the United States.†

The United States was finally at war with the Axis. The status quo in Europe and in Asia had been challenged and was being upset. America had been unable to preserve it short of war. The need now was to defeat the Axis on the field of battle, a task of staggering proportions but one that carried with it great opportunities for the extension of American power and influence. The United States was quick to grasp them, even while saving the world from the unimaginable horror of being ruled by Hitler and the Japanese Army.

* One of the most persistent myths in American history is that F.D.R. knew the attack on Pearl Harbor was coming but refused to give the commanders in Hawaii advance notice. In fact, Washington gave the military in Hawaii plenty of warning about the imminent outbreak of hostilities. There was no specific warning about an attack on Pearl Harbor because no one imagined the Japanese were capable of such a daring raid. MAGIC was no help because the Japanese fleet maintained radio silence.

† An inexplicable action. No one has ever explained why Hitler did it. He was not required to do so by the terms of the Tripartite Pact, he did not discuss his action with his own military leaders or foreign office, nor indeed with anyone of consequence. Thus Hitler, after a long string of successes, made two fatal errors between June and December of 1941—the invasion of Russia and the declaration of war against the United States.

[2]

The War in Europe

Give me allies to fight against!
NAPOLEON

There is only one thing worse than fighting with allies, and
that is fighting without them.

SIR WINSTON CHURCHILL

The Grand Alliance of World War II, sometimes called the
"Strange Alliance," joined together Britain, the world's
greatest colonial power led by Churchill, an imperialist determined to maintain the British Empire; with Russia, the
world's only Communist nation, led by Stalin, a revolutionary determined to maintain and expand Communism;
with the United States, the world's greatest capitalist power,
led by Roosevelt, a capitalist who frequently criticized colonialism and was no friend of Communism. Only Hitler
could have brought them together, and only the threat of
Nazi Germany could have held them together through four
years of war. The Big Three mistrusted each other, but
each of the partners knew he needed both of the others.
Neither Britain and America together nor any other combination of two was powerful enough to defeat Germany.
It took all three great nations to do the job.

So the Grand Alliance was successful. Despite many stresses
and strains, it held together to the end, an unprecedented
achievement. In the process, however, nerves were stretched
almost to the breaking point.

The process began in January 1942 when Churchill and
his military leaders came to Washington to discuss strategy.

Churchill presented the British view. He advocated a series of operations around the periphery of Hitler's European fortress, combined with bombing raids against Germany itself and encouragement to Resistance forces in the occupied countries, but no direct invasion. He would let the Continentals do their own fighting, just as the great British statesmen of the past had done. It was a mark of how greatly Churchill—the world's leading anti-Bolshevik—loathed and feared Hitler. The Europeans who were willing to fight Hitler, whether they were Russians, Frenchmen in the Resistance, Yugoslavs, or Greeks, were mostly on the political Left, either Socialists or, more often, Communists. Churchill's policy would have given a tremendous boost to the forces of the Left in Europe, but that was better than a Nazi victory.

The American military opposed Churchill's policy, although not on political grounds. Army Chief of Staff George C. Marshall felt that the concept was risky rather than safe, and that it would waste lives and material rather than save them. To leave the Red Army to face the bulk of the Wehrmacht, as Churchill advocated in effect, was to court disaster. Marshall was not at all sure that the Russians could survive unaided, and he thought it would be the greatest military blunder in all of history to allow an army of eight million fighting men to go down to defeat without doing anything to prevent it. For the Allies to avoid a confrontation with the Germans on the Continent in 1942 and 1943 might save British and American lives in the short run, but it might also lead to a complete victory for Hitler. Even if Churchill was right in supposing that the Red Army would hold out, Marshall believed that the effect would be to let the war drag on into 1944 or even 1945. The end result would be higher, not lower, Anglo-American casualties.

Marshall therefore proposed that the Anglo-Americans set as a goal for 1942 a buildup of American ground, air, and naval strength in the United Kingdom, with the aim of launching a massive cross-Channel invasion in the spring of 1943. Only thus, he argued, could the Americans bring

EUROPE IN 1985

their power to bear in a decisive manner, the Allies give significant help to the Russians, and the final aim of victory be quickly achieved.

There were two specific problems with Marshall's program of a 1942 buildup and a 1943 invasion: First, it would be of little help to the Russians in 1942, and second, it would mean that the United States would spend the whole year without engaging in any ground fighting with the Germans. The second point worried Roosevelt, for he wanted to get the American people to feel a sense of commitment in the struggle for Europe (well into 1942 public-opinion polls revealed that Americans were more eager to strike back at the Japanese than fight the Germans). The fastest way to do it was to get involved in the European fighting. The President therefore insisted that American troops engage German troops somewhere in 1942. But Roosevelt was also drawn to Churchill's concept of closing the ring, with its implication that the Russians would take the bulk of the casualties, and he was determined that the first American offensive should be successful, all of which made the periphery more tempting as a target than northwestern Europe.

Marshall proposed, as an addition to his program for a 1943 invasion, an emergency landing on the French coast in September 1942. The operation, code name SLEDGE-HAMMER, would be a suicide mission designed to take pressure off the Russians. It would go forward only if a Russian collapse seemed imminent. But although Marshall had no intention of starting SLEDGEHAMMER except as a last resort, he could and did hold it out to F.D.R. as an operation that would satisfy the President's demand for action in 1942. The obvious difficulty with SLEDGE-HAMMER was the risk, and Churchill countered with a proposal, code name TORCH, to invade French North Africa. This was certainly much safer than a cross-Channel attack in either 1942 or 1943, especially since it would be a surprise assault on the territory of a neutral nation. (North Africa was ruled by the French government at Vichy, under Marshal Henri Pétain; it was Fascist and pro-Nazi, but had declared its neutrality in the war.) TORCH dovetailed nicely with British political aims, since it would help the British reestablish their position in the Mediterranean.

Roosevelt had to choose between Marshall's and Churchill's proposals. The pressures on him, from all sides, were as tremendous as the stakes. Soviet Foreign Minister V. M. Molotov had visited him in the spring. F.D.R. had promised Molotov a second front in 1942. Although the President had tried not to be specific about where it would be opened, Molotov, like the rest of the world, thought of a second front only in terms of the plains of northwestern Europe. Roosevelt also knew that the hard-pressed Russians—facing nearly two hundred German divisions on a front that extended from Leningrad to the Caucasus, with huge areas, including their prime industrial and agricultural lands, under occupation, with millions of dead already, and with a desperate need for time in which to rebuild their industry and their army—regarded a second front as absolutely essential and as a clear test of the Western democracies' good faith. If the Anglo-Americans did nothing soon to draw off some German divisions, the Russians might conclude that it meant the Allies were willing to see Hitler win, in the East at least.

Roosevelt was never foolish enough to believe that anyone but the Nazis would benefit from a German victory over Russia, but he did have other concerns and pressures. America was far from full mobilization. Whatever Marshall's plans, the U.S. Army could not invade France alone. Even in combination with the British the United States would have taken heavy casualties. Churchill and his military were insistent about not going back onto the Continent in 1942, or indeed until everything had been well prepared, and they made North Africa sound attractive to the President. Churchill was willing to go to Moscow himself to explain TORCH to Stalin, and said he could convince the Soviets that TORCH did constitute a second front. Given British intransigence, it seemed to F.D.R. that for 1942 it was TORCH or nothing. He picked TORCH.

On July 28 Roosevelt gave his orders to Marshall. General

Dwight D. Eisenhower, commander of the American forces in Britain, commented bitterly that it could well go down as the "blackest day in history." Eisenhower and Marshall were convinced that the decision to launch a major invasion of French North Africa in November 1942 would have repercussions that would shape the whole course of the war, with implications that would stretch out far into the postwar world.

They were right. Once TORCH was successful, the temptation to build up the already existing base in Algeria and Tunisia and use it as a springboard for further operations was overwhelming. By far the greater part of the Anglo-American effort in 1942 and 1943 went into the Mediterranean, first in North Africa, then Sicily (July 1943), and finally Italy (September 1943). Impressive gains were made on the map, but there was no decisive or even significant destruction of German power.

The practical problems involved in launching a 1942 or even a 1943 invasion were enormous, perhaps insurmountable. It is quite possible that the British were right in arguing that a premature cross-Channel attack would simply result in a bloodbath. But political motives were paramount in the TORCH decision. Churchill wanted a strong British presence in the Mediterranean, while Roosevelt wanted a quick and relatively safe American involvement to boost morale at home. Both got what they needed from TORCH.

When TORCH was launched (November 8, 1942) the Americans scarcely knew what to anticipate. Because they believed that the French Army in Algeria, Morocco, and Tunisia was at heart anti-German, they hoped the invasion would be unopposed. American spies and secret agents had been operating in North Africa for two years. They were members of the Office of Strategic Services (O.S.S.), an organization created by F.D.R. at the beginning of the war, modeled after the British Secret Service. In setting up the O.S.S. Roosevelt told the man he selected to head the organization, William Donovan, that this was a no-holds-barred war and that the O.S.S. must fight the Gestapo with Gestapo techniques. Roosevelt then gave Donovan an unlimited budget (literally) from blind Congressional appropriations. Nevertheless, by European standards the O.S.S. was woefully amateur in its methods, techniques, ideology, and politics. Its agents represented a political rainbow of reactionary Ivy League sportsmen, radical Jewish intellectuals, members of the Communist Party, U.S.A., and every shade in between. All they had in common was idealism—and a hatred of Hitler.

Later in the war the O.S.S. did do some useful work, especially in combination with the British and the French underground behind German lines in Europe. But in 1942, in North Africa, the O.S.S. was out of its depth in the complexity of French politics. When Pétain had surrendered to the Germans, General Charles de Gaulle had refused to obey the Vichy government and instead had flown to London, where he denounced Pétain as a traitor and claimed that he, de Gaulle, was now head of a new French government that would continue the war. De Gaulle called his organization the Free French. Few Frenchmen in the colonial armies of France rallied to de Gaulle, however, because it was easier and safer for them to remain loyal to Pétain.

The Americans, although they were invading North Africa, did not want to fight the French. They preferred to make a deal. But Pétain had ordered resistance to any invasion, from whatever direction.

Admiral Jean Darlan, the commander in chief of Vichy's armed forces, was in Algiers when the invasion began. Thanks to clumsy O.S.S. work his own secret service was fully informed of the American plans. Darlan was bitterly anti-British, author of Vichy's anti-Semitic laws, and a willing collaborator with the Germans, but he was ready to double-cross Pétain. He agreed to a deal, which required the French to lay down their arms, in return for which the Allies would make Darlan Governor General of all French North Africa. General Henri Giraud would become head of the North African army. Within a few days the French officers obeyed Darlan's order to cease fire, and a week after the invasion Eisenhower flew to Algiers to approve the agreement.

Roosevelt, who had not expected to have to go so far in cooperating with Vichy, was taken aback. For some days he withheld approval, telling reporters that Eisenhower's deal with Darlan was simply an arrangement, temporary in nature, which by no means constituted a recognition of Darlan as head of the French North African government. But eventually F.D.R. gave his approval to the Darlan deal on the basis of military expediency.

The result was that in its first major foreign-policy venture in World War II, the United States gave its support to a man who stood for everything Roosevelt and Churchill had spoken out against. As much as Göring or Goebbels, Darlan was the antithesis of the principles the Allies were defending.

The Darlan deal raised a storm of protest in liberal circles in the United States and Britain. "What the hell are we fighting for?" radio commentator Edward R. Murrow demanded to know. Churchill's friends were aghast, Churchill himself hardly less so. De Gaulle and other critics of the Darlan deal raised serious questions: Did it mean that when the Allies went into Italy they would make a deal with Mussolini? If the opportunity presented itself, would they deal with Hitler or the German generals? Roosevelt rode out the storm by stressing the temporary nature of the deal. Darlan, increasingly indignant, complained that the Americans regarded him as a lemon to be squeezed dry then thrown away when its usefulness was over.

The controversy ended on Christmas Eve 1942, when a young Frenchman in Algiers assassinated Darlan. The assassination was part of a widespread conspiracy that involved more than two dozen men, but no positive evidence exists to show who was ultimately behind the plot to kill Darlan.

Whoever did it, the embarrassment of dealing with Darlan was over. As Eisenhower's deputy, General Mark Clark, put it, "Admiral Darlan's death was . . . an act of Providence. . . . His removal from the scene was like the lancing of a troublesome boil. He had served his purpose, and his death solved what could have been the very difficult problem of what to do with him in the future."

But deep-rooted Russian suspicions about American political intentions for liberated Europe increased. At the conclusion of the Casablanca Conference, in January 1943, Roosevelt tried to allay them. He announced that the Allied policy toward Germany and Japan, and by implication toward Italy, would be to demand unconditional surrender.

What did this mean? Roosevelt did not spell out the details. Presumably, unconditional surrender meant the Allies would fight until such time as the Axis governments put themselves unconditionally into the hands of the Allies, but beyond that nothing was known. What kind of governments would replace those of Mussolini, Tojo, and Hitler? Obviously there would be a period of military occupation, with control invested in an Allied military governor, but then what? F.D.R. did not say.

He did not because in all probability he did not know himself. Always the self-confident pragmatist, he was sure that he could handle situations as they arose. He would continue to make most of his decisions on the basis of military expediency. Meanwhile, he assured Stalin and the world that there would be no deals with Hitler and his gang, and that the Allies would fight on until the Axis governments surrendered, at which time he would settle everything and satisfy everyone. It was a brilliant stroke. By keeping war aims vague, he prevented bickering among the Allies.

Roosevelt's self-confidence was immense, but not always justified, as Franco-American relations soon demonstrated. At the beginning of 1943 Giraud was still leader of France's North African forces but even with American support he would not remain so for long. With British encouragement, de Gaulle came to Algiers, organized the French Committee of National Liberation, and joined Giraud as co-President. Giraud was a political innocent, however, and despite Roosevelt's efforts de Gaulle soon squeezed Giraud out of the French North African government altogether. By the end of 1943 F.D.R.'s French policy was a shambles and de Gaulle was in power.

The major Anglo-American military operations in 1943 were directed against Italy. The invasion of Sicily began in July, the assault on the Italian mainland followed in September. Even though Italy quit the war, it was not until mid-1944 that the Allies reached Rome, and the spring of 1945 before they controlled the whole of Italy. Heavy military commitments had been made for limited results. The Allies had tied down twenty German divisions in Italy, and they had obtained some additional airfields from which to send bombers against Germany, but that was all.

Political gains were more substantial. The Italian surrender had been arranged well in advance of the Allied invasion of the mainland, on terms that suited both the Anglo-Americans and the existing Italian governing structure but that left out altogether the interests of Italian Socialists and Communists, not to mention the Soviet Union. Two weeks after the landings at Sicily the Allies bombed Rome for the first time. As a result of the raid, and because of the deteriorating military situation, the Fascist Grand Council overthrew Mussolini. Marshal Pietro Badoglio replaced him. Badoglio and his associates had no intention of changing anything within Fascist Italy; their sole objective was to switch sides in the war so that they could be with the winners when it ended. The Anglo-Americans were willing enough to oblige.

The reason, again, was military expediency. German troops stationed in Italy outnumbered the invading forces nearly eight to one and the Germans and Italians combined had a twenty-to-one advantage.* Eisenhower felt he had to have, at a minimum, a neutral Italian Army, and to get it he was willing to make extensive concessions.

* Eisenhower was short of troops because the buildup in England for a 1944 cross-Channel assault had begun; as new American divisions completed their training and were shipped overseas, they went to England not North Africa.

The Italians were specific enough about the concessions they wanted to double-cross the Germans—protection from the Germans for the government in Rome, and to be allowed to declare war on Germany and join the Allies as a cobelligerent, thus avoiding the humiliation of signing an unconditional surrender. Eisenhower was willing to grant the requests and urged his superiors in Washington and London to do so, but this was too much for Churchill, whose government had been fighting Italy since June 1940, or Roosevelt, whose Casablanca announcement about unconditional surrender had supposedly meant no more deals with Fascists, which Badoglio and his associates certainly were. The heads of government therefore delayed making a decision, the talks bogged down, and through August 1943 little was accomplished.

Churchill and Roosevelt gradually gave Eisenhower permission to concede the central Italian demands. They wanted both stability in Italy and a neutral Italian army and were thus willing to deal with Badoglio to avoid social upheaval and possibly chaos. They finally allowed the Italian government to surrender with conditions, to stay in power, to retain administrative control of Italy, to retain the Italian monarchy, and eventually to join the Allies as cobelligerent.

The result was that by 1945 the same political groups that had run Italy before and during the war were still in power, backed by an Allied Control Council from which the Russians had been systematically excluded. Stalin had protested initially but did not press the point, for he recognized the value of the precedent—those who liberated a country from the Nazis could decide what happened there. He was more than willing to allow the Allies to shape the future in Italy in return for the same right in Eastern Europe.

The implication of Allied policy in Italy was that the liberating powers would be able to run the countries they overran, but what would happen to areas from which the Germans retreated without any direct Allied assault? The most important of these was Greece. The Germans could

not allow their troops in Greece to be cut off by the westward advance of the Red Army through the Balkans. When
the Nazis left there would be a vacuum in Greece. Churchill
feared that the Greek Communists would seize power. In
order to put the Greek government-in-exile (based in London) and the monarchy back in power, Churchill was determined to have British troops in Greece as soon as the
Germans pulled out.

In September 1943, when the Italians surrendered as the
Allies invaded Italy, Churchill wanted to put Allied troops
on Italian-controlled islands in the Aegean Sea, especially
Kos and Leros, as a prelude to an invasion of Rhodes. The
occupation of Rhodes, Churchill hoped, would bring Turkey into the war on the Allied side, provide a base for an
Allied invasion of the Balkans, and most importantly allow
the British to seize control in Greece.

The American military insisted that any operation aimed
toward Rhodes and eventually the Balkans would dissipate
Allied strength and delay the final victory. They feared
that involvement in Rhodes, Greece, Turkey, and the Balkans would draw off so many men, planes, and landing
craft that the 1944 invasion of France would have to be
postponed. Marshall and his colleagues would never agree
to another postponement of the cross-Channel attack. To
the Americans, a strong postwar position in Greece and
the Balkans was not worth the cost.

The British went into Greece alone when the Germans
withdrew late in 1944, they became involved in a civil war,
and reestablished the monarchy and former government
in Athens. The cost proved to be too high for the British,
however, and in 1947 they had to withdraw. They had kept
the Communists out of power for two years, but it had
proven too much for them and they finally had to turn to
the Americans. By 1947 the Americans had a new set of
assumptions about the world, which led to a different judgment about the importance of Greece.

American foreign policy in World War II was too complex and diverse to be encompassed by any generalization,

no matter how sweeping. In lieu of a policy, most political decisions were dictated by military necessity. If, for example, the Americans tried to promote a right-wing government in French North Africa and Italy, and allowed the British to do the same in Greece, it was equally true that the United States dropped arms and equipment to the Resistance in France, which was decidedly left-wing, and to Tito in Yugoslavia, who was leading a Communist revolution. Within occupied France the Americans had to deal with the Resistance or pass up any opportunity to hurt the Germans, since there was no one else fighting the Nazis, but in Yugoslavia there was an alternative to Tito in the form of a guerrilla force under General Draja Mikhailovitch, who supported the monarchy and the London-based Yugoslav government-in-exile. Eisenhower and the Americans followed the British lead in giving aid to Tito, however, because he was supposedly more effective than Mikhailovitch in fighting the Nazis. But it was not even completely true that America concentrated single-mindedly on defeating the Nazis, since nearly every senior American officer had warned the President that the 1942 North African invasion would delay the final victory. In that instance, and to a lesser extent with the invasions of Sicily and Italy, F.D.R. was responding more to domestic political pressures and Churchill's influence than to a desire to hasten Germany's defeat.

In January 1944 the confusion and drift that had characterized American policy came to an end. America was more fully mobilized than it had ever been. Eisenhower took command of the Allied Expeditionary Force (A.E.F.) in the United Kingdom and began the preparations for Operation OVERLORD, the cross-Channel assault. From that point on, a single question dominated American thought: Will this proposal help or hurt OVERLORD? OVERLORD had top priority and subsidiary operations were geared to it. America was now concentrating exclusively on the defeat of Germany. Postwar problems, for the most part, could be decided in the postwar period. In general, this was true until the very last day of the war.

And rightly so. OVERLORD was not only the supreme military act of the war by the Anglo-Americans, it was also the supreme political act. It was the ultimate expression of a permanent and fundamental goal of American foreign policy—to maintain the balance of power.

Examples of America's newly developed leadership and single-mindedness abound. Most involved the British, practically none the Russians, partly because the Americans had a close working relationship with the British and almost no contact with the Red Army, and partly because the British were more concerned with long-range questions than were the Americans. Three issues were especially important: what to do in the Mediterranean, what form the advance into Germany should take, and whether the objective should be the political center of Berlin or the German Army. On all three issues the Americans had their way. American preponderance in the Allied camp had become so great that, if necessary, the Americans could insist upon their judgment, while the British simply had to accept the decision with the best grace possible, for their contribution to Anglo-American resources was down to 25 percent of the whole.

American domination of the Alliance reflected, in turn, a new era in world history. The United States had replaced Great Britain as the dominant world power. By 1945 American production had reached levels that were scarcely believable. The United States was producing 45 percent of the world's arms and nearly 50 percent of the world's goods. Two-thirds of all the ships afloat were American built.

On the question of what to do in the Mediterranean, the Americans insisted on slowing down operations in Italy and using the troops instead to invade the south of France in order to provide a covering force for Eisenhower's right flank. The British objected, advocating instead operations into Austria and Yugoslavia, but they dared not argue their case on political grounds for they realized that Roosevelt would turn a deaf ear to the political case. As F.D.R. told Churchill, "My dear friend, I beg you to let us go ahead with our plan. For purely political reasons over here, I should never survive even a slight setback in OVERLORD if it were known that fairly large forces had been diverted to the Balkans." (That year, 1944, was an American Presidential-election year; F.D.R. was running for a fourth term.)

Churchill hoped to secure the British position in the Mediterranean by taking all of Italy and the Adriatic coast. He later declared that he was also interested in forestalling the Russians in central Europe, but he never used such an argument at the time. To the contrary, he repeatedly told Eisenhower—who bore the brunt of the argument on the American side—that he wanted to abandon the south of France attack and substitute for it an extended offensive in the Adriatic strictly as a military proposition. Eisenhower was convinced Churchill had Britain's postwar position in mind and told the Prime Minister that if he wished to change the orders (which directed Eisenhower to strike at the heart of Germany), he should talk to Roosevelt. On military grounds Eisenhower insisted on a landing in the south of France.

Churchill could not persuade Roosevelt to intervene, and the landing took place in August 1944, ending the Allies' opportunities to extend operations into Eastern Europe or the Balkans. The Americans had been willing to go as far east in the Mediterranean as Italy, but no farther. The possibility of the Soviet Union's postwar expansion into the Balkans or Eastern Europe did not seem to the Americans to be important enough at the time to justify a diversion from Germany.

A second great issue, fought out in September 1944, was the nature of the advance into Germany. Eisenhower directed an offensive on a broad front, with the American and British armies moving toward Germany more or less abreast. General Bernard L. Montgomery, commanding the British forces, argued for a single thrust into Germany, insisting that his plan promised a quick end to the war. Churchill supported Monty, partly because he wanted the British to have the glory of capturing Berlin, mainly because he wanted the Anglo-Americans as far east as possible when they linked up with the Red Army.

Eisenhower insisted on his own plan. He was absolutely

convinced that the broad front was militarily correct. Whether he was right or not depended upon one's priority. If the main goal were to insure a German defeat, Eisenhower's cautious approach was correct. But if the goal were to forestall a Russian advance into central Europe by an Allied liberation of Berlin, Prague, and Vienna, Monty's audacious program was better. Roles had been reversed. Eisenhower and Marshall, who in 1942 had been willing to accept any risk to go across the Channel, now adopted a dull, unimaginative, but thoroughly safe campaign. The British, who earlier had hesitated at the thought of confronting the Wehrmacht on the Continent, were now ready to take great risks to get the war over with and occupy Berlin.

The difference in approach, or sense of urgency, was well illustrated in December 1944 by the reaction to the German counteroffensive in the Ardennes. Eisenhower's armies, as a result of the broad-front advance, were fully committed and woefully short of reserves. Eisenhower sent an appeal to both London and Washington for additional manpower. Churchill, anxious to get the war over with, immediately ordered a new call-up from civilian life, one that reached deeply into Britain's remaining industrial force but provided Eisenhower with 250,000 more men. The American War Department, holding to F.D.R.'s view that the greatest contribution the United States could make was through industrial production, refused to call up any additional manpower. Eisenhower's Chief of Staff, Walter B. Smith, was furious. Comparing Washington to London, he told a staff meeting, "When I was tossing on my bed last night, the thought came to me, 'Should we not go on record to our Masters in Washington that if they want us to win the war over here they must find us another ten Divisions.' Look at Britain, about to produce another 25,000 men. If she can do that we should produce another 2,500,000."

Even without American reinforcements, the Allied armies overcame the crisis of the Battle of the Bulge and in the early spring of 1945 moved across the Rhine into Germany on a broad front. As immediate objectives Eisenhower recommended the encirclement of the industrial Ruhr and a drive to Dresden to link up with the Red Army in central Germany, which would cut Germany into two parts. Montgomery and Churchill objected. They wanted Eisenhower to give priority to supplies and air support for the British drive to Berlin, in order to get there before the Russians.

There has been much confusion about Churchill's advocacy of Berlin as a target. It is commonly asserted that he wanted to keep the Russians out of eastern Germany, to retain a united Germany, and to maintain Berlin's status as the capital, and that if only the Allies had captured the city there would be no Berlin problem today. This is nonsense. Aside from the military factors (it is probable that Eisenhower's men could never have taken Berlin ahead of the Red Army), these views do not remotely reflect the policies Churchill was advocating. He never thought in terms of denying to the Russians their position in East Europe generally or eastern Germany specifically, a position that had been agreed to much earlier. Once the 1943 cross-Channel attack had been scuttled, there never was the slightest chance that the Russians could be kept out of East Europe. Churchill realized this: His famous agreement with Stalin during their Moscow meetings in the fall of 1944 signified his recognition that Russian domination of East Europe was inevitable.

What Churchill did want from the capture of Berlin was much less grandiose. His major concern was prestige. He told Roosevelt that the Russians were going to liberate Vienna. "If they also take Berlin, will not their impression that they have been the overwhelming contributor to our common victory be unduly imprinted in their minds?"

Roosevelt would have none of it. His own major concerns, in the weeks before his death on April 12, were to create the United Nations (the San Francisco Conference to draw up the Charter began its sessions shortly thereafter), to insure the participation of the U.S.S.R. in the United Nations, and to maintain cordial relations with Stalin. He refused to take a hard line with Stalin on the Russian occupation of Poland or on Stalin's suspicions about the surrender of the German forces in Italy to the Western Allies. The President was not an experienced diplomat, and right to the end he had no clear goals for the postwar world. His sponsorship of the United Nations indicated that he had adopted Woodrow Wilson's belief in collective security, but the nature of the United Nations Roosevelt wanted, dominated as it was by the great nations on the Security Council, indicated that he retained a belief in spheres of influence for the great powers. So did his frequent remarks about the "Four Policemen," (China, Russia, Britain, and the United States).

But if much of Roosevelt's policy was cloudy, mystifying even his closest advisers, one thing was clear. To the exasperation of some members of the State Department, not to mention the Ambassador to Russia, W. Averell Harriman, the President refused to become a staunch anti-Soviet. Harriman, Churchill, and later Truman assumed that Russia would be unreasonable, grasping, probing, power hungry, and impossible to deal with except from a position of great strength and unrelenting firmness. F.D.R. rejected such assumptions. Furthermore, he seems to have felt it was only reasonable for the Russians to be uneasy about the nature of the governments on Russia's western frontier, and therefore was willing to consider Stalin's demands in East Europe. There was also an assumption, shared even by Churchill, that Stalin was stating the obvious when he remarked in early 1945 that "whoever occupies a territory also imposes on it his own social system." Churchill, who had taken the lead in establishing this principle in Italy and Greece, later denounced Stalin for practicing it in East Europe, but the evidence indicates that Roosevelt was realistic enough to accept the quid pro quo.

The nature of the alliance with Russia was generally confusing. After the Nazi invasion the Red Army became heroic, and Stalin appeared as a wise and generous leader in the American press. Whether this had a deep or lasting effect on a people who mistrusted and feared Communism as much as they did Fascism is doubtful. Behind the scenes, meanwhile, and especially in the State Department, anti-

Soviet feeling kept bubbling up. George Kennan, though a rather minor functionary in the State Department at the time, best expressed the mood two days after the Nazis invaded Russia in 1941: "We should do nothing at home to make it appear that we are following the course Churchill seems to have entered upon in extending moral support to the Russian cause. It seems to me that to welcome Russia as an associate in the defense of democracy would invite misunderstanding." Kennan felt that throughout Europe "Russia is generally more feared than Germany," and he implied that he agreed with this estimate of the relative dangers of Communism and Fascism.

The sentiment that Kennan expressed in 1941 may have been dominant in the State Department, but the Department was not setting policy. Roosevelt extended lend-lease to the Russians and gave moral support to Stalin. Bending to State Department pressure, he did refuse Stalin's request in 1941 for an agreement that would recognize Russian territorial gains under the Nazi-Soviet Pact, remarking that territorial questions could be settled at the end of the war. But beyond that issue Roosevelt concentrated on working together with Stalin against the common enemy. Kennan continued to protest. In 1944, when the Red Army had driven the Germans out of Russia and was preparing for the final offensive, Kennan argued that the time had come for a "full-fledged and realistic political showdown with the Soviet leaders." He wanted to confront them with "the choice between changing their policy completely and agreeing to collaborate in the establishment of truly independent countries in Eastern Europe or of forfeiting Western Allied support and sponsorship for the remaining phases of their war effort."

By this time Kennan was the chief adviser to the American Ambassador in Moscow, Harriman, who accepted Kennan's views. Harriman advised F.D.R. to cut back on or even eliminate lend-lease shipments to Russia. Roosevelt refused and the aid continued to flow, providing Russia with essential equipment, especially trucks. The West needed the Red Army at least as badly as the Russians needed lend-lease. Although Kennan had failed to see this, Marshall and Roosevelt were clear enough about who needed whom the most. Their greatest fear was precisely Kennan's greatest hope—that once the Red Army reached Russian borders, it would stop. The Germans could then have turned and marched west, confronting the Western Allies with the bulk of the Wehrmacht. Britain and America had not mobilized nearly enough ground troops to batter their way into Berlin against such opposition.

Further, there was the frightening possibility of new secret weapons. Germany had made rapid strides in military technology during the war, German propaganda continued to urge the people to hold on just a little longer until the new weapons were ready, and F.D.R. knew that the Germans were working on an atomic bomb. The V-weapons,* jet-propelled aircraft, and snorkel submarines were bad enough. To halt lend-lease to the Russians would slow the Red Army advance, giving the Germans more time to perfect their weapons, if it did not cause Stalin to withdraw from the war altogether.

The central dilemma of the war was embodied in these considerations. Until the end almost no one in power wanted Russia to stop its advance, but few Americans or British wanted Russia to dominate East Europe. It had to be one or the other. Roosevelt decided that the greater danger lay in an end to Russian offensives, and he continued to give Stalin aid and encouragement for the Russian drive to the west.

At his own level Eisenhower made his decision about Berlin on military grounds. He thought it was madness to send his forces dashing toward Berlin when there was little, if any, chance that they would arrive before the Red Army. He also needed a clearly recognizable demarcation line, so that when his forces met the Russians there would be no unfortunate incidents of the two allies mistakenly shooting at each other. He therefore informed Stalin that he would

---

* The "V" stood for Vengeance. These were the first rockets, or guided missiles.

halt when he reached the Elbe River. Churchill kept pestering him to push on eastward; finally Eisenhower wired the Combined Chiefs of Staff: "I am the first to admit that a war is waged in pursuance of political aims, and if the Combined Chiefs of Staff should decide that the Allied effort to take Berlin outweighs purely military considerations in this theater, I would cheerfully readjust my plans and my thinking so as to carry out such an operation." He was not, in other words, willing to risk the lives of a hundred thousand or more men for no military gain. The Combined Chiefs made no reply, and for Eisenhower, military considerations remained paramount.

While Eisenhower's forces occupied southern Germany, the Russians battered their way into Berlin, suffering heavy casualties, probably in excess of a hundred thousand. Herbert Feis points out that they gained "the first somber sense of triumph, the first awesome sight of the ruins, the first parades under the pall of smoke." Two months later they gave up to the West over half the city they had captured at such an enormous price. At the cost of not a single life, Great Britain and the United States had their sectors in Berlin, and they have been there ever since.

More important, the war ended without any sharp break with the Russians. There had been innumerable strains in the strange alliance, but the United States and Russia were still allies, and in May 1945 the possibility of continued cooperation was, if frail, alive. Much would depend on the attitude of the United States toward Soviet actions in East Europe. It was as certain as the sun's rising that Stalin would insist on Communist dictatorships controlled by Moscow. The economic and political leaders of the old regimes, landlords and factory owners, generals and aristocrats, would be thrown out, along with religious leaders and editors. With them would go some of the most cherished concepts in the West—freedom of speech, free elections, freedom of religion, and free enterprise. The men who ran the American government could not look with any approval on the suppression of precisely those liberties they had fought Hitler to uphold. President Harry S Truman (F.D.R.

had died in April 1945), his advisers, and the American
people would never be able to accept the forced commun-
ization of Eastern Europe without protest.

But the experience of World War II indicated that the
United States still had alternatives, that hostility was not
the only possible reaction to Stalin's probable moves. The
United States had demonstrated an ability to make realistic,
pragmatic responses to developing situations. America had
aided Tito and supported the French Resistance, had refused to get tough with the Russians, had made major decisions solely for the purpose of bringing about the fall of
Nazi Germany.

In the spring of 1945 America had enormously more
power, both absolutely and in relation to the rest of the
world, than she had possessed in 1941. To a lesser degree
that had also been the situation in 1918, but after World
War I America had disarmed and for the most part refused
to intervene in affairs outside the North American continent. She could do so again, and indeed Roosevelt had
privately confessed to Churchill that he doubted if he could
keep American troops in Europe for more than a year or
so after the conclusion of hostilities.

America was the victor. Her decisions would go far toward shaping the postwar world. In May 1945, she did not
have a firm idea of what those decisions would be. It was
still possible for the United States to travel down any one
of several roads.

[3]

The War in Asia

When the first atomic bomb went off, at Alamogordo, New Mexico, on July 16, 1945, the temperature at Ground Zero was 100 million degrees Fahrenheit, three times hotter than the interior of the sun and ten thousand times the heat on its surface. All life, plant and animal, within a mile radius of Ground Zero simply vanished. General Leslie Groves, director of the Manhattan Project, turned to his deputy and said, "The war's over. One or two of these things and Japan will be finished."

GORDON THOMAS and MAX MORGAN-WITTS, *Enola Gay*

One of the chief facts about the war in the Pacific was that when the shooting stopped the Americans did not have troops occupying the major nations of mainland Asia—Indochina, Korea, Burma, India, or China. Much of American foreign policy after the war was designed to compensate, to secure positions of strength for American armed forces on mainland Asia in order to shape the future there. In China, North Korea, and Indochina the attempt failed. America could not do after 1945 what she had been unable to do during the war.

America failed to get onto mainland Asia because she did not have enough manpower to carry on a large-scale land war in both Europe and Asia. There were other military limitations. It was approximately twice as far from the United States to Asia as it was to Europe, which meant that it took two ships going from the United States to Asia to do as much as one to Europe, and until the very last months of the war merchant shipping was in short supply. The United States devoted nearly 40 percent of its total effort

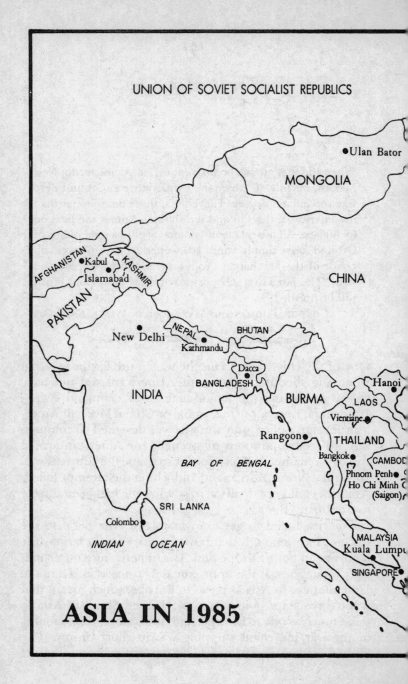

UNION OF SOVIET SOCIALIST REPUBLICS

●Ulan Bator

MONGOLIA

CHINA

AFGHANISTAN ●Kabul

KASHMIR

Islamabad

PAKISTAN

New Delhi

NEPAL

Kathmandu

BHUTAN

Dacca

BANGLADESH

BURMA

Hanoi

LAOS

Vientiane●

INDIA

Rangoon●

THAILAND

BAY OF BENGAL

Bangkok●

CAMBOD

Phnom Penh●

Ho Chi Minh

(Saigon)

SRI LANKA

Colombo●

MALAYSIA

Kuala Lumpu

INDIAN OCEAN

SINGAPORE

ASIA IN 1985

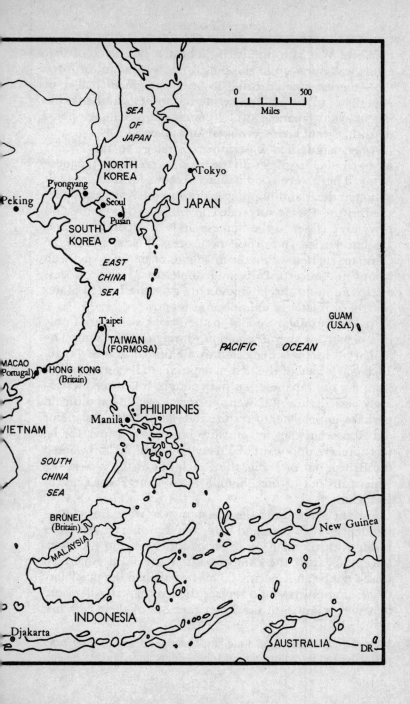

in World War II to the Pacific Theater, but much of that effort was eaten up in shipping, and the amount of force the Americans could bring to bear was much smaller in Asia than in Europe. As a result, the strategy in the Pacific was to avoid Japanese strong points and to initiate operations that would conserve men and material.

America pursued a peripheral strategy in the Pacific, never coming to grips with the main forces of the Japanese Army. There were good military reasons for doing so, but although the island-hopping campaign the Americans pursued in the Pacific succeeded in bringing the Army and Navy ever closer to the home islands of Japan, there was a political price. In Europe the process of closing in on the Germans carried with it the dividends of putting American troops in Antwerp, Paris, and Rome. In Asia the process of closing in on the Japanese only gave the United States control of relatively unimportant islands.

American military policy in the Pacific was geared only in a negative way to the nation's foreign-policy aims. The military effort was dedicated to the destruction of Japan. That was a goal of the first magnitude, to be sure, but just stopping the Japanese was not enough. It became increasingly clear as the war went on that it would be difficult, perhaps impossible, to restore the old order in Asia. Nor did Roosevelt want to return to business as usual, for he was a sincere opponent of old-style colonialism and wanted the British out of India, the Dutch out of the N.E.I., the Americans out of the Philippines, and the French out of Indochina.*

For the Americans the question was what form independence would take, and here, as in Europe, power would reside with the man on the spot with a gun in his hand. Except in Japan, the Philippines, and the N.E.I., that man would not be an American. This fact opened the possibility that Communists would replace the old colonial rulers and that they might shut the Americans out of their Asia just

* The United States had long since pledged itself to give independence to the Philippines on July 4, 1946, a pledge that it kept.

as thoroughly as did the Japanese. The challenge for American policy-makers was how to simultaneously drive out the Japanese, prevent the resurgence of European colonialism, and foster the growth of democratic, capitalist local governments, all without actually making the effort necessary to put the man with a gun on the spot. In China, Indochina, and North Korea it turned out to be an impossible challenge.

In Asia, American priorities combined with military necessities to shape events. The first priority, as in Europe, was the defeat of the enemy. Next came the elevation of China under Chiang Kai-shek and the Kuomintang Party to great power status, which required establishing Chiang's control in China, a control that was contested by the Communists under Mao Tse-tung, not to mention the Japanese, who held most of the China coast. Chiang was corrupt, inefficient, and dictatorial, but he was also friendly to the West. No matter how badly the Americans wanted Chiang to rule China, however, there was little they could do to support him without troops on the scene, and the military realities precluded sending large numbers of American troops to China.

At the end of the war the United States did have overwhelming force on all the major Asian island groups in contrast to the mainland. The strategy that put America there grew out of military necessity, personality conflict, and political motivation. After retreating from the Philippines in early 1942, the Americans established a base of operations in Australia. They already had one in the Central Pacific on Hawaii. Top Army and Navy officials did not get on well with one another. The result was a division of the area into two theaters of war, the Southwest Pacific and the Central Pacific; the Army under General Douglas MacArthur was responsible for the Southwest Pacific, and the Navy under Admiral Chester Nimitz was in charge in the Central Pacific. MacArthur's base was Australia; his strategy was to move northward through the N.E.I., the Philippines, and Formosa to get at Japan. Nimitz, in Hawaii, wanted to advance westward through the Central Pacific. In the end, both approaches were used.

When MacArthur reached Australia after his flight from Bataan (in February 1942) he announced "I shall return" to the Philippines.* Senior officers in the Navy objected; they felt that making the effort to get back into the Philippines was not worth the men and material required. Better by far, the Navy reasoned, to bypass the Philippines and go straight to Formosa, or to concentrate exclusively on the Central Pacific. MacArthur's critics, and their number was large, believed that the only reason the United States returned to the Philippines (in late 1944) was to enhance MacArthur's personal prestige.

MacArthur's egotism was great, but his desire to go back to the Philippines involved something more than personal satisfaction. MacArthur thought it would be madness for the United States ever to be involved in a land war in Asia, a military judgment that only reinforced his parallel belief that it was imperative for the United States to control the offshore islands, particularly the Philippines and Japan. The General knew that if the United States bypassed the Philippines, there was a danger that the Hukbalahap, a Communist-led guerrilla organization, would take power. It might be impossible to root them out. MacArthur's invasion of the Philippines solved this problem, and in 1946 the United States turned the destiny of the Philippines over to men who were friendly to America and allowed her to keep American military bases and investments.

In China, unlike the Philippines, the Americans did not have troops on the spot and could not control events. The United States hoped Chiang's Kuomintang Party would bring China into the modern world community both as a market and as a producer of raw materials. Americans realized that to accomplish this the Kuomintang would have

---

* The War Department liked the phrase but thought the statement should read, "We shall return," since presumably MacArthur would need help. MacArthur refused to change it, and "I shall return" it remained.

to be reformed and its policies liberalized. They encouraged Chiang to root out the rampant corruption, make an accommodation with Mao and the Communists, introduce some meaningful land reform, and modernize along Western lines.

The tactical mistakes made in attempting to implement this program were manifold, but more important was the strategic error. The program rested on the twin assumptions that Chiang wanted reform and that he could put it through, assumptions that turned out to be totally unwarranted. But most Americans regarded the Chinese Communists with horror, and there seemed to be no middle ground between Mao and Chiang. Events therefore ground on with what appeared to be a tragic inevitability. America sent huge loans to China, often in the form of direct cash, but with a foreboding of failure since they were really bribes to Chiang and his chief supporters, who threatened to quit the war against Japan otherwise. The possibility that the Chinese might surrender frightened Washington sufficiently to keep the money flowing.

Throughout the war the situation within the Kuomintang's armies was desperate. Senior officers lived in luxury while the enlisted men suffered from body-wracking diseases, seldom ate, were usually shoeless, and had insufficient equipment (one in three had a rifle, usually without ammunition). American officials wanted improvement, for it was imperative that China's vast manpower resources be used against Japan.

There was in addition the problem of the Chinese Communists. Chiang was using his only respectable troops against Mao, who in turn deployed a force of up to two million men. Full-scale civil war threatened, a war that would be dangerous to the Americans on two counts: It would reduce the potential forces that could be thrown against Japan, and it might lead to Chiang's overthrow and Mao's victory. The Americans therefore tried to force Chiang to bring the Communists into the government and to persuade Mao to cooperate with Chiang. Neither of the Chinese groups, however, would make any but the most impossible demands of the other, and nothing was accomplished.

During the last stages of the war Chiang was able to obtain Russian promises, honored for the most part, not to support the Chinese Communists and to urge Mao to unite with the Kuomintang. In return, Chiang leased Port Arthur to the Russians and made Dairen a free port, while recognizing Soviet control of Outer Mongolia. In Asia, as in Europe, Stalin was the extreme nationalist, basing his decisions solely on Russian interests and ignoring or selling out the Communist parties of the world. He regarded Mao as an adventurer whose wild schemes would anger the West and thus endanger Russian gains in the Far East. Mao regarded Stalin as a backstabber.

For two years, meanwhile, the hopeless American policy of trying to bring Mao and Chiang together continued, even though realism was not entirely absent from the upper reaches of the American government. After the war, when Truman sent Marshall to China in another attempt to bring the two Chinese leaders together, Secretary of War Stimson warned Marshall: "Remember that the Generalissimo [Chiang] has never honestly backed a thorough union with the Chinese Communists. He could not, for his administration is a mere surface veneer (more or less rotten) over a mass of the Chinese people beneath him." Despite this realism, and despite the proclaimed neutrality of the Marshall mission, America continued to give material support to Chiang. It was never enough, primarily because nothing short of a total American occupation of China would have been sufficient to prevent Mao's eventual victory. Such an occupation would have required millions of American soldiers, far more than the nation was willing to send even to Europe, and there never was the slightest possibility that either the American people or government were willing to make the sacrifice required to save the Kuomintang.

Stalin's willingness to cooperate in Asia with the Americans extended beyond China. Roosevelt first met with Stalin in late 1943, in Teheran, Iran. The American President's dislike of de Gaulle reinforced his general opposition to European colonialism and led to his proposal for Indochina. Roosevelt suggested that Laos, Cambodia, and Vietnam be placed under a four-power trusteeship after the war (the powers being China, the United States, Russia, and Britain). Stalin immediately endorsed the proposal, adding that Indochinese independence might follow in two or three decades. Only the British, fearful for their own empire, objected to thus snatching away a colony from France.

The situation within Vietnam did not lend itself to an easy solution. The Japanese had allowed the French to maintain civil control of Indochina until March 1945, when they gave limited encouragement to Vietnamese nationalism by replacing the French with a royal puppet government under the Bao Dai. The Viet Minh then went into active resistance. Their leader, Ho Chi Minh, told Washington that he wanted independence within five to ten years, land reform, a democracy based on universal suffrage, and national purchase of French holdings. He had worked closely with O.S.S. agents during the war (primarily rescuing downed American pilots) and had copied the Vietnamese Declaration of Independence from the American document. After the war this availed Ho nothing, for the American position toward French colonialism changed. Whatever Roosevelt's personal feelings toward de Gaulle, good relations with France were imperative if Communism were to be thwarted in Europe, still the main theater, and relations with France would turn in large part on the American attitude toward Indochina.

There was, in addition, the general American fear of Communism in Asia, of which Ho was obviously a part and potentially a leader. The Americans therefore agreed, in August 1945, that in Indochina the British would accept the Japanese surrender south of the 16th parallel, while Chiang's troops would do so to the north. The British held the southern position until de Gaulle could send troops to Saigon, while Chiang's troops looted with abandon until the French returned to Hanoi. America had taken its hard line with Japan in 1941 in large part because of the Japanese occupation of Indochina, and it was at least consistent

that at the end of the war she would move again to prevent
Southeast Asia from falling into unfriendly hands, distasteful as French colonial rule might be.

Many American decisions in World War II—such as allowing the French to reoccupy Indochina—were made
quickly and without the benefit of deep analysis, because
they concerned issues with a relatively low priority. In some
cases these decisions had serious repercussions, as in Vietnam and the agreement to divide Korea. The Russians were
to occupy Korea north of the thirty-eighth parallel and the
Americans the area south of that line. Both agreed that
this was merely a matter of convenience—that the Japanese
colony eventually would be reunited and given its independence—and both seem to have meant it at the time,
although neither gave Korea a great deal of thought.

The most important American decision of the war, however —to build and then use an atomic bomb—was thoroughly examined and discussed in the highest levels of the
government. The Manhattan Project, the best-kept secret
of the war, began in 1939, with the sole purpose of harnessing the energy of the atom to produce a bomb that
could be carried by aircraft, and to succeed before the
Germans could. J. Robert Oppenheimer, one of the emi-
nent scientists on the Project, later recalled, "We always
assumed if they were needed they would be used." The
tendency was to regard the bomb as simply another military
weapon.

By mid-1945 the military situation dominated thinking
about the bomb, because although Japan had clearly lost
the war, she was far from crushed. She had lost most of
her Pacific empire and fleet, to be sure, but she still retained
control of much of China, most of Southeast Asia, and all
of Korea and Manchuria. Her army was more or less intact,
and her air force—based on the kamikazes—was a major
threat. Japan had an army estimated at up to two million
men in Manchuria available for the defense of the home
islands, with some 5,350 kamikaze planes ready for use
with 7,000 more in storage. There were also thousands of

kamikaze PT boats and more than enough young volunteers to steer the planes and boats. An American invasion of the home islands would be a bloody affair. Stimson wished to avoid it not only because he feared the casualties but also because he did not wish to inaugurate a race war in the Pacific, where the white man was so badly outnumbered.

A key factor was the Red Army. If Stalin would declare war, Japan might quit without a last-ditch fight. Contemplating the possibility, on June 18, 1945, General Marshall noted, "The impact of Russian entry on the already hopeless Japanese may well be the decisive action levering them into capitulation." The U.S. Navy thought the Japanese could be starved into submission through a blockade, and the Army Air Force argued that even without the atomic bomb the enemy could be forced through bombing to surrender (the recently developed napalm was being used in raids on Tokyo with fearful effectiveness), but Truman and Marshall could not accept these optimistic forecasts. If the United States wanted an unconditional surrender, it must first destroy the Japanese Army. Since in the early summer of 1945 the atomic bomb had not yet been tested, it appeared that the only way to destroy the Japanese Army was to fight it, and in Marshall's view it was preferable to have the Red Army do it than the American Army.

There was another alternative. However strong the Japanese Army, whatever cost the enemy could force the United States to pay to overrun the home islands, Japan was a defeated nation and her leaders knew it. They could delay but not prevent the final defeat. Japan was fighting on to avoid the humiliation of unconditional surrender. She wanted some explicit conditions before her capitulation. A few Japanese leaders dreamed of holding onto conquered territory on the mainland, but most were realistic enough to know that Japan would lose control of all but her home islands. What they did want was some guarantee of eventual self-rule, and more immediately a guarantee that the Emperor would remain sacrosanct, both physically and in his official position (the American press was carrying demands by some politicians that the Emperor be tried as a war criminal and punished).

American leaders knew that the Japanese were trying to find a way out with honor. They had also agreed among themselves that the Emperor had to stay, since his elimination would bring on social chaos in Japan. For reasons of domestic morale and politics, however, and because they did want to humiliate the enemy who had humiliated them in the Pearl Harbor attack, the Americans decided not to inform the Japanese of their intentions about the Emperor.

At the February 1945 meetings with the Russians at Yalta the Americans pressed Stalin to promise to enter the Pacific war and offered to force Chiang to make concessions to the Russians on the Sino-Soviet border in return. Stalin agreed to come in three months after the conclusion of hostilities in Europe—he would need that much time to shift troops from Germany to Manchuria. When in July the Big Three met again at Potsdam, outside Berlin, the Americans remained as anxious as ever to have the Red Army in the Pacific.

Then came the successful test of the first atomic bomb. It inaugurated a new era in the world's history and in the tools of American foreign policy. No longer, or so it seemed, would the United States have to rely on mass armies, either those of its allies or its own. The atomic bomb had the great advantage of being cheaper than mass armies—and much quicker. The Americans immediately began to use the bomb as an instrument of diplomacy. As Churchill summed up the American attitude on July 23, "It was now no longer necessary for the Russians to come into the Japanese war; the new explosive alone was sufficient to settle the matter." Later the same day, reporting on a conversation with Secretary of State James Byrnes, Churchill declared, "It is quite clear that the United States do not at the present time desire Russian participation in the war against Japan." And that evening Stimson recorded that even Marshall, who had pushed hardest for Russian entry, "felt, as I felt sure he would, that now with our new weapon we would not need the assistance of the Russians to conquer Japan."

At Potsdam Truman casually informed Stalin that the United States had a "new weapon" and was pleased when the Soviet leader did not press him for details. The Big Three then agreed to retain the Emperor after Japanese surrender but refused to let the Japanese know this. Instead, they issued the Potsdam Declaration, calling again for unconditional surrender on pain of great destruction. The Japanese rejected the demand as it contained no guarantee on the Emperor, and Truman gave the order to drop the bomb.

What was the great hurry? This question has bothered nearly everyone who has examined the controversy raging around the decision to use the bomb. The importance of the question stems from three related factors: (1) the United States had no major operations planned before November 1, 1945, so there was plenty of time to wait and see what effect the anticipated Russian declaration of war would have on the Japanese, or to see if the Japanese peace feelers were serious; (2) the bomb was not planned for use against a military target, so it would not change the military situation; and (3) the Americans expected the Russians to enter the war on or about August 8, but they dropped the bomb on August 6. When the Japanese did not surrender immediately, they dropped a second bomb on August 9. The British physicist P. M. S. Blackett, and later others, charged that the sequence of events demonstrated that the use of the bomb was "the first major operation of the cold diplomatic war with Russia." Its primary purpose was to keep Russia out of the Far Eastern postwar settlement rather than to save American lives.

A parallel interpretation claims that the American intention was to impress the Russians with the power of the bomb and to make it clear to them that the United States would not hesitate to use it. America had already deployed the bulk of her troops out of Western Europe, as had the British, so that by August of 1945 the Red Army in East Europe was the most powerful force in all Europe. To those concerned about a possible Russian advance across the Elbe

River, the bomb seemed a perfect deterrent.

These interpretations are not necessarily wrong; they are just too limited. They tend to ignore or underestimate Japan's remaining power of resistance, especially the terrifying kamikazes. While it is true that Roosevelt's death allowed anti-Soviet sentiment to bubble up in Washington, it is not at all clear that anti-Soviet advisers were controlling events. In any case, if their motive was to keep the Russians out of the Far Eastern settlement, the Americans could have done that by negotiating a conditional surrender in July and probably earlier, long before the Soviets were ready to declare war.

Nearly every individual who participated in the decision to use the bomb had his own motive. Some were concerned with the kamikazes, others wanted to punish the Japanese for Pearl Harbor, while there were those who said that the actual use of the bomb was the only way to justify to Congress and the people the expenditure of $2 billion to produce it. Life came cheap in the world of 1945. The Anglo-Americans at Dresden had slaughtered thousands of women and children in air raids that had no discernible military purpose. To kill a few more "Japs" seemed natural enough, and the racial factor in the decision cannot be ignored. The British military writer B. H. Liddell Hart later charged that the United States would never have used the bomb against the white people in Berlin.

But the simplest explanation is perhaps the most convincing. The bomb was there. Japan was not surrendering. No one in the government thought seriously about not using it. To drop it as soon as it was ready seemed natural, the obvious thing to do. As Truman later put it, "The final decision of where and when to use the atomic bomb was up to me. Let there be no mistake about it. I regarded the bomb as a military weapon and never had any doubt that it should be used."

Unfortunately, the bomb dropped on Hiroshima did not bring an immediate Japanese response. The Russians, meanwhile, declared war on August 8 and the Red Army moved forward in Manchuria and Southern Sakhalin. The

Japanese Manchurian army surrendered. In order to prod the Japanese, on August 9 the United States dropped a second bomb, on Nagasaki, which insured that the Japanese government would surrender to the Americans. Even after the second bomb, however, the Japanese insisted on a guarantee about Emperor Hirohito's safety. Truman decided he would have to give it, the United States made the required promise, and Japan finally surrendered.

American troops occupied Japan, excluding the Russians, not to mention the Australians and the British. Even though MacArthur, who headed the occupation, was supposed to be a Supreme Allied Commander responsible to all the governments that had been at war with Japan, in fact he took his orders only from the United States government. The conclusion of the war therefore found the United States either occupying, controlling, or exerting strong influence in four of the five major industrial areas of the world—Western Europe, Great Britain, Japan, and the United States itself. Only the Soviet Union operated outside the American orbit.

It was an ironic conclusion. Of the Big Three powers, the United States had made the least relative sacrifices but had gained by far the most. Roosevelt's policy of avoiding direct confrontation with the armies of the Axis had saved thousands of lives, while his insistence on maintaining the civilian economy at relatively high levels had strengthened the domestic economy. The United States was the only nation in the world with capital resources available to solve the problems of postwar reconstruction. She could use this capital to dictate the form of reconstruction and to extend the areas of her own influence. America had, in addition, the atomic bomb. In 1945 it seemed the ultimate weapon, and American politicians, ignoring the scientists' warnings that others would soon make their own bombs, believed that they had a secret that would insure American military dominance for decades.

There were problems. One existed on mainland Asia. Except in South Korea, the United States had no significant numbers of troops on the mainland. Whatever influence

she wished to exert could be effected only through the
French, British, Dutch, and Chinese Nationalists, all of whom
were intensely unpopular with the great masses of Asians.
The Japanese had shattered the image of the white man
in the Orient. Asians had come to believe that they could
control their own lives and resources. They wanted the
white man out—out of Indochina, out of India, out of
Malaya, out of the N.E.I., out of the Philippines. American
foreign policy would either have to adjust to this historic
development or her influence would wane.

America's chief assets were her military and economic
strength, but she had another asset to call upon, one that
was less tangible but potentially more valuable. In September 1945 America's prestige, like its relative power in the
world, had never been higher. The United States had provided the tools and the men to save Europe and Russia
from Hitler and his Nazis. The United States had driven
the Italians out of their African colonies and thrown the
Japanese out of China, Indochina, the N.E.I., the Philippines, Burma, and Korea. America had asked nothing for
itself in return. Ho Chi Minh hailed the Americans as the
true friends of the oppressed of the earth. So did such
dissimilar men as Charles de Gaulle, Churchill, and on one
occasion even Stalin himself. In a world full of hatred,
death, destruction, deception, and double-dealing, the
United States at the end of World War II was almost uni-
versally regarded as the disinterested champion of justice,
freedom, and democracy. American prestige would never
be as high again.

The Beginnings of the Cold War

While the British and Americans held firmly . . . the whole
position in Africa and the Mediterranean . . . and the whole
of Western Germany, . . . they undertook by negotiation and
diplomatic pressure to reduce Russia's position in Eastern
Europe—which the Soviet Union had won because the Red
Army had defeated two thirds of the German Army.

WALTER LIPPMANN

There is no satisfactory date to mark the beginning of the
Cold War, but the issue that gave it life and shaped its early
course was East Europe. For centuries East and West have
struggled with each other for control of the huge area
running from the Baltic to the Balkans, an area rich in
human and industrial resources and strategically vital to
both sides, either to Russia as a buffer against the West, or
to Germany and France as the gateway for an invasion of
Russia. Neither the West nor the East has been willing to
allow East Europe to be strong, independent, or neutral.
Russia and the West have each wanted the area to be aligned
with them. The United States participated in this process
in 1919, when President Woodrow Wilson took the lead in
breaking up the Austro-Hungarian Empire and establishing independent, Western-oriented governments designed, in part, to hold the Soviet Union in check. The
attempt ultimately failed because of the inability of the
capitalist states to stick together, a failure helped along by
American refusal in the thirties to participate in European
politics.

A climax came at the 1939 Munich conference. For three
years Stalin had sought to form an alliance with Britain

and France, but the democracies would do anything to avoid getting into bed with the Soviets, with the result being that they slept with the Nazis instead. Stalin, no more ready than the West to take on Hitler alone, in 1939 signed the Nazi-Soviet Pact, which provided for a division of East Europe between Germany and Russia. They soon began fighting over the spoils, however, and in 1941 Hitler took all of East Europe then drove deep into Soviet territory. The British and French, meanwhile, had tried to redeem their abandonment of East Europe by declaring war when Hitler invaded Poland, but the aid they gave to the defense of Poland was useless. In the conflict that followed the West made no significant contribution to the liberation of East Europe, and when the end came the Red Army was in sole possession of the area east of a line drawn from Stettin on the Baltic to Trieste on the Adriatic.

Russia controlled East Europe. This crucial result of World War II destroyed the Grand Alliance and gave birth to the Cold War.

America was unwilling to accept Russian domination of East Europe. Although the Americans were ready to admit that Stalin had earned the right to have the major say in the politics of the region, and that Russian security demanded friendly governments there, they were not prepared to abandon East Europe altogether. They persisted in insisting that it was possible to have East European governments that were both democratic and friendly to Russia. Nearly every important American leader acknowledged that East Europe could no longer maintain an anti-Soviet position, but at the same time they all wished to promote democracy, freedom of religion and speech, and free enterprise. As Secretary of State James Byrnes put it, "Our objective is a government [in Poland] both friendly to the Soviet Union and representative of all the democratic elements of the country."

It was an impossible program. Given the traditions, prejudices, economics, and social structures of East Europe, any freely elected government would certainly be anti-Russian. It may be that F.D.R. realized this fact, but if so was unwilling to explain it to the American people. When he reported on the Yalta conference in February 1945, he emphasized Stalin's agreement to hold free elections in East Europe. Roosevelt's report fed soaring American expectations about the shape of postwar East Europe. Poland, Bulgaria, Rumania, and the rest of the region would become, it was believed, democratic capitalist states closely tied to the West. There never was the slightest possibility that this would happen, but when it failed to occur, millions of Americans were outraged. They demanded liberation and rollback, and hurled insults at the Russians, while professional anti-Communists searched for the betrayers of East Europe and found them in the highest circles of American government, including, in the minds of some, President Roosevelt himself.

The struggle centered on Poland. There were two separate but related questions: Who would control Poland? and What would the Polish boundary be? The British had tried to answer the first question by sponsoring a government-in-exile in London, in which the Church, the Polish Army officer corps, and the landlords were dominant. The Americans had answered the second in early 1942 by refusing to discuss, as Stalin wished to do, the boundary question in East Europe. The United States insisted that such discussion had to be postponed until Hitler was crushed, partly because F.D.R. did not want to enter into any secret agreements that could later be denounced, but mainly because Stalin was demanding Russia's 1941 frontiers, which had extended Soviet influence into East Europe as a result of the Nazi-Soviet Pact. Given the general desire at Yalta to hold the Grand Alliance together, based on mutual need, the Big Three tried to find a face-saving formula. The Russians had created an alternative to the London-based Polish government-in-exile, the so-called Lublin government, which was a Soviet puppet. In January 1945 Stalin had recognized the Lublin Poles as the sole government of Poland. At Yalta a month later Churchill and Roosevelt tried to retrieve the situation by insisting on free elections and a broadly based Polish government that would include

major figures from the London government. They believed
that they had achieved a miracle when Stalin agreed to
"free and unfettered elections as soon as possible on the
basis of universal suffrage and secret ballot," and also to
"reorganize" the Polish government by bringing in Poles
from London. Had these promises been kept, democratic
forces in Poland probably would have power, thereby giving the West the best possible result. Stalin, however, had
no intention of giving up Poland, and he never accepted
the Western interpretation of the Yalta agreements—that
they meant what they said. It is possible that he did not
fully realize that the West was serious, for he may have felt
that all that was required was a face-saving formula, which
he was willing enough to give. But if he thought the West
would accept without protest his violations of the agreement, he was wrong.

Both sides wanted a friendly government in Poland for
solid strategic reasons. Poland is a corridor that leads both
ways. As Stalin put it at Yalta, "For the Russian people, the
question of Poland is not only a question of honor but also
a question of security. Throughout history, Poland has been
the corridor through which the enemy has passed into Russia. Twice in the last thirty years our enemies, the Germans,
have passed through this corridor. . . . Poland is not only
a question of honor but of life and death for the Soviet
Union." The West saw Poland in reverse, as the outpost of
European civilization holding back the hordes of Asians
ready to overrun the Continent. This great fear, a constant
in European history, was heightened in 1945 because of
the vacuum in Germany and because of the Red Army, by
then incomparably the strongest power in all Europe. If
the Red Army remained intact, if it occupied Poland and
East Germany, if the United States demobilized, and if
Poland fell into Communist hands—all of which seemed
probable in February 1945—then there would be nothing
to prevent the Russians from overrunning all Europe.

Because Stalin's concerns were less for the Russo-Polish
boundary than for the Polish-German boundary and the
nature of the Polish government, he agreed to relatively

limited Russian gains at Poland's expense, while insisting that Poland be compensated by taking huge hunks of German territory. He intended to move Poland's western borders all the way to the Oder-Neisse line, taking not only East Prussia and all of Silesia but also Pomerania, back to and including Stettin. From six to nine million Germans would have to be evicted. The Anglo-Americans were alarmed, but there was little they could do about it. Considering German treatment of the Poles, it was difficult to argue that Stalin's proposal was anything less than fair, and in any case what mattered was not so much the frontiers of Poland as who would rule in Poland. By leaving the boundary question in abeyance and emphasizing Stalin's promise to hold free elections, Roosevelt came away from Yalta with a feeling of triumph.

Stalin quickly began to shatter the American illusion. He refused to reorganize the Polish government in any significant way, suppressed freedom of speech, assembly, religion, and the press in Poland, and made no move to hold the promised free elections. To a greater or lesser extent the Soviets followed this pattern in the rest of East Europe, making it perfectly clear that now that they held the region they would not give it up. They shut the West out completely. By any standard the Soviet actions were high-handed, their suppressions brutal.

The West was shocked and felt betrayed. Stalin either failed to realize this or felt he had no choice. Time and again, at Yalta and later, Stalin emphasized Russia's security problem, her need to protect herself from Germany and the West by controlling the nations on her border, but increasingly Americans dismissed his statements as lies and denounced him as a paranoid whose aim was world conquest. Millions of American voters of East European origin, aided by the Catholic Church and military men who were worried about the new strategic balance in Europe, decided that standing up to Stalin was as important as standing up to Hitler.

One of the first, and surely the most important, of those to feel these impulses was President Truman. His inclina-

tion was to take a hard line with the Russians, an attitude
that was supported by senior American officials stationed
in Moscow. A week and a day after Truman assumed office,
on April 20, 1945, he met with Ambassador Harriman to
discuss America's relations with the Soviet Union, which by
then were at a critical stage, with the war coming to an end
and new policies required.

Harriman had just come from Moscow, where his chief
intellectual adviser was George Kennan, one of the leading
anti-Soviets in the Foreign Service. Kennan was opposed
to the denazification policy the Americans intended to apply to Germany because he felt the Germans would soon
be joining the United States in opposition to Russia. But
Kennan stopped short of a call to arms. He believed the
Russians would never be able to maintain their hegemony
over East Europe, that United States–Russian postwar collaboration was unnecessary when what was needed was just
a clear recognition of each side's sphere of influence, that
Stalin had no intention of marching farther west, and most
of all that "it was idle for us to hope that we could have
any influence on the course of events in the area to which
Russian hegemony had already been effectively extended."
When Harry Hopkins, Roosevelt's trusted adviser, asked
Kennan what the United States should do about the Russian
domination of Poland, Kennan merely remarked that "we
should accept no share of the responsibility." "Then you
think it's just sin," Hopkins rejoined, "and we should be
agin it."

"That's just about right," Kennan replied.

Such a do-nothing policy could have been adopted; the
indications were that this was the line F.D.R. intended to
follow. The President felt that postwar collaboration could
be achieved through the United Nations. To get Stalin's
cooperation Roosevelt was willing to overlook much, or,
like Kennan, to adopt a realistic attitude toward developments in Poland.

Harriman, however, rejected the do-nothing policy. According to Truman, at their April 20 meeting Harriman
"said that certain elements around Stalin misinterpreted

our generosity and our desire to cooperate as an indication of softness, so that the Soviet government could do as it pleased without risking challenge from the United States." But he emphasized that the Soviets would need American economic aid to reconstruct their country, so "we could stand firm on important issues without running serious risks." Truman stopped Harriman to inform him that he was "not afraid of the Russians," and that he "intended to be firm," for "the Russians needed us more than we needed them." Truman's statement is a key to much that followed. American postwar policy was based, in part, on the belief that no matter what the United States did or said, the Russians could not protest because they had to have American money.

Harriman then warned that the West was faced with a "barbarian invasion of Europe." After continuing in this vein for some time, he finally added that in international negotiations "there is give-and-take, and both sides make concessions." Truman argued for the lion's share. He would not, he said, "expect one hundred percent of what we proposed," but he did feel that "we should be able to get eighty-five percent."

As a first practical step to secure 85 percent, Truman promised to tell Soviet Foreign Minister Molotov, who would soon be in Washington, that the Soviets had to immediately hold free elections in Poland. Truman added that he intended to put it to Molotov "in words of one syllable." At the conclusion of the meeting Harriman confessed that he had rushed to Washington because he was afraid that Truman did not understand the true nature of the Soviet problem. "I am greatly relieved," Harriman said, "to discover . . . we see eye to eye on the situation."

Two days later Truman met with Molotov. For the most part it was a diplomatic function and the two men were cordial. Truman did point out that he wanted free elections in Poland "because of the effect on American public opinion." Molotov said he understood that point, but added that Truman should understand that Poland was "even more important for the Soviet Union," since Poland was far from America but bordered on Russia. Truman brushed that aside and insisted that Molotov recognize that America was making Poland a test case, "the symbol of the future development of our international relations."

The next afternoon, April 23, 1945, Truman held his first major foreign-policy conference. Secretary of State Edward Stettinius, Secretary of War Stimson, Secretary of the Navy James Forrestal, Admirals William Leahy and Ernest King, General Marshall, Ambassador Harriman, and others attended. The subject was Poland. Truman set the tone by declaring that it was obvious "that our agreements with the Soviet Union had so far been a one-way street and that this could not continue." He then asked each man present to state his views.

Stimson began by saying that unless the United States fully understood "how seriously the Russians took this Polish question we might be heading into very dangerous waters . . ." Forrestal took the opposite view; he said it was his profound conviction that "if the Russians were to be rigid in their attitude we had better have a showdown with them now rather than later." Harriman, too, thought the United States should be firm on Poland. Stimson thought "the Russians perhaps were being more realistic than we were in regard to their own security," and Leahy added that he never expected the Soviets to sponsor free elections in Poland. General Marshall, who favored a cautious policy with regard to Poland, wanted to avoid a break with the Soviets since it was imperative to get Russian help in the Pacific war.

Truman, who was to meet with Molotov at 5:30 P.M., still could go either way. His senior advisers were split. He could acquiesce in Soviet actions in Poland, or he could continue to demand 85 percent.

Truman decided upon the latter course. When Molotov arrived the President shouted at him in the language of a Missouri mule driver. The interpreter said "he had never heard a top official get such a scolding." At the end Truman told Molotov that "there was only one thing to do": Stalin had to reorganize the Polish government by bringing in elements from the London Poles, and he had to hold elections. Molotov finally remarked, "I have never been talked to like that in my life." Truman replied, "Carry out your agreements and you won't get talked to like that."

The Russians were puzzled as well as upset, as Stalin indicated on April 24 in a letter to Churchill and Truman. "Poland borders on the Soviet Union which cannot be said about Great Britain or the U.S.A.," he began. Turning to complaints about Soviet actions in Poland, he remarked, "I do not know whether a genuinely representative Government has been established in Greece, or whether the Belgium Government is a genuinely democratic one. The Soviet Union was not consulted when those Governments were being formed, nor did it claim the right to interfere in those matters, because it realizes how important Belgium and Greece are to the security of Great Britain." He said he could not understand why in the West "no attempt is made to consider the interests of the Soviet Union in terms of security as well."

It was difficult for other outsiders, not just Stalin, to understand the American position. Throughout the war Americans had denounced sphere-of-influence and balance-of-power concepts, calling instead for a new era of peace backed by the collective security of the United Nations, an organization open to all democratic nations. Yet in practice the United States maintained a near hegemony over Central and South America (through the instrument of military dictatorships in most cases). It was true that free elections in East Europe would result in anti-Soviet governments, but it was equally true that free elections in Latin America probably would bring power to anti-American governments.

This inner contradiction was recognized by some leading Americans. In May 1945 Stimson talked on the telephone with his assistant, John J. McCloy, about how to square the American sphere of influence in the Western hemisphere with the United Nations concept. Stimson and McCloy agreed that allowing the Soviets to form a sphere of influence in East Europe would raise the risk of war and destroy the effectiveness of the U.N. They also agreed that American domination of Latin America should be preserved. "I think," said Stimson, "that it's not asking too much to have our little region over here which never has bothered anybody." McCloy felt "we ought to have our cake and eat it too: . . . we ought to be free to operate under this regional arrangement in South America, at the same time intervene promptly in Europe; we oughtn't to give away either asset." The United States, successfully, insisted that the U.N. Charter make provision for regional security groupings, which in practice meant a continuation of American influence in Latin America.

The country was not willing to give Stalin a quid pro quo in East Europe. Truman's attitude toward the Polish issue was a compound of many elements. In terms of domestic politics, there were millions of Americans of East European parentage, along with countless Catholic voters, who were enraged by Soviet actions, and Truman had to take their views into account. Churchill was bombarding the President with hard-line telegrams, and Truman had great respect for the Prime Minister. Harriman, the man on the spot in Moscow, had persuaded Truman that no matter how tough the United States got, the Russians would have to yield, for without American aid they could never reconstruct. Truman had recently been briefed on the Manhattan Project, where the atomic bomb was nearing completion, which added to his sense of power. Certainly ideology cannot be ignored. Men like Truman, Harriman, and Kennan were appalled by Russian brutality and Communist denial of the basic Western freedoms.

Truman, Harriman, and others viewed the United States as the chief defender of Western civilization. There were racist undertones to the policy, because insofar as the term Western civilization applied to the colored peoples of the world it meant white man's rule. Western Europe's day was over or ending, and the only white men left to take over in Southeast Asia and the Pacific as well as to hold the line in East Europe were the Americans. But again, most of all, Americans of all classes and shades of opinion were outraged by the Russian actions in East Europe.

Of all the ingredients in the policy mix—such as anti-Communism, the equating of Stalin with Hitler, economic motives, and concerns over military security and democracy—the element that gave body to it all was a sense of awesome power. By every index available, save that of men in arms, the United States was the strongest nation in the world. Many Americans, including leading figures in the government, believed that they could use their power to order the world in the direction of democratic capitalism on the American model.

But it could not be, for a reason that most Americans did not like to think about, seldom discussed, and frequently ignored. This was the simple fact that however great America's military and productive power was, it had limits. Six percent of the world's people could not run the lives of the remaining 94 percent. In practice this led to restraints on what America tried to do—for example, America's disapproval of Stalin's actions in East Europe was always verbal, and no troops ever set forth on a crusade to liberate Poland. But caution in action led to a general frustration, felt not only by millions of ordinary Americans but by the President himself. Truman had unprecedented power at his fingertips and a program for the world that he believed was self-evidently good. Yet he could not block Soviet expansion.

American influence would never be as great as American power. Over the next two decades American leaders and the American people were forced to learn that bitter lesson. American power was vaster than anyone else's, but in many cases it was not usable power and thus could not be translated into diplomatic victory. Vietnam would be the ultimate proof of America's inability to force others to do as she wished, but the process began much earlier, in 1945, with Truman's attempt to shape the course of events in East Europe.

Truman rejected the do-nothing advice of Stimson, Kennan, Leahy, and Marshall at the April 23, 1945, policy conference. Instead, he adopted the get-tough policy of

Harriman and Forrestal, primarily because he accepted their view that the Soviet Union was a barbaric nation bent on world conquest. But although he insisted on making an issue out of Poland, he never felt that Poland was important enough to risk World War III. Truman did not threaten to use force to impose his views. In part, this was because he still thought he could make Stalin behave by applying economic pressure. The world was weary of war, the American people were demanding demobilization, and the Red Army in Europe was too powerful for Truman even to consider war. He was, therefore, following a policy that was doomed to failure because the President would be satisfied with nothing less than 85 percent. Given Truman's view of the Soviet Union and his desire to spread American ideals and influence around the globe, he felt he could demand no less. But Stalin would not retreat and the Grand Alliance broke up. Resources that might have been used to reconstruct a war-torn world went instead into new armaments.

On May 8, 1945, Truman suddenly revealed the main outline of America's plan to use economic pressure to force compliance with its demands. On V-E Day he signed an executive order that terminated lend-lease shipments to America's allies and he placed an embargo on all shipments to Russia and other European countries. Some ships headed for Russia were turned around and brought back to port for unloading. There had been no warning to either Russia or Britain, the two principal recipients, and both countries had been planning their reconstruction on the basis of a continuation of lend-lease. In a grand understatement, Secretary of State Stettinius, then in San Francisco for the U.N. organizational meeting, said the order was "particularly untimely and did not help Soviet-American relations." Stalin was irate, and Truman sent Harry Hopkins to Moscow to pacify him. It was Hopkins's job to explain to Stalin that the whole thing was a terrible mistake. Truman countermanded his lend-lease order and the flow of supplies resumed.

Stalin accepted the explanation, but as Stettinius's remark indicated, the mistake was not one of policy but one of timing. The United States had no intention of continuing to send supplies to either Russia or Britain once she no longer needed their help in the Pacific war. Even the manner in which lend-lease shipments were resumed showed as much, for only material that would be used against Japan was sent. No supplies that could be used for reconstruction were put on the cargo ships. What Stettinius found "incredible" was not the termination of lend-lease itself but that America had revealed the policy change before the Soviets declared war on Japan.

In the end the policy of applying economic pressure, pursued so actively, failed. In January 1945 Stalin had asked for a $6-billion loan. The State Department refused to discuss the request unless, as Harriman put it, Stalin became more receptive to American demands in Europe. Aid should go to the Soviets, Harriman said, only if they agreed to "work cooperatively with us on international problems in accordance with our standards. . . ." Later in 1945 the Soviets asked for a $1-billion loan. The United States government "lost" the request. When it was finally "found," months later, the State Department offered to discuss the loan if the Soviets would pledge "non-discrimination in international commerce," allowing American investment and goods into the Russian sphere of influence. Stalin rejected the offer. Instead the Soviets announced a new five-year plan to rebuild heavy industry and to ensure "the technical and economic independence of the Soviet Union." The Russians would rebuild through forced savings at home, at the expense of their own citizens, and by taking whatever they could move out of the areas in East Europe they occupied.

In his discussions with Stalin on Poland, Hopkins could not influence the Soviet dictator. The United States had to recognize the Russian puppet government or break relations, so in June Truman accepted the inevitable and the United States established relations with the Communist government of Poland. America continued to try to force Poland to accept, as the State Department put it, "a policy of equal opportunity for us in trade, investments and access to sources of information," but there was never any chance that the policy would succeed. America had suffered what she considered to be a major defeat, which caused much resentment and was not forgotten.

Hopkins's other major task was to ensure Soviet entry into the Pacific war. On May 28 he jubilantly cabled Truman, "The Soviet Army will be properly deployed on the Manchurian position by August 8th." There was, naturally, a price. Stalin expected Truman to see to it that Chiang would keep the promises Roosevelt had made at Yalta; in return Stalin would support Chiang's leadership in China. President Truman had no objections. Hopkins also said Stalin expected to share in the occupation of Japan and he wanted an agreement with the Anglo-Americans to establish zones of occupation in Japan, a demand to which Truman did not reply. Such an agreement could, however, be worked out at Potsdam, where the Big Three had arranged to meet in July 1945.

At Potsdam, Truman said, his "immediate purpose was to get the Russians into the war against Japan as soon as possible," for he realized that "Russia's entry into the war would mean the saving of hundreds of thousands of American casualties." American lives could be saved, however, only by substituting for them Russian lives, which Stalin was not going to sacrifice for nothing. Truman recognized this, which indicated that he was willing to make concessions in return for the Soviet aid, an attitude reinforced by his second objective at Potsdam, "to come out with a working relationship" with the Russians "to prevent another world catastrophe."

As soon as the meeting began, however, irreconcilable differences emerged. Truman proposed as an agenda item an agreement reorganizing the governments of Rumania and Bulgaria with a view to early free elections. Stalin instead proposed to discuss the questions of German reparations, trusteeships for Russia (among other things, he wanted a share of the Italian colonies in Africa), an end to the Franco regime in Spain, and a settlement of Poland's western frontier on the Oder-Neisse line, with a liquidation of the London government-in-exile. Arguments went on and on, with some minor agreements reached, but nothing important could be settled. Everyone did as they pleased in the areas they controlled and disapproved of what the other side was doing.

Snipping and jabbing were the hallmarks of Potsdam. The Russians had given the Poles administrative control of eastern Germany. Truman and Churchill protested that Polish control meant the forced evacuation or death of millions of Germans, as well as a unilateral decision by Russia to bring another occupying power into Germany. Stalin shrugged off their criticism, saying that all the Germans had already left the territory and that the frontier had been determined at Yalta, neither of which was true. The Soviets wanted to participate with Turkey in the control of the Black Sea straits. Truman proposed an international guarantee that the straits would be open to all nations at all times, as a substitute for fortification or Russian participation in the control of the straits. Molotov asked if the Suez Canal were to be operated under such a principle. Churchill said the question of Suez had not been raised. Molotov retorted, "I'm raising it." Churchill explained that the British had operated Suez for some seventy years without complaints. Molotov replied that there had been many complaints: "You should ask Egypt."

The major issue at Potsdam was Germany. At Yalta the Big Three had agreed to divide Germany into four zones (one to the French), with each area governed by the local military commander. Together, the generals formed the Allied Control Council (A.C.C.) which would lay down rules for reuniting Germany. The A.C.C. would be governed by a rule of unanimity, a rule that proved disastrous for reunification, since the Anglo-Americans wanted one outcome, the French and Russians another. England and the United States aimed to create a politically whole Germany that would have self-sufficient industry; the other two occupying powers wanted to keep Germany divided and weak. No reconciliation of such divergent views was possible and at Potsdam none was really attempted. The

Americans did agree that German industry should not exceed a certain level, but within less than a year they violated the agreement.

Potsdam did try to deal with the problem of German reparations. Since the United States had already indicated that it would not continue lend-lease after the war nor extend a loan to the Soviet Union, for Stalin the question of German reparations was crucial. Geography was against him, however, because the prime industrial area of Germany, the Ruhr, was in the British zone. His advantage was that the Ruhr could not feed itself and he controlled the major agricultural regions of Germany. In the end a deal was made: The West recognized the Oder-Neisse line as Germany's eastern border, and Stalin accepted 25 percent of German capital equipment from the Western zones as his share of reparations. Fifteen percent of this figure was to be in exchange for food from eastern Germany. Stalin also got carte blanche on reparations from the Russian zone, which he quickly stripped.

Perhaps more important than the agreements and arguments at Potsdam was the attitude Truman took back to the White House. At Potsdam, he later recorded, he learned that the only thing the Russians understood was force. He decided he would no longer "take chances in a joint setup with the Russians," since they were impossible to get along with. The immediate result of this decision was Truman's determination "that I would not allow the Russians any part in the control of Japan. . . . As I reflected on the situation during my trip home, I made up my mind that General MacArthur would be given complete command and control after victory in Japan." In the Pacific, at least, Truman was going to ask for, and get, more than the 85 percent he said he wanted.

The successful test of the atomic bomb, which took place while the President was at Potsdam, encouraged him to take a harder line. The notion was widespread in high American governmental circles that American possession of the atomic bomb would, in Stimson's words, result in "less barbarous relations with the Russians," or as Byrnes put it in June 1945, the bomb "would make Russia more manageable in Europe."

The bomb, coupled with the financial position the United States enjoyed, gave Truman and his chief advisers a feeling of awesome power. From Potsdam on, the bomb was the constant factor in the American approach to the Soviet Union. The new policy was aptly described by Stimson as wearing "this weapon rather ostentatiously on our hip," which he himself later came to admit had fed "their suspicions and their distrust of our purposes and motives. . . ."

The bomb appeared to be a godsend to the Americans. They could impose their will on any recalcitrant nation merely by threatening to use it. Stopping aggression would be simplicity itself—just drop the bomb. America could retain a powerful position in Europe without having to maintain a mass army there. One of the great fears in American military circles was that, having smashed Germany, the West now had to confront the Red Army, and the only nation capable of doing so was the United States. But in the United States domestic political realities precluded the maintenance of a large, conscripted, standing army in postwar Europe. The Republican Party, soon to take control of Congress, meanwhile had made it clear that taxes had to be cut and the budget balanced. The administration would have neither the men nor the money to engage actively in war.

The bomb seemed to solve all these problems. America could fight a cold war without demanding any sacrifices of her citizens. The Red Army was neutralized, even overcome. America's leaders hoped that through a judicious use of financial credit and the veiled threat of the bomb the United States could shape the postwar world. In the fall of 1945 Truman met with de Gaulle, who was worried about the intentions of General Lucius Clay, head of the American occupation zone in Germany, to reunify Germany and to raise its levels of production. De Gaulle was also concerned about the Red Army in Central Europe. Truman off-handedly remarked that there was nothing to fear. If any nation did become aggressive, he explained, the United States would use the atomic bomb to stop it.

The strategy would later be called massive retaliation. The trouble with it was that even as early as 1945 it bore little relation to reality. The atomic bombs of the 1945–49 period were not powerful enough to deter the Russians, nor did America have enough of them to institute a true massive retaliation program. These truths were only gradually realized by the politicians but they colored the military situation from the beginning. Even had the U.S. Air Force been able to deliver all the bombs available in 1947 or 1948, they were hardly sufficient to destroy Russia.

Should the Russians realize the West's worst fears and march across the Elbe, the most that bombs could achieve would be retaliation on principal Russian population centers, which would kill tens of thousands but which would not hamstring the Russian war machine. Stalin could match American destruction of Moscow with Soviet occupation of Western Europe. The Red Army was just as effective a deterrent as the atomic bomb.

There was a psychological as well as a military problem involved in massive retaliation. Whatever the limitations on the bomb, the world regarded it as the ultimate weapon, an attitude the American press and politicians encouraged. In the end this backfired since it meant the bomb could only be used in the most extreme situation imaginable. It was easier for the United States to threaten to use the bomb to punish aggression than to find an aggression serious enough to justify its use. When in 1948 the Communists took over Czechoslovakia, for example, no responsible American official thought the outrage serious enough to start dropping bombs on Moscow, but because the United States had put its faith in the bomb there were no other tools available to punish the aggressor. The United States, therefore, could do nothing. This helplessness had been clear, in fact, as early as 1945.

American possession of the bomb had no noticeable effect on Stalin's policy in East Europe. He and Molotov continued to do as they pleased, refusing to hold elections or to allow Western observers to travel freely in East Eu-

rope. At Foreign Ministers' meetings the Russians continued to insist that the West had to recognize the puppet
governments in East Europe before peace treaties could be
written. Byrnes's hope that the bomb would "make Russia
more manageable" proved abortive, and by the summer of
1946 both sides had accepted the fact of a divided Europe.

Russian mistrust of the West, added to Stalin's determination to maintain a tight grip on his satellites, had grown
so great that Molotov refused to consider seriously Secretary of State Byrnes's proposal that the Big Four powers
sign a treaty unifying Germany and guaranteeing German
demilitarization, an offer sincerely made and one that represented the best hope of solving the German problem.
Instead, the Soviets stopped removing machinery from East
Germany and began instead to utilize the skilled German
manpower to produce finished goods in their zone, goods
they then shipped to the Soviet Union. On May 3, 1946,
meanwhile, General Clay unilaterally informed the Russians that they could expect no more reparations from the
Western zones. Later that year, at Stuttgart, Secretary Byrnes
gave a highly publicized speech in which he announced
that Germany must develop exports in order to become
self-sustaining. Byrnes said the Germans should be given
primary responsibility for running their domestic affairs
and allowed to increase their industrial productivity (policies Clay had already been putting into practice), and emphasized that the American presence in Central Europe
would not be withdrawn.

Solutions acceptable to both East and West were hard to
find in 1946. This impasse applied especially to the atomic
bomb. Whatever the limitations on the size and number of
nuclear weapons in the first half decade of the atomic age,
it was obvious that the growth potential was almost unlimited. Control of the bomb was crucial to the future welfare
of the world. How to get the weapon under control was
not so clear. On the one hand, the United States had a
monopoly, something no nation would ever give up lightly.
On the other hand, all the atomic scientists agreed that it
was only a question of time before the Soviets developed

the bomb. If the Russians got atomic weapons on their own, and if they continued to be treated as just another military weapon to be used by sovereign nations as they saw fit, the world would live in continual terror.

What made a solution especially difficult was the postwar atmosphere in which America and Russia made their proposals for atomic control. There were almost daily crises in Germany among the occupying powers. Tension dominated the Middle East, reaching its peak in Iran and Turkey. According to the terms of a 1942 occupation treaty, the Russians were required to withdraw their forces from Iran six months after the end of the war. They refused to do so because Stalin wanted oil concessions from the Iranian government. To apply pressure, the Russians supported a revolt in northern Iran. As the crisis moved forward, Byrnes sent a strong note (March 6, 1946) to Moscow demanding immediate Russian withdrawal. Three weeks later Iran and the U.S.S.R. announced that the Soviet occupation troops would be pulled out of northern Iran and that a joint Iranian-Soviet oil company would be formed by treaty, subject to ratification by the Persian parliament. On May 6 the Russians withdrew; early in 1947 the parliament rejected the oil-company treaty.

The reaction to this major Soviet diplomatic defeat illustrated how far apart the former allies had drifted. To the Russians it seemed only fair that they be allowed to participate in the exploitation of Iranian oil. To be forced out showed that the West was up to its old tricks of encircling the Soviet Union and doing everything it could to keep it weak. To the Americans the crisis proved once again that the Soviets were bent on world conquest.

Churchill interpreted these and other events for the benefit of the American public on March 5, 1946, in a speech at Fulton, Missouri, with Truman on the platform beside him. Churchill declared that "from Stettin in the Baltic to Trieste in the Adriatic, an iron curtain has descended across the Continent." He wanted to lift that curtain, to liberate East Europe, and to hold the Russians back elsewhere, as in Iran and Turkey. He suggested that a fraternal association of the English-speaking peoples, operating outside the United Nations, should do it. Their tool would be the atomic bomb, which Churchill said "God has willed" to the United States alone.

Churchill's speech did not help American efforts, then being undertaken, to find an acceptable solution to international control of the bomb. Stalin reacted with the full fury of a wounded animal at bay. He compared Churchill and his "friends" in America to Hitler, charging that like Hitler they held a racial theory that proposed world rule for the English-speaking peoples. Stalin said Churchill's speech was "a call to war with the Soviet Union." He reminded the West that twice in the recent past Germany had attacked Russia through East European countries that had "governments inimical to the Soviet Union." Within three weeks of Churchill's iron curtain speech the Soviets rejected membership in the World Bank and in the International Monetary Fund, announced the start of a new five-year plan designed to make Russia self-sufficient in the event of another war, built up the pressure on Iran, and mounted an intense ideological effort to eliminate all Western influences within the Soviet Union.

But Stalin was no more ready for war than Truman, as events in Turkey showed. The issue there was control of the Dardanelles. In August 1946 Stalin demanded of the Turks equal partnership in running the Straits. This participation was an ancient Russian dream. But Under Secretary of State Dean Acheson interpreted the demand as a Soviet attempt to dominate Turkey, threaten Greece, and intimidate the remainder of the Middle East. He advised a showdown. Truman agreed: "We might as well find out whether the Russians were bent on world conquest now as in five years or ten years." The United States told the Turks to stand firm. To back them up, Truman sent the most modern American aircraft carrier through the Straits. The Soviets backed down.

In this atmosphere of threat and counterthreat, bluff and counterbluff, achieving workable international control of atomic weapons was almost hopeless. Still, the Americans tried. On March 16, 1946, the United States released a plan, the Acheson-Lilienthal proposal, which called for international control to be reached through a series of stages. The proposal was an honest attempt to avoid the horrors of a world in which Russia and the United States rattled nuclear-tipped sabers at each other. It did not, however, satisfy the Soviets, for during the transitional stages the Acheson-Lilienthal proposal reserved to the United States full control of its own bombs. "Should there be a breakdown in the plan at any time during the transition," Acheson declared, "we shall be in a favorable position with regard to atomic weapons." The Soviets, meanwhile, would not be allowed to develop their own bomb.

Given the tension in Soviet-American relations, it was unthinkable that the United States could go further in sharing the bomb; it was equally unthinkable that the Russians could accept. The Soviet counterproposal called for an end to the production and use of atomic weapons and insisted on the destruction within three months of all existing stocks of atomic bombs. Only then would they discuss international control.

No way could be found out of the impasse. In April 1946 Truman appointed Bernard Baruch, financier and adviser to Presidents, as the American delegate to the U.N. Atomic Energy Commission. Baruch thought the Acheson-Lilienthal proposal had gone much too far because it contained no reference to Russia's veto power. Baruch wanted majority rule at all stages, which meant that the Soviets could not veto the use of the bomb against themselves if violations were discovered, nor could they prevent inspection teams roaming at will through their country. It could hardly have been expected that they would accept Baruch's proposal.

Baruch, however, insisted upon the elimination of the veto. He was backed by Army Chief of Staff Eisenhower, who advised him that only through effective international control of atomic energy could there be any hope of preventing atomic war, but who also insisted that national security required that methods of such control be tested and proven before the United States gave up its monopoly. "If we enter too hurriedly into an international agreement to abolish all atomic weapons," Eisenhower pointed out, "we may find ourselves in the position of having no restraining means in the world capable of effective action if a great power violates the agreement." He warned that the Russians might deliberately avoid the use of atomic weapons and undertake aggression with other—but equally decisive—weapons.

This was the central dilemma for the United States in its efforts to get some international control of atomic energy before it was too late, an issue more important by far than the veto or inspection. The question Eisenhower raised was straightforward enough: If the United States gave up the atomic bomb, how could it stop the Red Army? The only alternatives to American possession of the bomb were to build up a mass army or get the Russians to demobilize, and in 1946 there was little chance of doing either one. Both sides made various concessions but neither would back down on the crucial points. America insisted on retaining the bomb until it was satisfied with the effectiveness of international control, and the Russians would not give up the veto.

The only hope of eliminating the bomb, which in the political atmosphere of 1946 was never very great, was gone. America would not give up its monopoly as long as the Red Army was intact and the Russians would never demobilize as long as the Americans had the bomb. In a relatively short period of time the Russians would have their own bomb; eventually the United States would be maintaining a large standing army. An arms race unprecedented in the world's history would be under way. This would force a qualitative change in American foreign policy and in international relations generally. Every crisis would strike terror into the hearts of people everywhere. There would be no security, no defense. Much of American foreign policy after Baruch's proposal had been a search for a viable method of using the bomb to achieve overseas goals. The bomb had already failed America once, in East Europe, where the Soviets refused to behave. How effectively it could be used elsewhere remained to be seen. Russian probes toward Iran and Turkey had been met and stopped. By the end of 1946 spheres of influence in Europe were clearly drawn, but elsewhere what belonged to whom was uncertain. Perhaps, as with Iran and Turkey, there would have to be a confrontation at each point around the world until the line was drawn and accepted everywhere. The Cold War would meanwhile continue to be fought under the shadow of the mushroom-shaped cloud.

[5]

The Truman Doctrine and
the Marshall Plan

At the present moment in world history nearly every nation must choose between alternative ways of life. . . . One way of life is based upon the will of the majority, and is distinguished by free institutions, representative government, free elections, guarantees of individual liberty, freedom of speech and religion, and freedom from political oppression. The second way of life is based upon the will of a minority forcibly imposed upon the majority. It relies upon terror and oppression, a controlled press and radio, fixed elections, and the suppression of personal freedoms. I believe that it must be the policy of the United States to support free peoples who are resisting attempted subjugation by armed minorities or by outside pressures.

HARRY S TRUMAN
March 12, 1947

There are limits to the extent that even the most powerful nation can project its influence beyond its borders. In a democracy one of the most important limitations is the mood on the domestic scene, which involves both a general perception of a need to exert influence and a willingness to make the sacrifices required to generate usable power. In the United States, at the beginning of 1947, neither was present. If there was no retreat to isolation as in 1919, there was a popular feeling that America could handle her foreign problems through possession of the atomic bomb. In November 1946 the Republicans had won control of Congress by emphasizing a modified version of Warren Har-

ding's return to normalcy—demobilization, business as usual,
a cutback in the role and spending of the government, and
lower taxes. These domestic facts severely restricted the
Truman Administration's ability to carry on the Cold War.

By the beginning of 1947 the United States had almost
completed the most rapid demobilization in the history of
the world. The Army had been cut from 8 million to 1
million men; the Navy from 3.5 million to less than 1 million; the Air Force from over two hundred to less than fifty
effective combat groups. As General Marshall later recalled, "I remember, when I was Secretary of State I was
being pressed constantly, particularly when in Moscow
[March, 1947], by radio message after radio message to
give the Russians hell. . . . When I got back, I was getting
the same appeal in relation to the Far East and China. At
that time, my facilities for giving them hell—and I am a
soldier and know something about the ability to give hell—
was 1⅓ divisions over the entire United States. That is quite
a proposition when you deal with somebody with over 260
and you have 1⅓."

Foreign policy and military policy were moving in opposite directions. Truman and his advisers wanted to meet
the Communist challenge wherever it appeared, but except
for the atomic bomb they had nothing with which to meet
it. Stimson and Forrestal, among others, urged Truman to
stop the demobilization process by dramatically warning
the nation about the scope of the Soviet threat. In January
1946 Secretary of the Navy Forrestal advised the President
to call in "the heads of the important news services and the
leading newspapers . . . and state to them the seriousness
of the present situation and the need for making the country aware of its implications abroad." Throughout 1946 he
pressed Truman, but the results were meager, for Truman
wanted a balanced budget and was enough of a politician
to realize that the public would not support higher taxes
for a larger military establishment.

Simultaneous with the decrease in military force there
was an increasing fear in Washington of the scope and
nature of the Soviet threat. In a speech at the National War

College in mid-1947 William C. Bullitt of the State Department neatly summed up the attitudes then dominant in Washington. "The Soviet Union's assault upon the West is at about the stage of Hitler's maneuvering into Czechoslovakia," he asserted, which immediately linked Stalin with Hitler. "The final aim of Russia is world conquest," which outlined the scope of the problem. The Soviet method, however, differed from Hitler's and was potentially more dangerous. Because of the American atomic monopoly, the Russians would not inaugurate large-scale war but would rather avoid armed conflict while advancing their aims through internal subversion.

Since the challenge was worldwide, it had to be met everywhere, at once. As one step Bullitt advocated a "European Federation of Democratic States" in order to "face up to Russia." He was thinking primarily in terms of a military organization, under American leadership, supplied with American arms. Meeting the Russian threat by arming Europeans was in practice a continuation of the wartime policy of lend-lease. Another part of the response was to provide economic and technical aid to threatened nations. There was general agreement in the American government that Communism thrived on chaos and poverty; the way to respond to it was to promote stability and prosperity through economic aid.

At the end of 1946 most discussion of the optimum American response to the Soviet challenge revolved around three possibilities: build up America's own military resources; send military aid to threatened nations; give economic and technical assistance to needy peoples. These proposals were not mutually exclusive, and most officials wanted a combination of the three, with an emphasis on one. All rested on Bullitt's assumptions about the nature of the threat, and all would cost money.

The Republican Congress controlled the money and it saw no pressing reason to spend it on any of those courses. Neither did a majority of the American people. In January 1947 there was a popular feeling that postwar tensions with the Russians were easing, based primarily on the completion of peace treaties signed by the Big Three with the Eastern European countries that had fought alongside Hitler. These treaties constituted a practical recognition by the United States of the Soviet sphere of influence in East Europe, for they all were signed with Communist satellite governments. Robert Taft, a prominent Republican in the Senate and leader of the drive for economy in government, expressed the current mood when he objected to any attempt by the administration to divide the world into Communist and anti-Communist zones, for "I do not want war with Russia." The Democrats accused Taft—and other Republicans who resisted joining a crusade against Communism—of isolationism, but despite the negative connotations of the label there was no denying that a majority of the American people did not want to embark on a crusade.

To obtain the economic and military resources to carry out an aggressive foreign policy, Truman had to convince the bulk of the voters of the reality and magnitude of the Soviet threat. To do that, he needed a dramatic issue. Greece stood near the top of the list of potential trouble spots. Great Britain had been supporting the Royalist government there, but a severe storm in January 1947 had raised havoc with an already weak British economy and underscored the impossibility of Britain's continuing to play a leading world role. As early as September 1946 the American government had quietly prepared programs for military aid for Greece. In January 1947 the State Department sent an economic mission to Greece to see what could be done, and in February the Department began intensified planning to provide military aid. The United States was prepared to move into Greece whenever the British pulled out.

In January 1947 Secretary of State Byrnes resigned; his successor was General Marshall. Marshall's first task was to prepare for a meeting of the Council of Foreign Ministers in Moscow to begin on March 10, and he was spending most of his time on the German problem, the main issue on the agenda of the Moscow conference.

While Marshall prepared for Moscow, events in Greece

rushed forward. In January 1947 Truman sent the Greek government an offer to provide advisers and funds for a program of economic stabilization. The Greek government had already complained in the United Nations that the insurgents were receiving outside assistance, and a U.N. mission had gone to Greece to investigate. Truman had sent his own agent to make a report. The damaged British economy, meanwhile, made it increasingly doubtful that Britain could maintain its forty thousand troops in Greece. On February 3 the American Ambassador in Athens reported a rumor that the British would be pulling out soon. On February 18 Truman's personal representative in Greece cabled that everything pointed to an impending move by the Communists to seize the country, and two days later the American Embassy in London reported that the British Treasury could give no further aid to Greece. The stage was set.

On February 21, 1947, the British Ambassador to the United States informed the State Department that London would no longer provide aid to Greece or Turkey. Britain would pull out by the end of March. To Secretary Marshall this "was tantamount to British abdication from the Middle East with obvious implications as to their successor." Within five days the State Department had consulted with the War Department, held meetings of its own, and was ready to move. Under Secretary Dean Acheson took the lead, as Marshall was busy preparing for the Moscow conference. On February 26 Truman, Marshall, and Acheson met to discuss the result of the studies of the experts.

Acheson made the presentation. He emphasized that if Greece were lost, Turkey would be untenable. Russia would move in and take control of the Dardanelles, with the "clearest implications" for the Middle East. Morale would sink in Italy, Germany, and France. Acheson was describing what would later be called the domino theory, which held that if one nation fell to the Communists, its neighbors would surely follow. In this case, Acheson said one rotten apple would infect the whole barrel. Put in those terms, the administration had no choice but to act vigorously and quickly. Truman felt, he later told his Cabinet, that "he was faced with a decision more serious than had ever confronted any President," which took in quite a lot of ground and was in any case overly dramatic in its implications, for it implied that he was tossing in bed at night trying to decide what to do. Actually, he had long since made the decision and the real task was to sell the program to Congress.

On February 27 Truman called in the congressional leaders of both parties, with the exception of Senator Taft, leader of the isolationists, who was not invited. Instead Truman concentrated on Senator Arthur Vandenberg, a Republican "isolationist turned internationalist" who, as chairman of the Senate Foreign Relations Committee, was one of architects of the bipartisan foreign policy. Truman described the Greek situation in dark terms, then said he wanted to ask Congress for $250 million for Greece and $150 million for Turkey. Most, if not all, of what he said was news to the Congressmen, but the way in which he outlined the issues, coupled with Vandenberg's support for the policy, won them over.

During the following weeks the State, Navy, and War Departments worked out the details of the aid program while Vandenberg and the other congressional leaders built support in Congress for the new policy. Not until March 7 did Truman go before his Cabinet to explain developments; there, perhaps unexpectedly, he found some opposition. Although Forrestal wanted a full mobilization for the struggle with the Russians, others were not so convinced. The Secretary of Labor objected to pulling British chestnuts out of the fire. Someone wondered if it was good policy to support the corrupt, inefficient, right-wing Greek government. Most of all, however, the Cabinet was concerned about the way the public would receive such a sharp break with America's historic foreign policy, especially as it promised to be so expensive. As Truman laconically put it in his *Memoirs,* "There was considerable discussion on the best method to apprise the American people of the issues involved."

The State Department, meanwhile, was preparing a message for Truman to deliver to the Congress and the nation. He was unhappy with the early drafts, for "I wanted no hedging in this speech. This was America's answer to the surge of expansion of Communist tyranny. It had to be clear and free of hesitation or double talk." Truman told Acheson to have the speech toughened, simplified, and expanded to cover more than just Greece and Turkey. Truman's strategy was to explain aid to Greece not in terms of supporting monarchy but rather as part of a worldwide program for freedom.

George Kennan saw one of the revised drafts. Kennan had risen in prestige and power in the State Department since the end of the war and Marshall had just named him head of a new Policy Planning Staff. His rise was due in part to a seven-thousand-word telegram which he sent from Moscow, warning of the Soviet Union's postwar intentions. The warning was well received. Truman read it, and Forrestal had it reproduced and made it required reading for thousands of senior officers. Kennan's analysis provided the intellectual justification for a policy of containment, and Kennan was widely understood in Washington to be the father of that policy.

Despite all this, Kennan was upset when he read the speech Truman was to deliver to the Congress. First, he saw no need for any military aid to Turkey, where no military threat existed. So too in Greece—Kennan was all for helping the Greek government but thought it should be done through political and economic aid. In his view the Soviet threat was primarily political. Kennan was also upset at the way in which Truman had seized the opportunity to declare a worldwide, open-ended doctrine, when what was called for was a simple declaration of aid to a single nation. Truman was preparing to use terms, Kennan later remarked, "more grandiose and more sweeping than anything that I, at least, had ever envisaged." Kennan protested, but to no avail. He was told that it was too late to change the speech.

The point Kennan had missed was the need to rally the public in support of a policy that broke sharply with America's past. Kennan was not a politician—in fact he had hardly been in the United States through most of his adult life—while Truman was *the* expert on domestic politics. Like the President, Kennan wanted to stop the Communists, but he wanted to do so in a realistic way, at little cost, and with minimal commitments. Truman realized that he could never get the economy-minded Republicans—and the public that stood behind them—to shell out tax dollars to support the king of Greece. Truman had to describe the Greek situation in universal terms, good versus evil, to get support for containment.

On March 10, the day the Moscow conference opened, Truman completed preparation of the ground for his speech by calling in, once again, the congressional leaders. This meeting was larger than the earlier one, and this time Senator Taft was among those present. He listened quietly as Acheson and Truman talked for two hours. Vandenberg "expressed his complete agreement" with the new policy. Bipartisanship had won; everything was ready. At 1:00 P.M. on March 12, 1947, Truman stepped to the rostrum in the hall of the House of Representatives to address a joint session of the Congress. The speech was also carried on nationwide radio. Truman asked for immediate aid for Greece and Turkey, then explained his reasoning: "I believe that it must be the policy of the United States to support free peoples who are resisting attempted subjugation by armed minorities or by outside pressures."

The statement was all-encompassing. In a single sentence Truman had defined American policy for the next generation. Whenever and wherever an anti-Communist government was threatened, by indigenous insurgents, foreign invasion, or even diplomatic pressure (as with Turkey), the United States would supply political, economic, and most of all military aid. The Truman Doctrine came close to shutting the door against any revolution, since the terms "free peoples" and "anti-Communist" were thought to be synonymous. All the Greek government, or any dictatorship, had to do to get American aid was to claim that its opponents were Communist.

It has often been noted that Americans expect their wars to be grand heroic crusades on a worldwide scale, a struggle between light and darkness with the fate of the world hanging on the outcome. The Truman Doctrine met that requirement. At one of the meetings between the President and the congressional leaders, Vandenburg had warned Truman that if he wanted the public to support containment, he would have to "scare hell out of the American people." Truman did. He painted in dark hues the "totalitarian regimes" that threatened to snuff out freedom everywhere. The time had come, he said, when "nearly every nation must choose between alternative ways of life." The President escalated the long, historic struggle between the Left and the Right in Greece for political power, and the equally historic Russian urge for control of the Dardanelles, into a universal conflict between freedom and slavery. It was a very broad jump indeed.

It was also brilliant. There were outbursts of protest. Walter Lippmann, dean of the newspaper columnists, attacked Truman for bypassing the United Nations and for the open-ended nature of his pledge of assistance. Lippmann also questioned the wisdom of helping the reactionary Greek government. Some Congressmen resented the crisis treatment to which they had been subjected—Truman talked as if there had been another Pearl Harbor. A British diplomat was surprised by the "enormous hullaballoo" that accompanied the speech and by the fact "that the policy of aid to Greece was made to seem hardly less than a declaration of war on the Soviet Union." But despite the protests, the plain fact was that Truman had struck a responsive chord with the majority of his countrymen. As they had done on December 7, 1941, so again on March 12, 1947, the American people rallied behind their leader in a cause that transcended national, economic, social, and military interests: the cause of freedom itself.

On May 15, 1947, Congress appropriated $400 million for Greece and Turkey. By later standards the sum was small, but nevertheless America had taken an immense stride. For the first time in its history the United States had chosen to intervene during a period of general peace in the affairs of peoples outside North and South America. The symbolic act could not have been more significant. The commitment had been made. It would take years to persuade Congress and the public to provide all the enormous funds needed for the new policy, but having accepted the premises of the Truman Doctrine there would be no turning back.

Simultaneous with the announcement of the Truman Doctrine, the Moscow conference of foreign ministers failed—indeed, it was doomed before it began. Positions on Germany had hardened. Neither the Americans nor the Soviets had any intention of working toward a peace treaty with Germany and German reunification, except on their own terms, which they knew in advance were unacceptable to the other side. All anyone could do at Moscow was issue propaganda.

The immediate situation in Europe was acute. When Marshall returned from Moscow he reported that "the patient [Europe] is sinking while the doctors deliberate." "Agreement was impossible" at Moscow, Marshall reported in a radio talk to the nation on April 28, because the Soviet proposals "would have established in Germany a centralized government adapted to the seizure of absolute control." As General Clay later put it, "the principal result was to convince the three foreign ministers representing the Western Powers of the intransigence of the Soviet position." This in turn "led them to work more closely together in the future," which meant it speeded the process of unifying the Western zones and bringing western Germany into the budding alliance against the Soviets.

While in Europe Marshall had been shaken by the seriousness and urgency of the plight of Western Europe, where economic recovery from the ravages of war had been slow. Total economic disintegration appeared to be imminent; the great storm in Britain had only emphasized the danger. The Secretary of State's discussion with the Russians, according to Kennan, "had compelled him to recognize, however reluctantly, that the idea of approaching the solution to Europe's problems in collaboration with the Russians was a pipe dream." Stalin, Marshall had concluded, wanted the European economy to come crashing down.

The Truman Doctrine had cleared the way for a massive American aid program to Europe. Marshall ordered Kennan and the Policy Planning Staff to draw one up. Round-the-clock meetings began. The general aim was to revive the economy of Western Europe, which was imperative for both economic and military reasons. As Acheson explained, American exports were running at $16 billion a year, imports at less than $8 billion. Most of the exports went to Europe. If the Europeans were to pay for them, they had to have dollars, which they could only get by producing goods America could import. Otherwise, America's export market would dry up. Militarily, only with a healthy economy could Europe support the troops necessary to stop the Red Army.

The key was Germany. To get European production rolling again, Germany's coal mines and steel mills had to be worked at maximum capacity. Kennan emphasized this point, saying "it is imperatively urgent today that the improvement of economic conditions and the revival of productive capacity in the west of Germany be made the primary object of our policy . . . and be given top priority." It would have been absurd to expect the Russians to cooperate in the revival of Germany without themselves controlling the Ruhr, and indeed Kennan had no such expectations. The problem was that if the United States went ahead on its German program, the division of Europe would be complete, and responsibility for the split would rest with the United States.

There would be no progress in Europe without including Germany, and there could be no improvement in Germany without antagonizing the Russians. What to do about the Soviets thus became a prime consideration. Kennan insisted that the United States should "play it straight" by inviting the Russians to participate in any Europe-wide recovery program. "We would not ourselves draw a line of division through Europe." He recognized the dangers. "What if," he himself asked, "the Russians spiked it" by accepting the invitation and "trying to link it to Russian participation in the administration of the Ruhr?" Kennan's answer was straightforward: "In that case I think we can only say 'no' to the whole business as pleasantly and firmly as we know how. . . ."

Even in making an offer to the Russians, Kennan wanted strict controls. He insisted that the Russians would have to open their economic records for American scrutiny, and he wanted the East European economy integrated into that of Western Europe. Despite Marshall's famous sentence stating that the policy was "directed not against any country or doctrine but against hunger, poverty, desperation and chaos," in fact Kennan and the State Department did not want Soviet participation and did all they could to prevent it while making it appear that a genuine offer was being made.

Kennan applied the same formula in a more general way to the Soviet satellites. Insofar as they were free to accept the American offer and integrate their economies into those of the West, Kennan was willing to offer them aid. He insisted, however, that it be done in such a way that they would "either exclude themselves by unwillingness to accept the proposed conditions or agree to abandon the exclusive orientation of their economies."

A final aim of Kennan's Policy Planning Staff was "to correct what seemed to us to be the two main misimpressions that had been created in connection with the Truman Doctrine." These were the notions that America's foreign policy was a defensive reaction to Communist pressure, and that the Doctrine was a blank check to give aid to any area of the world threatened by the Communists. Truman was more nearly correct, however, in stating that the Doctrine and the Marshall Plan "are two halves of the same walnut." The emphasis in Greece and Turkey was military, while initially in West Europe it was economic, but both were designed to contain the Soviets.

On June 5, 1947, speaking at Harvard University, Marshall announced his plan. The general proposals, like the man himself, were high-minded. He recognized the Continent-wide nature of the problem. Marshall recalled the disruption of Europe's economy because of the war and the destructive rule of the Nazis. Europe could not feed itself, so it was using up scarce foreign credits to buy food. If the United States did not provide help, "economic, social and political deterioration of a very grave character" would result, with serious consequences for the American economy. The assistance should not be piecemeal but "should provide a cure rather than a mere palliative." He asked the European nations to gather themselves together, draw up a plan, and submit it to the United States.

The reaction in Western Europe was enthusiastic. Even traditional fears of Germany quieted. Although Marshall had made it clear that "the restoration of Europe involves the restoration of Germany," the French were anxious to go ahead, for the Marshall Plan tied Germany to Western Europe generally and offered vast sums to everyone. French Foreign Minister Georges Bidault began meetings in Paris. He neglected to invite the Russians to participate, but pressure from the powerful French Communist Party made him change his mind. On June 26 Molotov arrived in Paris with eighty-nine economic experts and clerks, which indicated that the Russians were seriously considering the proposal, as indeed they had to. As the American Ambassador to Moscow, General Walter B. Smith, said, "they were confronted with two unpalatable alternatives." They were afraid of a Western bloc and realized that "to refrain from participation in the Paris Conference would be tantamount to forcing the formation of such a bloc." On the other hand, if they joined up, "they would create the possibility of a certain amount of economic penetration by the western democracies among the satellite states."

Molotov spent three days at the conference, most of it on the telephone talking to Stalin in Moscow. He finally proposed that each nation establish its own recovery program. The French and British refused. They insisted on following the American line of making the program Europewide. Molotov angrily walked out, warning that a revived Germany would dominate Western Europe, and that the

Plan would divide "Europe into two groups of states." He returned to Moscow, where within a week the Soviets announced a "Molotov Plan" for their satellites. The Poles and Czechs, who had wanted to participate in Paris, had to inform the West that they could not join the Marshall Plan because "it might be construed as an action against the Soviet Union."

All that remained was for the Western Europeans to work out the details of a plan and for the American Congress to accept it. At the end of August the sixteen Western European nations represented at Paris presented a plan calling for $28 billion over a four-year period. After thorough examination the Truman Administration accepted the program and Truman presented it to Congress on December 19, although he reduced the proposed amount to $17 billion.

Despite the reductions, the Plan faced a hostile Congress, and 1948 was a Presidential election year. Some Republicans did not want to give Truman a major diplomatic triumph or throw American dollars away. They called the Plan a gigantic "international W.P.A.," a "bold Socialist blue-print," and a plain waste of American money. But Vandenberg ardently championed the bill. In presenting it to the Senate he called it a "calculated risk" to "help stop World War III before it starts." The area covered by the Plan, he declared, contained "270,000,000 people of the stock which has largely made America. . . . This vast friendly segment of the earth must not collapse. The iron curtain must not come to the rims of the Atlantic either by aggression or by default." Administration witnesses before Congressional committees considering the Plan underscored Vandenberg's emphasis on containment. They pointed out that a rejuvenated Europe could produce strategic goods that the United States could buy and stockpile, preserve Western control over Middle Eastern oil supplies, and free Europeans from economic problems so they could help the United States militarily.

Indeed, as Walter LaFeber has pointed out, the Plan offered all things to all people. Those who feared a slump in exports and a resulting depression within the United States could envision a continued vigorous export trade; those who thought Communist expansion would result from economic chaos saw salvation in an integrated, healthy European economy; those who thought the real threat was the Red Army fairly drooled at the thought of reviving Germany and then rebuilding the Wehrmacht. For the humanitarian the Plan offered long-term aid to war-torn Europe.

Still the Plan met intense opposition. Senator Taft proclaimed that American money should not be poured into a "European T.V.A." Like many of his Republican colleagues, he was deeply disturbed at European steps toward socialism, and he feared that the Europeans might use Marshall Plan money to nationalize basic industries, including American-owned plants. The Republican-dominated Congress would not budge. Committee meetings ground on, with no results.

All in all, 1947 had been a frustrating year for the new foreign policy. In Greece guerrilla warfare raged on despite increased American military assistance to the government. The Chinese Communists continued to push Chiang back. Russia retained her grip on East Europe; indeed, she strengthened it, for immediately after Molotov left the Paris Conference he announced the formation of the Communist Information Bureau (Cominform), a replacement for the old Communist International, abolished during World War II. In Hungary the Soviets purged left-wing anti-Communist political leaders, rigged the elections on August 31, 1947, and destroyed all anti-Communist opposition. Truman had been forced by the Republicans and the public generally to call off the peacetime drafting of young men into the armed services and demobilization continued, which left the administration with inadequate tools to pursue the policy of containment.

Truman was even unable to achieve unification of the armed forces, a proposal designed to make them more efficient and cheaper. In July 1947 Congress finally passed the National Security Act, which provided for a single Department of Defense to replace the three independently run services, gave statutory status to the Joint Chiefs of Staff, established a National Security Council to advise the President, and created a Central Intelligence Agency to gather information and to correlate and evaluate intelligence activities around the world. Truman appointed the leading anti-Communist in his Cabinet, Forrestal, as the first Secretary of Defense, but the act as a whole fell far short of what he, Marshall, and Army Chief of Staff Eisenhower had wanted. They had envisioned the creation of a single armed force, small but efficient, that could move quickly to trouble spots or be expanded rapidly through the draft. Instead they got a loosely federated system with an independent Air Force, and no draft.

The Air Force doctrine was to punish misbehavior through strategic bombing, including the atomic bomb, which made the new service popular with Congress, since massive retaliation seemed a cheap way of providing for national defense. Taft and some other Senators indicated that they were nearly ready to abolish the Army and Navy and concentrate funds on the Air Force. This doctrine, however, did not fit in at all with containment; mass bombardment from the air clearly was not an effective answer to the problems raised in Greece or Hungary or even China. It did appear to be a good way to protect the United States from any mass assault, which indicated that its proponents were retreating to isolation and had not fully accepted the doctrine of containment, with its implication of an active military policy around the world.

The alternative to an American armed force that could stand up to the Communists was one manned by Europeans, but this too had so far failed. The Greek government and army showed scarcely any improvement. In Western Europe, proposing the Marshall Plan had helped to draw a line across the Continent, but the unwillingness of Congress to appropriate money had left the area much too weak to support any sizable armed forces. The last, faint hope of redeeming Eastern Europe through the economic policies of the Marshall Plan had gone aglimmering when Molotov walked out of the Paris Conference. Indeed, the Molotov Plan and the Cominform had made the situation worse.

The Marshall Plan had now become the keystone to containment, and on January 2, 1948, Truman tried to get some action from Congress by dropping the $17 billion request and asking instead for $6.8 billion to cover the first fifteen months of the Plan's operation. He got no immediate response.

Then came the Communist coup in Czechoslovakia.

Soviet and American troops had jointly occupied Czechoslovakia after the war. Both sides pulled out on December 1, 1945, although the Soviets kept a number of divisions on Czechoslovakia's borders. Czechoslovakia was, in addition, caught between Poland and eastern Germany on the north and Hungary on the south, which made Soviet influence there pervasive.

In May 1946 Czechoslovakia held her first postwar elections. The Communists won 38 percent of the vote and Klement Gottwald, who had spent World War II in Moscow, became the Prime Minister. Neither the President, Eduard Benes, nor the Foreign Minister, Jan Masaryk, were Communist, and both were greatly admired in the West. They tried to maintain a balance between East and West, but the polarization of Europe—particularly after the Paris Conference—made the success of their policy increasingly doubtful. The end came in February 1948 when Gottwald refused to cooperate with Benes on a plan to reorganize the police and the Cabinet broke up. Gottwald issued an ultimatum for a new government under his power and a Soviet mission flew to Prague to demand Benes' surrender. On February 25, 1948, Benes capitulated and the Communists assumed control. Two weeks later they assassinated Masaryk.

The Czechoslovakian coup did two things absolutely necessary for the adoption of the containment policy. First, as Truman noted, it "sent a shock throughout the civilized world." Americans had regarded Czechoslovakia as a model democracy. Nearly everyone remembered, and discussed, Hitler and Munich. It seemed the same play was about to be performed, ten years later, with new actors. Second, the coup dramatically illustrated the limitations of current American policy, for not only could the United States do nothing to help save Czechoslovakia, it was doing nothing to prevent similar occurrences in the remainder of Europe.

Events now began to rush forward. On March 5, 1948, Clay sent a telegram from Germany. Although "I have felt and held that war was unlikely for at least ten years," the General began, "within the last few weeks, I have felt a subtle change in the Soviet attitude which . . . gives me a feeling that it may come with dramatic suddenness." The Soviet officials in Germany had adopted a new attitude, "faintly contemptuous, slightly arrogant, and certainly assured." On March 11 Marshall described the situation as "very, very serious." Three days later the Senate endorsed the Marshall Plan by a vote of 69 to 17.

In Washington, London, and Paris there was a real war scare. In Europe, France, Britain, and the Benelux countries held a series of meetings in Brussels and on March 16, 1948, signed the Brussels Union, pledging mutual defense arrangements. In the United States Averell Harriman warned: "There are aggressive forces in the world coming from the Soviet Union which are just as destructive in their effect on the world and our own way of life as Hitler was, and I think are a greater menace than Hitler was."

On March 17 Truman, noting "the grave events in Europe . . . moving so swiftly," canceled an engagement in New York and instead went before Congress. The President declared that the Soviet Union was the "one nation" that was blocking all efforts toward peace. America must, he said, meet "this growing menace . . . to the very survival of freedom." He welcomed the Brussels Treaty and promised to extend American aid to the signatories "to help them to protect themselves."

Truman asked for an immediate favorable vote in the House on the Marshall Plan, but that was only a beginning. He also wanted a resumption of selective service. Even after the Czech coup, however, Congress was not willing to respond wholeheartedly to a call to arms. The House gave Truman the Marshall Plan on March 31 (although it appropriated $4 billion, not the $6.8 billion Truman had requested), but it refused to resume the draft.

The Czech coup had another immediate result with immense long-range consequences. At the end of the war Truman had abolished the O.S.S., on the grounds that a Gestapo-like organization was incompatible with American traditions and values. In 1947 Truman had agreed to the creation of the Central Intelligence Agency (C.I.A.) as part of the National Defense Act of that year, but the C.I.A. was not given authority to carry out covert operations abroad. It was restricted to gathering and analyzing intelligence. After the Czech coup Forrestal set about raising money from his Wall Street friends to create a private clandestine organization to carry out covert actions abroad. Allen Dulles, Deputy Director of the new C.I.A., insisted that his organization had to have exclusive control of any such activities. In June 1948 the Truman Administration authorized the C.I.A. to engage in a broad range of covert operations directed against the Soviet Union and Communists elsewhere, including political and economic warfare and paramilitary activities.

The immediate fear was the upcoming election in Italy. The Communist Party was strong there, and thanks to the Russians it had plenty of money to spend in the campaign. The C.I.A. countered by placing a few million dollars in the hands of the anti-Communist Christian Democrats, who ended up winning the election. This result, quite naturally, delighted the C.I.A. and impressed the administration. To have kept Italy out of Communist hands for a relatively minuscule amount of money was a great bargain.

The C.I.A. was off and running, to the eventual dismay of the two men most responsible for giving it a covert mission, Kennan and Truman. Kennan had thought that the C.I.A. might intervene in an occasional European election; in 1975 he confessed to a Congressional committee, "It did not work out at all the way I had conceived it." And in

1963, Truman himself had said, "I never had any thought that when I set up the C.I.A. that it would be injected into peacetime cloak-and-dagger operations." Truman's lament was disingenuous, however. He wanted to contain the Communists, and like his successors, he found it convenient to turn the unsavory aspects of the job over to the C.I.A. and then not ask embarrassing questions.

Congressional action on the draft, meanwhile, had indicated that the politicians would not use American boys to contain the Russians. The implementation of the policy of containment was still in debate. One of the administration's promises about the Marshall Plan, however, had been that it would strengthen Europe's economy to the point where the Europeans could man their own barricades. With invaluable assistance from Soviet actions in Czechoslovakia, the administration had gotten agreement on a policy. The Truman Doctrine and the Marshall Plan had set forth some of the details of containment in Europe. The rest could now be worked out. Events in Berlin would help speed the process.

Containment Tested

We are going to stay, period.

HARRY S TRUMAN

In July 1947, when George Kennan's influence within the government was at its peak, he published an article in the journal *Foreign Affairs* entitled "The Sources of Soviet Conduct" and signed only "By X." Its author was soon widely known; its reception nothing short of spectacular. It quickly became the quasi-official statement of American foreign policy.

Kennan argued that the Soviets were motivated by two beliefs: (1) the innate antagonism between capitalism and socialism, and (2) the infallibility of the Kremlin. Their goal was world conquest, but because of the Soviet theory of the inevitability of the eventual fall of capitalism they were in no hurry and had no timetable. The Kremlin's "political action is a fluid stream which moves constantly, wherever it is permitted to move, toward a given goal. Its main concern is to make sure that it has filled every nook and cranny available to it in the basin of world power."

Kennan was an intellectual and he filled the X article with qualifications, although he would later complain that he had not qualified sufficiently and that therefore his article had been misread. He did not believe the Russians posed any serious military threat nor that they wanted war. The challenge Kennan saw was a political and economic one, which should be met on those grounds by "long term, patient but firm and vigilant containment."

The sentence in Mr. X's article that was most frequently quoted, however, and the one that became the touchstone of American policy, declared that what was needed was "the adroit and vigilant application of counter-force at a series of constantly shifting geographical and political points, corresponding to the shifts and maneuvers of Soviet policy." This implied (and most readers thought this was what Kennan meant) that crisis would follow crisis around the world, as the Soviet-masterminded conspiracy used its agents to accelerate the flow of Communist power into "every nook and cranny." It also implied that the threat was military, which made it the responsibility of the United States to meet and throw it back wherever it appeared. Containment meant building up the military strength of America and her allies, and a willingness to stand up to the Russians wherever they applied pressure.

The first test came in Berlin. It had been expected, for the Americans, knowing in advance what the Russian reaction would be, had pushed ahead with plans to join together the three Western German zones. Because neither of the superpowers dared let the other control all of Germany, the Americans had decided to abandon all pretense of unifying Germany and accept its division into two parts. In June 1948 the Western powers indicated that they intended to go ahead with the formation of a West German government.

Simultaneously, the American Joint Chiefs proposed a military alliance with the Brussels powers. They urged the establishment of a central military command for the new organization with an American supreme commander. At the time there were about twelve ill-equipped and poorly trained divisions in all Western Europe; military plans called for a withdrawal to the Pyrenees if the Red Army marched. The Joint Chiefs wanted eighty-five divisions, which was almost as many as the United States had mobilized for World War II, and they could obviously be had only through extensive rearmament of Western Europe. Unspoken but implicitly understood by everyone involved in the discussions was the fact that the only way to get the required number of men in arms was to use German troops. Because of British, Benelux, and especially French fears, however, this could not be broached at once. The first step was to form a Western Union without Germany but at the same time continue efforts toward West German independence.

Even in the United States, acceptance of the program would not be easy. There were three major objections: the cost; the abandonment of America's historic position of no entangling alliances; and doubts about the wisdom of rearming the Germans. Truman would need all the help he could get. Senator Vandenberg responded handsomely. In early June 1948 he introduced a resolution in the Senate that encouraged "the progressive development of regional and other collective arrangements" for defense and promised to promote the "association of the United States" with such organizations. Vandenberg explicitly repudiated the idea that the United States should help in building up a sizable force-in-being. On June 11 the Vandenberg Resolution breezed through the Senate by a vote of 64 to 4.

At the beginning of the summer of 1948 the Soviets were thus faced with a series of what they considered threatening developments. The Marshall Plan was beginning to draw the Western European nations closer together. France, Britain, and the Benelux nations had signed a military pact that the United States had officially welcomed and had indicated it intended to join. Americans were already beginning to talk of bringing others into the proposed organization, among them Canada, Portugal, Denmark, Iceland, Norway, and Italy. Since these countries could contribute little or nothing to ground defense, the Soviets judged that the Americans wanted them included in order to use their territory for air and sea bases. Equally ominous was the Western determination to give independence to West Germany. In the long run this could only mean that the West intended to merge West Germany into the proposed anti-Soviet military organization.

Adding to Stalin's difficulties, Marshal Tito in Yugoslavia struck out on an independent course—breaking decisively with Stalin. Truman extended American economic aid to Tito, thus widening the split in the supposedly monolithic Communist bloc. Stalin tried to topple Tito, failed, and in despair expelled Yugoslavia from the Cominform. The example Tito had set, however, could not be so easily dismissed.

Soviet foreign policy, based on an occupied and divided Germany, a weakened Western Europe, and tight control of East Europe, faced total collapse. Whether Stalin had expansive plans is unclear and at least doubtful, but what had happened threatened the security of the Soviet Union itself. The victor in the war was being hemmed in by the West, with the vanquished playing a key role in the new coalition. Worst of all was the Western listening post and outpost in the heart of the Soviet security belt, the Western sector in Berlin.

Stalin responded by arguing that since the West had abandoned the idea of German reunification, there was no longer any point to maintaining Berlin as the future capital of all Germany. The Western powers, through the logic of their own acts, ought to retire to their own zones. The Russians clamped down a total blockade on all ground and water traffic to Berlin. The British joined the Americans in a counterblockade on the movement of goods from the east into western Germany.

In the West there was sentiment to abandon Berlin. For many, it seemed foolish to risk World War III for the sake of the ex-Nazis, especially since there was some force to Stalin's argument that if the West was going to create a West German nation it had no business staying in eastern Germany. Clay and Truman quickly scotched such talk. As Clay told the War Department, "We have lost Czechoslovakia. Norway is threatened. We retreat from Berlin. When Berlin falls, western Germany will be next." Then all Europe would go Communist. The Americans felt they could not give an inch. Marshall declared, "We had the alternative of following a firm policy in Berlin or accepting the consequences of failure of the rest of our European policy," a statement that described equally well Stalin's feelings. Truman provided the last word in a succinct, simple declaration: "We are going to stay, period."

Clay wanted to shoot his way through the Russian blockade. He thought the United States might just as well find out immediately whether the Russians wanted war or not. Given the ten-to-one disparity of ground strength in Europe, Army Chief of Staff Omar Bradley was able to convince Truman that there must be a better way. It was found with air transport, which soon began flying round-the-clock missions into Berlin, supplying up to thirteen thousand tons of goods per day. In an amazing performance American flyers undertook to supply a great city completely from the air, and somehow managed to do it. The Berlin airlift caught the imagination of the world and made the Russians look absolutely awful as they tried to starve out women and children.

The war scare continued. On July 15 the National Security Council decided to send two groups of B-29s to Britain; B-29s were known around the world as the bombers that carried atomic weapons. In his diary Forrestal noted the rationale: (1) it would show the American public "how seriously the government . . . views the current sequence of events"; (2) it would give the air force experience and "would accustom the British" to the presence of the U.S. Air Force; and (3) "we have the opportunity *now* of sending these planes, and once sent they would become somewhat of an accepted fixture," whereas if America waited, the British might change their minds about the wisdom of having American bombers on their soil.

On July 21 Forrestal formally requested that Truman turn over custody of the bomb to the air force so that the generals could decide when and where to use it. At the time the civilian Atomic Energy Commission (A.E.C.) controlled the bomb. A.E.C. head David Lilienthal objected to Forrestal's request on the grounds that the atomic bomb was not simply another weapon. Truman agreed, saying "the responsibility for the use of the bomb was his and that was the responsibility he proposed to keep."

So the military did not get everything out of the crisis that it wanted, but it had made giant strides. The principle of American forward bases in Europe had been established; it was obvious that if they were to be effective they would have to be scattered and that there would have to be more of them. Meanwhile, the need for a closer military connection with Western Europe had been emphasized. The draft was reintroduced and the army began to build up. To Kennan's great discomfort the economic orientation of the Marshall Plan had been nearly forgotten, as containment took on a narrow military look.

Truman, triumphant after his reelection (foreign policy had not been an issue between the major parties in the 1948 campaign), pledged in his Inaugural Address to aid those European nations willing to defend themselves, while the new Secretary of State, Dean Acheson, pushed forward a treaty with the Europeans. On April 4, 1949, the North Atlantic Treaty was signed in Washington. Britain, France, Belgium, the Netherlands, Italy, Portugal, Denmark, Iceland, Norway, Canada, and the United States pledged themselves to mutual assistance in case of aggression against any of the signatories.

The NATO Treaty signified the beginning of a new era. In the nineteenth century America had broken the bonds of a colonial, extractive economy and become a great industrial power thanks in large part to private European loans. In the first forty-five years of the twentieth century the United States had gradually achieved a position of equality with Europe. The Marshall Plan, followed by NATO, began in earnest an era of American military, political, and economic dominance over Europe.

In the spring of 1949 Truman enjoyed success after success. NATO was followed by a victory in Berlin—on May 12 the Russians lifted the blockade. They had decided—as Clay had felt they would—that the counterblockade was hurting them more than they were injuring the West, and they realized there was no longer any hope of stopping the movement toward a West German government (the Bonn Republic came into being on May 23, 1949).

It had been a good spring for the President, but trouble lay ahead. The end of the war scare, combined with the fear that NATO was going to cost a good deal of money, began to put an end to bipartisanship in foreign policy.

The old issues, buried since Truman's dramatic speech on Greece, reemerged. Should the United States be a world policeman? How much should it pay to play such a role? And, at bottom, what was the nature and extent of the Soviet threat and how should it be met? Thoughtful Republicans, led by Senator Taft, began to question the wisdom of provoking the Soviets thousands of miles from America's shores. In the committee meetings to consider ratification of the NATO Treaty, Congressmen began to ask embarrassing questions about the purpose of NATO.

Senator Henry Cabot Lodge wanted to know if NATO was the beginning of a series of regional organizations designed to hem in the Russians. Acheson reassured him by stressing that no one in the administration contemplated following NATO with "a Mediterranean pact, and then a Pacific pact, and so forth." Other Senators wondered why the United States did not rely upon the United Nations. One reason was the Russian veto; another was that the Europeans required some sort of special guarantee. Acheson explained that "unity in Europe requires the continuing association and support of the United States. Without it free Europe would split apart."

All these arguments had appeal, but serious questions remained. Could not as much be accomplished through the Marshall Plan? Why permanently split Europe, thereby abandoning all hope of ever reopening relations with East Europe? What was the substance of the military guarantees that Americans were making or supporting?

The last question was crucial. The West already had adequate power with the atomic bomb. NATO as it stood added nothing to this power. The ground figures remained the same, with the Russians enjoying a ten-to-one advantage. Did the Secretary of State plan to send "substantial" numbers of American troops to Europe? Acheson responded, "The answer to that question, Senator, is a clear and absolute 'No.' " Did he plan to put Germans back in uniform? "We are very clear," Acheson replied, "that the disarmament and demilitarization of Germany must be complete and absolute."

This deepened the mystery rather than clarifying it. What would NATO do? The problem, as French Premier Henri Queuille put it in a much-quoted statement, was easily described: "We know that once Western Europe was occupied, America would again come to our aid and eventually we would again be liberated. But the process would be terrible. The next time you probably would be liberating a corpse." The solution was not so easily seen. In the absence of an imminent attack, neither the Europeans nor the Americans were remotely prepared to undertake the rearmament effort on the required scale to match the Red Army. The Europeans were unwilling to jeopardize their economic revival by building new standing armies.

Each side was trying to carry water on both shoulders. In order to persuade their peoples of the necessity of accepting a provocative alliance, the governments had to insist that the alliance could defend them from invasion. But the governments also had to simultaneously insist that no intolerable sacrifices would be required. As Robert Osgood noted, "these two assurances could only be fulfilled, if at all, by the participation of West Germany in the alliance, but for political reasons this measure was no more acceptable to the European countries than a massive rearmament effort."

German rearmament was also politically unacceptable in the United States, and the administration continued to insist that it had no intention of encouraging a German buildup. Nor, the Senators were assured, would NATO lead to an arms race or require the Americans to provide military material to the Europeans. Taft was still opposed to the Treaty but was persuaded to vote for it after the Senate specifically repudiated any obligation either to build up the armed forces of the eleven allies or to extend to them continued economic aid for the twenty-year period covered by the Treaty. The Senate then ratified the NATO pact by a vote of 84 to 12.

On July 23, 1949, Truman signed the North Atlantic Treaty. It marked the high point of bipartisanship and of containment in Europe. It also completed one phase of the revolution in American foreign policy. America had entered an entangling alliance. American security thereafter could be immediately and drastically affected by changes in the overseas balance of power over which the United States could not exercise much effective control. It meant that the United States was guaranteeing the maintenance of foreign social structures and governments for the next twenty years. It committed the United States to close peacetime military collaboration with the armed services of foreign nations. It signified the extent both of America's break with her past and of her determination to halt Communist expansion.

The presence of Italy (and later Greece and Turkey) among the members of the alliance made a misnomer of the words "North Atlantic" in the title; Portugal's presence weakened the assertion that it was an alliance in defense of democracy. Even weaker was the claim that NATO represented a pact between equals, for the United States had no intention of sharing the control of its atomic weapons with its NATO partners, and the bomb was the only weapon that gave NATO's military pretensions validity. Acheson's denials to the contrary notwithstanding, the Treaty paved the way for German rearmament. It also underscored the European orientation of Truman's foreign policy, an orientation for which he would soon have to pay a price.

First, however, it was the Senate's turn to pay. On the very day that the President signed the NATO Treaty he presented the bill to Congress. All the assurances that the Treaty would not inaugurate an arms race or cost the United States anything were brushed aside. Truman sent to Congress a Mutual Defense Assistance Bill asking for $1.5 billion for European military aid. The President described the object in modest terms: "The military assistance which we propose for these countries will be limited to that which is necessary to help them create mobile defensive forces"; in other words, to equip and bring up to strength Europe's twelve or so divisions.

There was immediate opposition. Such a limited program would hardly give a "tangible assurance" to the peo-

ples of Western Europe that they would be protected from
the Red Army. The Military Assistance Program of 1949
was, obviously, only a small down payment on a large, long-
term investment. Senator Taft and other skeptics said this
would never do, for the military assistance would be large
enough only to provoke the Russians and precipitate an
arms race without being adequate to halt the Red Army.
Taft charged that the administration was committing the
United States to a futile, obsolete, and bankrupt strategy
of defending Europe by large-scale land warfare. He much
preferred a unilateral American defense of Europe through
building up the American air force and stepping up the
production of atomic bombs.

This got to the heart of the matter, for in point of fact
the meaning of NATO was that the United States promised
to use the bomb to deter a Russian attack. The only alternative was to build up Western ground strength to match
the Red Army, a politically impossible task.

The United States's promise to use the bomb to deter
Russian aggression made sense only if the Americans had
bases in Europe from which to deliver the bombs and if
the Americans retained their nuclear monopoly. The great
need was bases for American bombers, which was the first
and most important accomplishment of NATO. This, however, could have been accomplished through bilateral
agreements and did not require a multinational treaty; it
also did not require military aid to the NATO countries.
Opposition to Truman's Military Assistance Program continued.

Then, on September 22, 1949, the President announced
that the Soviets had exploded an atomic bomb. "This is
now a different world," Vandenberg painfully recorded.
It was indeed. The urge to do something, anything, was
irrepressible. Six days later Congress sent the NATO appropriations to the President for his approval. Truman
ordered the development of the hydrogen bomb accelerated. Nothing, however, could change the fact that America's promise to defend Europe with the bomb had been
dissipated almost before it had been given. If the Russians

could make the bomb, they surely could develop the means to deliver it, first to Western European targets and then to the United States itself. The Soviets now had two trumps, the bomb and the Red Army, to the West's one.

German remilitarization and Western European rearmament was the obvious way to counter the Red Army threat. The Americans could pay the bill, in an updated version of lend-lease. But the Europeans were suspicious, and France especially so. Europeans could see little point in accepting American arms if it also meant accepting American orders, the central problem in NATO both then and later. A strategy that uses American equipment and European lives to counter the Red Army has little appeal to the Europeans, especially since only the Americans can decide when or where to use the troops, only the Americans can pull the nuclear trigger, and the battlefield where Russia and America fight it out is Europe.

If the Europeans would not rearm, the Americans would have to do so themselves. Here the problem, as Samuel Huntington stated it, was "Could a democracy arm to deter or could it only arm to respond?" An election year was coming up. The House was changing Truman's tax-revision bill into a tax-reduction bill. The Soviet threat was largely theoretical—the Red Army had not marched beyond the position it held in May of 1945, not even into Czechoslovakia. How much support, if any beyond what they were already paying, would the American people give to a policy of deterrence designed to forestall a threat that could only with difficulty be seen to endanger American security? Billions of dollars would be needed. Even if the taxpayers agreed to pay the bill, could the economy afford it? These were serious questions, but so were the ones on the other side. Could America afford not to rearm? Would not the failure to do so automatically abandon Western Europe to the Communists? It seemed to many in the government that it would.

In Asia the problem had reached crisis proportions. Mao's troops were on the verge of driving Chiang off the mainland. American support for Chiang had been limited and halting, partly because of the Europe-first orientation of the Truman Administration, mainly because of the budget ceilings within which the Congress forced the government to operate. That Chiang could have been "saved," that one of the great historic events of the century could have been reversed by a few million or even billion more dollars of aid, is one of the will-o'-the-wisps popular among the Asia-first wing of the Republican Party. It is patent nonsense. The point was, however, that millions of Americans believed that more aid would have saved Chiang. A great nation had been "lost" to Communism because Congress was stingy.

This widespread attitude underscored one of the basic assumptions of American foreign policy during the Cold War. Americans high and low implicitly assumed that with good policies and enough will, the United States could control events anywhere. If things did go wrong, if Poland or China did fall to the enemy, it could only happen because of mistakes, not because there were areas of the world in which what America did or wanted made little difference. The assumption that in the end every situation was controllable and could be made to come out as the United States wished—what Senator William Fulbright later called "the arrogance of power"—colored almost all foreign-policy decisions in the early Cold War. It also prepared the way for the right-wing charge that the Truman Administration was shot through with traitors, for there could be no other explanation for American failures.

The roots of the assumption were deep and complex. The American belief that the United States was different from and better than other countries was part of it. American success in 1917–1918 and 1941–1945 contributed to the conceit that the United States could order the world. So did the awesome feeling of power that came with a monopoly of the atomic bomb, American productivity, and the American military position at the conclusion of World War II. There were racial connotations to the idea. Although most Americans were too sophisticated to talk about the "white man's burden" and the "little brown brothers," they still believed in white superiority.

Given all the power America had at her disposal, given American goodwill, and given the eagerness of peoples everywhere to follow the American example, how could it be that East Europe and China fell to the Communists? The junior Senator from Wisconsin, Joseph R. McCarthy, had one answer. On February 9, 1950, in a speech at Wheeling, West Virginia, he declared, "I have in my hand 57 cases of individuals [in the State Department] who would appear to be either card-carrying members or certainly loyal to the Communist Party, but who nevertheless are helping to shape our foreign policy." A few days later the figure had gone up to 205 Communists in the Department; at another time the figure was 81. The charge, however, was consistent—America had been betrayed.

McCarthy's charges came less than eight weeks after Chiang fled to Formosa, five days before the Soviet Union and Communist China signed a thirty-year mutual-aid treaty, and three weeks before Klaus Fuchs was found guilty of giving atomic secrets to agents of the Soviet Union. The last was, perhaps, the most important cause of the spectacular popularity of McCarthy and of the forces he represented, for it seemed to be the only explanation of how the backward Russians matched America's achievements in atomic development so quickly. McCarthyism swept the country. The Republicans suddenly had an issue that could bring them, after twenty years ("twenty years of treason," according to McCarthy), back to power.

McCarthy never had a majority of the public behind him, but he nevertheless enjoyed broad support, and the threat he represented was real. The Federal government, to fight back, strengthened and extended its loyalty investigations. At times it seemed that everyone in America was checking on everyone else for possible Communist leanings. Millions of Americans agreed with McCarthy's basic premise— America had failed in the Cold War not because of inherent limitations on her power, nor because of her refusal to rearm, but because of internal treason. Even those public figures who did speak out against McCarthy, and their numbers were few, objected to his methods, not his assumptions. The opponents also wanted to ferret out the guilty, but they insisted that the rights of the innocent should be protected.

There was an Alice in Wonderland quality to the entire uproar. Truman Administration officials, up to and including Acheson, had to defend themselves from charges that began with their being soft on Communism and escalated to treason. The Democrats were bewildered and angry. With some justice, they wondered what more they could have done to stand up to the Russians, especially in view of the funds available, funds drastically limited by the very Republicans who now demanded blood for the State Department's shortcomings. Chickens had come home to roost. From the time Truman had "scared hell out of the American people" in March of 1947 to the explosion of the Russian bomb and the loss of China, Democratic officials in the State Department had been stressing the worldwide threat of Communism along with the danger of internal subversion in foreign governments. McCarthy and his adherents followed the same path, only they went further along it.

There was in McCarthyism an appeal to the inland prejudice against the eastern-seaboard establishment and the things it stood for in the popular mind—the New Deal, among others. Antiintellectualism was always prominent in the movement. McCarthy drew strong support from those Asia-firsters who had been opposed to the trend of American foreign policy, with its European orientation, at least since the early days of World War II. Americans of East European origin were among the first to flock to McCarthy's standard; much of the Catholic Church in America came with them. Above all, McCarthy provided a simple answer to those who were frustrated as America seemed to suffer defeat after defeat in the Cold War.

One of the appeals of the McCarthy explanation of the world situation was that it would not cost much to set things right. All that was required was to eliminate the Communists in the State Department. Few of McCarthy's supporters, and none of those like Senator Taft who tolerated him, were ready to go to war with Russia to liberate the satellites or to send millions of American troops to China to restore Chiang. They did want to root out those who had sold out America at Yalta, Potsdam, and in China; then, with honest patriots in the State Department, world events would develop in accordance with American wishes.

The Administration could not accept such a limited program for the Cold War, but it too wanted the same results. It was difficult, however, to develop a comprehensive program in this atmosphere of fear, even hysteria. Nevertheless, something had to be done. China had been lost. Russia did have the bomb. The Europeans were not willing to assume the burden of rearmament. The McCarthy assault was there. The United States had practically no usable ground power. And the President, primarily for domestic political purposes, was still trying to cut the budget. His new Secretary of Defense, Louis Johnson, had set out to "cut the fat" from the Defense Department. He began by canceling the Navy's supercarrier. Truman set a limit of $13 billion for defense in the upcoming budget, by no stretch of the imagination enough to support a get-tough-with-the-Russians stance. American foreign policy had arrived at a crossroads.

On January 30, 1950, President Truman had authorized the State and Defense Departments "to make an over-all review and re-assessment of American foreign and defense policy in the light of the loss of China, the Soviet mastery of atomic energy and the prospect of the fusion bomb." Through February, March, and early April, as events whirled around it, a State-Defense committee met. By April 12 it had a report ready, which Truman sent to the National Security Council. It came back as an N.S.C. policy paper, number 68; it was, as Walter LaFeber says, "one of the key historical documents of the Cold War." N.S.C. 68, Senator Henry Jackson declared, was "the first comprehensive statement of a national strategy."

As one of the principal authors stated, N.S.C. 68 advocated "an immediate and large-scale build-up in our military and general strength and that of our allies with the intention of righting the power balance and in the hope that through means other than all-out war we could induce a change in the nature of the Soviet system." How the change was to be brought about was unclear, except that it would not be through war. N.S.C. 68 postulated that while the West waited for the Soviets to mellow, the United States should rearm and thereby prevent any Russian expansion. The program did not look to the liberation of China or of Eastern Europe, but it did call on the United States to assume unilaterally the defense of the non-Communist world.

N.S.C. 68 represented the practical extension of the Truman Doctrine, which had been worldwide in its implications but limited to Europe in its application. The document provided the justification for America's assuming the role of world policeman and came close to saying that all change was directed by the Communists and should therefore be resisted. N.S.C. 68 also assumed that if America were willing to try, it could stop change. This was satisfying to the McCarthyites, but the willingness to abandon East Europe, China, and Russia to Communism was not. The McCarthyites, however, had no very clear idea on how to liberate the enslaved peoples either.

N.S.C. 68 was realistic in assessing what it would cost America to become the world policeman. State Department officials estimated that defense expenditures of $35 billion a year would be required to implement the program of rearming America and NATO. Eventually, more could be spent, for N.S.C. 68 declared that the United States was so rich it could use 20 percent of its gross national product for arms without suffering national bankruptcy. In 1950 this would have been $50 billion.

That was a great deal of money, even for Americans. It was necessary, however, because the danger was so great. The document foresaw "an indefinite period of tension and danger" and warned that by 1954 the Soviet Union would have the nuclear capability to destroy the United States. America had to undertake "a bold and massive program" of rebuilding the West until it far surpassed the Soviet bloc; only thus could it stand at the "political and material center with other free nations in variable orbits around it." The United States could no longer ask, "How much security can we afford?" nor could it attempt to "distinguish between national and global security."

Truman recognized, as he later wrote, that N.S.C. 68 "meant a great military effort in time of peace. It meant doubling or tripling the budget, increasing taxes heavily, and imposing various kinds of economic controls. It meant a great change in our normal peacetime way of doing things." He refused to allow publication of N.S.C. 68 and indicated that he would do nothing about revising the budget until after the congressional elections. He realized that without a major crisis there was little chance of selling the program to the Congress or the public. He himself had only two and a half years to serve, while N.S.C. 68 contemplated a long-term program. If the Republicans entered the White House, the chances were that their main concern would be to lower the budget, in which case the nation would have to wait for the return of the Democrats to really get N.S.C. 68 rolling. Thus when Truman received N.S.C. 68 in its final form in early June, 1950, he made no commitment. What he would have done with it had not other events intruded is problematical.

While Truman was studying the paper, he may have noted a sentence that declared it should be American policy to meet "each fresh challenge promptly and unequivocally." If so, he was about to have an opportunity to put it into practice. The crisis that would allow him to implement N.S.C. 68 was at hand.

[7]

Korea

[An all-out war with China] would be the wrong war at the
wrong time in the wrong place against the wrong enemy.

GENERAL OMAR BRADLEY

Truman had pried the money for containment in Europe
from a reluctant Congress only with the help of the crises
in Greece and Czechoslovakia. In June 1950 he badly needed
another crisis, one that would allow him to prove to the
American people that he and the Democratic Party were
not soft on Communism, to extend containment to Asia,
to shore up Chiang's position on Formosa, to retain American bases in Japan, and most of all to rearm America and
NATO. The whole package envisioned in N.S.C. 68, in
short, could be wrapped up and tied with a ribbon by an
Asian crisis.

The possibilities were there. In China Mao's armies were
being deployed for an assault on Formosa, where the remnants of Chiang's forces had retreated. The United States
had stopped all aid to Chiang, thereby arousing the fury
of the Republicans. Truman was under intense pressure
to resume the shipment of supplies to the Nationalist Chinese.
Former President Herbert Hoover joined with Senator Taft
in demanding that the U.S. Pacific Fleet be used to prevent
an invasion of Formosa.

In Japan the United States was preparing to write a unilateral peace treaty with that country, complete with agreements that would give the United States military bases in
Japan on a long-term basis. But in early 1950 the Japanese
Communist Party staged a series of violent demonstrations
against American military personnel in Tokyo. Even mod-

erate Japanese politicians were wary of granting base rights to the American forces. The U.S. Air Force was confronted with the possibility of losing its closest airfields to eastern Russia.

In Korea all was tension. Postwar Soviet-American efforts to unify the country, where American troops had occupied the area south of the thirty-eighth parallel and Russia the area to the north, had achieved nothing. In 1947 the United States had submitted the Korean question to the U.N. General Assembly for disposition. Russia refused to go along. Elections were held anyway in South Korea in May 1948 under U.N. supervision. Syngman Rhee became President of the Republic of Korea. The Russians set up a Communist puppet government in North Korea. Both the United States and the Soviets withdrew their occupation troops; both continued to give military aid to their respective sides, although the Russians did so on a larger scale.

Rhee was a petty dictator and thus an embarrassment to the United States. In April 1950 Acheson told Rhee flatly that he had to hold elections. Rhee agreed, but his own party collected only 48 seats in the Assembly, with 120 going to other parties, mostly on the Left. The new Assembly immediately began to press for unification, even if on North Korean terms. Rhee was on the verge of losing control of his government.

Rhee's position was also tenuous because he was losing American backing, despite having held the elections. On May 2, 1950, Senator Tom Connally, Chairman of the Senate Foreign Relations Committee, said he was afraid that South Korea would have to be abandoned. He thought the Communists were going to overrun Korea when they got ready, just as they "probably will overrun Formosa." Connally said that he did not think Korea was "very greatly important. It has been testified before us that Japan, Okinawa, and the Philippines make the chain of defense which is absolutely necessary." His statement was widely reported in the United States and Japan, causing consternation in both MacArthur's headquarters in Tokyo and in Rhee's capital, Seoul. Connally's position was consistent with the entire policy of the Truman Administration to date,* but it ran counter to the thoughts just then being set down in N.S.C. 68, and with the concurrent rise of McCarthyism, the abandonment of Rhee and Chiang was rapidly becoming a political liability of the first magnitude.

By June 1950 a series of desperate needs had come together. Truman had to have a crisis to sell the N.S.C. 68 program; Chiang could not hold on in Formosa nor Rhee in South Korea without an American commitment; the U.S. Air Force and Navy needed a justification to retain their bases in Japan; the Democrats had to prove to the Mc-Carthyites that they could stand up to the Communists in Asia as well as in Europe. The needs were met on June 25, 1950, when North Korean troops crossed the thirty-eighth parallel in force.

Truman was ready with his countermeasures. Within hours of the attack he ordered MacArthur to send supplies to the South Koreans. He also sent the U.S. Seventh Fleet to the Formosan Straits to prevent a possible Chinese invasion of Formosa, and he promised additional assistance to counter-revolutionary forces in the Philippines and Indochina.

These were sweeping policy decisions. Using the Seventh Fleet to protect Formosa constituted a complete reversal of policy with respect to the Chinese civil war. Having MacArthur ship supplies to Rhee's troops carried with it the implication that the United States would defend South Korea. Among other things, the decision carried with it the possibility of the introduction of American troops into the battle, for it was already doubtful that the South Koreans would be able to hold out alone.

Since 1941 the United States had pursued a military policy of avoiding ground warfare on mainland Asia. When the country pulled out of Korea in 1948 there were no American troops stationed anywhere on the Continent. Truman was on the verge of changing the policy and extending American military power to the Asian mainland.

* Secretary of State Acheson had made identical remarks in February 1950.

N.S.C. 68 had declared that the United States must be prepared to meet "each fresh challenge promptly and unequivocally." It would have been difficult to better Truman's record in the forty-eight hours following the North Korean invasion.

On June 25, the day the attack began, the United States launched a massive diplomatic counterattack. In the Security Council she pushed through a resolution branding the North Koreans as aggressors, demanding a cessation of hostilities, and requesting a withdrawal behind the thirty-eighth parallel. The resolution's sweeping nature gave the United States the advantage of United Nations approval and support for military action in Korea. This was the first time ever that an international organization had actually taken concrete steps to halt and punish aggression (Russia failed to veto the resolution because she was boycotting the United Nations at the time because it refused to give Chiang's seat on the Security Council to Mao), and it lifted spirits throughout the country. Despite the U.N. involvement, however, the overwhelming bulk of equipment used in Korea and the overwhelming number of non-Korean fighting men came from the United States.

They came almost immediately. On June 26, the day after the assault, in a statement released at noon from the White House, the President formally extended the Truman Doctrine to the Pacific by pledging the United States to military intervention against any further expansion of Communist rule in Asia. He announced that he was extending military aid to the French, who were fighting Ho Chi Minh and the Viet Minh in Indochina, and to the Philippines, where the Huks continued to challenge the government. Truman also ordered the Seventh Fleet to "prevent any attack on Formosa," declaring that the determination of Formosa's future status "must await the restoration of security in the Pacific, a peace settlement with Japan, or consideration by the United Nations." America had thus become involved in the Chinese civil war, the Philippines' insurrection, and the war of national liberation in Indochina, in one day.

Simultaneously the United States entered the Korean

War. Truman announced that he had "ordered United
States air and sea forces to give the Korean Government
troops cover and support." His Air Force advisers had convinced him that America's bombers would be able to stop
the aggression in Korea by destroying the Communist supply lines. Truman believed that it was possible to defeat
the North Koreans without any commitment of American
ground troops, just as he evidently expected that the French
could defeat Ho Chi Minh without having to use American
soldiers.

Truman tried to limit the sweeping nature of his actions
by carefully refraining from linking the Russians to the
Korean attack. On the day of his White House announcement Truman sent a note to Moscow assuring Stalin that
American objectives were limited and expressing the hope
that the Soviets would help in restoring the status quo ante
bellum. This implied that all the United States wished to
do was to contain, not destroy, North Korea.

The underlying assumption of Truman's approach to
the war was that Communist aggression in Asia could be
stopped at a fairly low cost in lives. American money and
equipment would do the job in Indochina and the Philippines; the American Navy would save Chiang; American
bombers would force the North Koreans to pull back. Much
of this was wishful thinking. It was partly based on the
American Air Force's strategic doctrine and its misreading
of the lessons of air power in World War II, partly on the
racist attitude that Asians could not stand up to Western
guns, and partly on the widespread notion that Communist
governments had no genuine support. Lacking popularity,
the Communists would be afraid to commit their troops to
battle, and if they did, the troops would not fight.

The question of who would fight and who would not was
quickly answered. The North Koreans drove the South
Koreans down the peninsula in a headlong retreat. American bombing missions slowed the aggressors not at all. The
South Koreans fell back in such a panic that two days after
Truman sent in the Air Force he was faced with another
major decision: He would either have to send in American

troops to save the position, which meant accepting a much higher cost for the war than he had bargained for, or else face the loss of all Korea, at a time when the Republicans were screaming, "Who lost China?"

On June 30 Truman ordered United States troops stationed in Japan to proceed to Korea. America was now at war on the mainland. The President promised that more troops would soon be on their way from the United States. In an attempt to keep the war and its cost limited, he emphasized that the United States aimed only "to restore peace and . . . the border." At the United Nations the Americans announced that their purpose was the simple one of restoring the thirty-eighth parallel as the dividing line. The policy, in other words, was containment, not rollback.

It had been arrived at unilaterally, for Truman had not consulted his European or Asian allies before acting, not to mention Congress. Indeed, the unilateral nature of his response to the world crisis was always clear. Once again, as in F.D.R.'s war on the Atlantic in the summer of 1941, the United States found itself at war without the Constitutionally required congressional declaration of war.

In Korea, American reinforcements arrived just in time, and together with the South Koreans they held on in the Pusan bridgehead through June and July. By the beginning of August it was clear that MacArthur would not be forced out of Korea and that when MacArthur's troops broke out of the perimeter they would be able to destroy the North Korean Army.

In Washington there was a surge of optimism. Perhaps it was possible to do more than contain the Communists. MacArthur wanted to reunify Korea, an idea that found great favor in the White House. It would mean rollback, not containment, and thus represented a major policy change, but the opportunity was too tempting to pass up. On September 1 Truman announced that the Koreans had a right to be "free, independent, and united." Pyongyang, the Americans boasted, would be "the first Iron Curtain capital" to be liberated. This seemed to imply that others would follow.

The risks were obvious. Truman moved to minimize them by building up American military strength. Congress had voted all the funds he had requested for defense since June; on September 9 he announced that the rapid increase in the Army would continue and that he was sending "substantial" numbers of new troops to Europe. Simultaneously, Acheson met with the British and French Foreign Ministers at the Waldorf-Astoria Hotel in New York City. On September 12 he dropped—as one official called it—"the bomb at the Waldorf." The United States proposed to create ten German divisions. French and British protests were loud and numerous but Acheson insisted. To make German rearmament on such a scale palatable to the Europeans, the United States sent four divisions to Europe, and three months later Truman appointed Eisenhower, who was extremely popular and trusted in Europe, as the Supreme Commander of an integrated NATO force.

With the French and British taken care of, German rearmament under way, and Congress willing to vote funds for defense, the Truman-Acheson foreign policy was rolling. On September 15 MacArthur successfully outflanked the North Koreans with an amphibious landing at Inchon, far up the Korean peninsula. In a little more than a week MacArthur's troops were in the capital, Seoul, and they had cut off the bulk of the North Korean forces around Pusan. On September 27 the Joint Chiefs ordered MacArthur to destroy the enemy army and authorized him to conduct military operations north of the thirty-eighth parallel. On October 7 American troops crossed the parallel. The same day the United Nations approved (47 to 5) an American resolution endorsing the action.

MacArthur's broad authority to invade North Korea, it is important to note, came after full discussion and consideration in the highest levels of the American government. Truman later implied, and millions believed, that MacArthur had gone ahead on his own, that it was the general in the field, not the government at home, that had changed the political objective of the war in the middle of the con-

flict. Such was never the case. Truman, with the full con-
currence of the State and Defense Departments and the
Joint Chiefs, made the decision to liberate North Korea
and accept the risks involved.

The Chinese issued a series of warnings, culminating
with a statement to India for transmission to the United
States, that China would not "sit back with folded hands
and let the Americans come to the border." When even
this was discounted, the Chinese publicly stated on October
10 that if the Americans continued north, they would enter
the conflict. The Russians were more cautious, but when
on October 9 some American jet aircraft strafed a Soviet
airfield only a few miles from Vladivostok, they sent a strong
protest to Washington. Truman immediately decided to fly
to the Pacific to see MacArthur and make sure he restrained
the Air Force. Fighting Chinese forces in Korea was one
thing, war with Russia another. The Americans were willing
to try to liberate Pyongyang, but they were not ready to
liberate Moscow.

The Truman-MacArthur meeting at Wake Island in October accomplished its main purpose, for the Air Force
thereafter confined its activities to the Korean peninsula.
More important was what it revealed. Commentators have
concentrated almost exclusively on MacArthur's statement
that the Chinese would not dare enter the war. On this
point everybody, not just MacArthur, was wrong. Other
differences between Truman and MacArthur were more
those of method than of goals. MacArthur was excessively
dramatic in the way he put things and he had a milliennial
quality about him, but like Truman his immediate aim was
to liberate North Korea. At various times he indicated that
he also wanted to help Chiang back onto the mainland, a
long-range goal that Truman had not accepted as realistic,
but for the immediate future the General and the President
were together. They differed on means. MacArthur was
not at all sure he could unify Korea without striking at the
Chinese bases across the Yalu. Truman, more concerned
about Europe and the dangers there, especially since nei-

ther the German nor the American rearmament programs were yet well under way, insisted on keeping limits on the area of military operations.

Even this difference, however, was not made clear at Wake Island, for the Chinese had not been seen nor were they expected in Korea. MacArthur flew back to Tokyo to direct the last offensive. By October 25 his forces reached the Yalu at Chosan. That day Chinese "volunteers" struck South Korean and American troops around the Choshin Reservoir. After hard fighting MacArthur's units fell back. The Chinese then retired. They had, by their actions, transmitted two messages: (1) they would not allow MacArthur's forces to proceed unmolested to the Yalu, and (2) their main concern continued to be Formosa, and like Truman they wanted to limit the fighting in Korea. The second message was reinforced by Peking's acceptance of an invitation to come to the United Nations to discuss the Formosa situation and, hopefully, the Korean War.

Truman and Acheson, like their more bombastic commander in the field, were not ready to accept a negotiated peace. They discounted Chinese intervention, continued to dream of liberating North Korea, and had no intention of abandoning the recent commitment to Chiang's defense. A negotiated settlement with the Chinese would bring the wrath of the Republicans on their heads, and congressional elections were only a few days away. If peace came, there would be no N.S.C. 68 and American foreign policy would be back where it was before the Korean War—much bluster and little muscle.

MacArthur planned to launch another ground offensive on November 15, which would have coincided with the announced date of arrival of the Chinese delegates at the United Nations. The delegates, however, were delayed. On November 11 MacArthur learned of the delay, and later that the Chinese delegation would arrive at the United Nations on November 24. MacArthur put off his offensive, finally beginning it on the morning of November 24. Thus the headlines that greeted the Chinese delegates when they arrived at the United Nations declared that MacArthur promised to have the boys "home by Christmas," after they had all been to the Yalu. The Americans were once again marching to the Chinese border, this time in greater force.

Europeans were incensed. The French government charged that MacArthur had "launched his offensive at this time to wreck the negotiations" and the British *New Statesman* declared that MacArthur had "acted in defiance of all common sense, and in such a way as to provoke the most peace-loving nation." The Chinese delegation at the United Nations soon packed its bags and returned to Peking, taking with it only what it had brought plus some additional bitterness.

The failure of the negotiations did not upset Truman, but the failure of the offensive did. MacArthur had advanced on two widely separated routes, with his middle wide open. How he could have done so, given the earlier Chinese intervention, remains a mystery to military analysts. The Chinese poured thousands of troops into the gap and soon sent MacArthur's men fleeing for their lives. In two weeks the Chinese cleared much of North Korea, isolated MacArthur's units into three bridgeheads, and completely reversed the military situation.

The Americans, who had walked into the disaster together, split badly on the question of how to get out. MacArthur said he now faced "an entirely new war" and indicated that the only solution was to strike at China itself. But war against China might well mean war against Russia, which Truman was not prepared to accept. Instead, the administration decided to return to the pre-Inchon policy of restoring the status quo ante bellum in Korea while building NATO strength in Europe. All talk of liberating iron curtain capitals disappeared. Never again would the United States attempt by force of arms to free a Communist state.

A lesson had been learned, but not fully accepted immediately, and it was enormously frustrating. Just how frustrating became clear on November 30, when at a press conference Truman called for a worldwide mobilization against Communism and, in response to a question, de-

clared that if military action against China was authorized
by the United Nations, MacArthur might be empowered
to use the atomic bomb at his discretion. Truman casually
added that there had always been active consideration of
the bomb's use, for after all it was one of America's military
weapons.

Much alarmed, British Prime Minister Attlee flew to
Washington, fearful that Truman really would use the bomb
for the third time in five years against an Asian people.
Attlee, in a series of meetings, hammered away at the
Americans. There was much talk in Washington (and Tokyo) of pulling out of Korea altogether. Attlee thought that
if this were done the humiliation of defeat would lead the
Americans to an all-out war with China. He suspected that
such a development was exactly what MacArthur had in
mind. Truman, Acheson, Bradley, and the newly appointed Secretary of Defense, General Marshall, all assured
Attlee that every effort would be made to stay in Korea
and then promised that as long as MacArthur held on there
would be no atomic bombs dropped.

With Attlee's departure, Truman and Acheson quickened the pace of their policy. They accomplished so much
that by the end of January 1951 only the most extreme
McCarthyite could complain that they were ignoring the
Communist threat. Truman put the nation on a Cold War
footing. He got emergency powers from Congress to ex-
pedite war mobilization, reintroduced selective service, submitted a $50-billion defense budget that followed the
guidelines of N.S.C. 68, sent two more divisions (a total of
six) to Europe, doubled the number of air groups to ninety-
five, obtained new bases in Morocco, Libya, and Saudi Arabia, increased the Army by 50 percent to 3.5 million men,
pushed forward the Japanese peace treaty, stepped up aid
to the French in Vietnam, initiated the process of adding
Greece and Turkey to NATO, and began discussions with
Franco that led to American aid to Fascist Spain in return
for military bases there.

Truman's accomplishments were breathtaking. He had
given the United States a thermonuclear bomb (March 1951)

and rearmed Germany. He pushed through a peace treaty with Japan (signed in September 1951) that excluded the Russians and gave the Americans military bases, allowed for Japanese rearmament and unlimited industrialization, and encouraged a Japanese boom by dismissing British, Australian, Chinese, and other demands for reparations. Truman extended American bases around the world, hemming in both Russia and China. He had learned, in November of 1950, not to push beyond the iron and bamboo curtains, but he had made sure that if any Communist showed his head on the free side of the line, someone—usually an American—would be there to shoot him.

There had to be a price. It was best summed up by Walter Millis, himself a Cold Warrior and a great admirer of Forrestal. The Truman Administration, Millis wrote, left behind it "an enormously expanded military establishment, beyond anything we had ever contemplated in time of peace. . . . It evoked a huge and apparently permanent armament industry, now wholly dependent . . . on government contracts. The Department of Defense had become without question the biggest industrial management operation in the world; the great private operations, like General Motors, du Pont, the leading airplane manufacturers had assumed positions of monopoly power . . ." The Administration produced thermonuclear supergiant weapons, families of lesser atomic bombs, guided missiles, the B-52 jet bomber, new supercarriers and tanks and other heavy weapons. It had increased the risk of war while making war immeasurably more dangerous.

One other thing bothered Millis. For all that the Truman Administration accomplished, "what it failed to do was to combine these men and weapons into a practicable structure of military policy competent to meet the new political and military problems that now stood grimly before us. We were to face them in a large measure of bewilderment as to where the true paths of military policy might lead."

Millis might have added that the bewilderment extended to foreign policy, as there was no way to split sharply the activities of the soldiers and the diplomats. Truman gave

America power and a policy, but it seemed to many that with all the power he had generated, and the justification he had given for the policy, the policy itself was much too modest. Containment had never been very satisfying emotionally, built as it was on the constant reiteration of the Communist threat and the propaganda line that divided the world into areas that were free and those that were enslaved. Millions of Americans wanted to accept their Christian obligation and free the slaves. Other millions wanted to destroy, not just contain, the Communist threat, on the grounds that if it were allowed to exist, the Cold War would go on forever, at a constantly increased cost. There were those who felt that the only justification for a garrison state was the old one of putting it on a temporary basis, which was to say, to fight a war to destroy the threat.

This criticism of the Truman-Acheson foreign policy, which centered around the towering figure of MacArthur, turned Attlee's criticism on its head. The Prime Minister had warned the Americans that they could not do it all alone, not forever anyway. He said they would either have to fight all out in Asia or negotiate, and he urged them to negotiate. MacArthur wanted to fight all out. American liberals and self-styled realists derided MacArthur and his followers for the simplicity of their views, but there was no denying MacArthur's appeal or the frustration built into the containment program, an appeal and a frustration based on Truman's and Acheson's own descriptions of the world scene.

If America made permanent Cold War its policy, with a commitment to continuous military superiority to back an attitude of unrelenting hostility toward China and Russia, without ever doing anything to destroy the Communist nations, it would be accepting permanent tension, permanent risk, and a permanent postponement of the social and economic promises of the New Deal.

The difference in outlook soon erupted into one of the great emotional events of American history. In January and February 1951 MacArthur resumed the offensive and drove the Chinese and North Koreans back. By March he was again at the thirty-eighth parallel. The administration, having been burned once, was ready to negotiate. MacArthur sabotaged the efforts to obtain a ceasefire by crossing the parallel and by demanding an unconditional surrender from the Chinese. Truman was furious. He decided to remove the General at the first opportunity.

It came shortly. On April 5 Representative Joseph W. Martin, Jr., Republican, read to the House a letter from MacArthur calling for a new foreign policy. The General wanted to reunify Korea, unleash Chiang for an attack on the mainland, and fight Communism in Asia rather than in Europe. "Here in Asia," he said, "is where the communist conspirators have elected to make their play for global conquest. Here we fight Europe's war with arms while the diplomats there still fight it with words."

Aside from the problem of a soldier challenging Presidential supremacy by trying to set foreign policy, the debate centered on Europe-first versus Asia-first. This, however, was not the root question, for the choice of a battleground was simply one of methods, not policies. MacArthur was not challenging only, or even primarily, the Europe-first priority, but rather the doctrine of containment. Initially he had a large majority of the people with him. After Truman relieved him MacArthur returned to the United States to receive a welcome that would have made Caesar envious. Public opinion polls showed that three out of every four Americans disapproved of the way Truman was conducting the war.

The American people seemed to be rejecting containment, and Truman had rejected victory; that left only Attlee's alternative of peace. Even Attlee, however, had wanted peace only in Asia, and as Truman pointed out to him time and again, Congress would not accept a policy of intervention in Europe and isolation in Asia. As it was, Truman was in trouble because he spent most of the money Congress voted for defense on NATO at a time when most Americans assumed that the effort was going into Korea. If the Korean War came to a sudden end, so would N.S.C. 68 and the entire program that went with it.

It was necessary to keep the small war going until rearmament was complete. This was the meaning of the American rejection of a Soviet offer on June 23 for a pure and simple military armistice in the field. The Russians had *not* demanded the three political conditions on which the Chinese and North Koreans had laid such stress: withdrawal of American troops from Korea; the return of Formosa to China; and the seating of the Peking government in the United Nations. Presumably Russia had the power to enforce what amounted to a surrender on China and North Korea. Certainly Stalin thought so and certainly this fitted in with the American beliefs about the nature of monolithic Communism. No one ever found out because, as journalist I. F. Stone wrote, the American leaders regarded the possibility of peace talks "as a kind of diabolic plot against rearmament." Republican leader Thomas Dewey said, "Every time the Soviets make a peace move, I get scared. . . . Every time Stalin smiles, beware." Within a week the Secretary of Defense, the Chairman of the Joint Chiefs, the Chief of Naval Operations, the Defense Mobilizer, Averell Harriman, and General Eisenhower had all warned against any letdown in the mobilization effort. On July 4 Truman said that even if the Korean War should end, "we face a long period of world tension and great international danger." MacArthur joined the chorus.

The pressure from the United Nations and the NATO allies to negotiate could not be totally ignored, however, and on July 10, 1951, peace talks—without a ceasefire— began. They broke down on July 12. For the remainder of the year they were on again, off again. The front lines began to stabilize around the thirty-eighth parallel while American casualties dropped to an "acceptable" weekly total. The war, and rearmament, continued.

Truman had won. Administration witnesses at the MacArthur hearings in the Senate (held to examine foreign policy and MacArthur's dismissal) argued convincingly that America could neither destroy Russia or China nor allow them to expand. Public opinion swung back to Truman. America remained committed to containment and per-

manent Cold War. MacArthur's alternative of victory, like
Attlee's of peace in Asia, had been rejected. America girded
for the long haul.

The Cold War would be fought Truman's way. There
would be clashes on the periphery but none between the
major powers. America would extend her positions of
strength around the Communist empire. The military-
industrial complex in the United States would become a
major social and economic force. The United States would
make no settlement, no compromise with Russia or China,
nor would she consult her allies on major decisions. America would build up the mightiest armed force the world
had ever known and, if necessary, defend the barricades
of freedom alone.

When Truman became President he led a nation anxious
to return to traditional civil-military relations and the historic American foreign policy of noninvolvement. When
he left the White House his legacy was an American presence on every continent of the world and an enormously
expanded armament industry. Yet so successfully had he
scared hell out of the American people, the only critics to
receive any attention in the mass media were those who
thought Truman had not gone far enough in standing up
to the Communists. For all his troubles, Truman had
triumphed.

8

Eisenhower, Dulles, and the Irreconcilable Conflict

It is now clear that we are facing an implacable enemy whose avowed objective is world domination by whatever means and at whatever cost. There are no rules in such a game. Hitherto acceptable norms of human conduct do not apply. We must develop effective espionage and counterespionage services and must learn to subvert, sabotage and destroy our enemies by more clever, more sophisticated, and more effective methods than those used against us.

> The Doolittle Committee,
> charged by President Eisenhower
> in 1955 to investigate and
> report to him on the activities
> of the C.I.A.

"We can never rest," General Eisenhower declared during his 1952 campaign for the Presidency, "until the enslaved nations of the world have in the fullness of freedom the right to choose their own path, for then, and then only, can we say that there is a possible way of living peacefully and permanently with communism in the world." Like most campaign statements, Eisenhower's bowed to both sides of the political spectrum. For the bold he indicated a policy of liberation, while the cautious could take comfort in his willingness to someday live peacefully with the Communists. Since the Americans believed, however, that no one would freely choose Communism, Eisenhower's statement had a major internal contradiction.

The emphasis, therefore, was on liberation. John Foster Dulles, the Republican expert on foreign policy, author of the Japanese peace treaty, and soon to be Secretary of State, was more explicit than Ike. Containment, he charged, was a treadmill policy "which, at best might perhaps keep us in the same place until we drop exhausted." It cost far too much in taxes and was "not designed to win victory conclusively." One plank in the Republican platform damned containment as "negative, futile and immoral," for it abandoned "countless human beings to a despotism and Godless terrorism." It hinted that the Republicans, once in power, would roll back the atheistic tide. Rollback would come not only in East Europe but also in Asia. The platform denounced the "Asia last" policy of the Democrats and said, "We have no intention to sacrifice the East to gain time for the West."

The Eisenhower landslide of 1952 was a compound of many factors, the chief being the General's enormous personal popularity. Corruption in the Truman Administration and the McCarthy charges of Communist infiltration into the government also helped ("There are no Communists in the Republican Party," one platform plank declared). So did Ike's promise to go to Korea and end the war there, not through victory but through negotiation. But one of the major appeals of the Eisenhower-Dulles team was its rejection of containment. The Republican pledge to do something about Communist enslavement —it was never very clear exactly what—brought millions of former Democratic voters into the Republican fold, especially those of East European descent. Eisenhower reaped where McCarthy sowed. Far from rejecting internationalism and retreating to isolationism, the Republicans were proposing to go beyond containment. They would be more internationalist than Truman.

Republican promises to liberate the enslaved, like nineteenth-century abolitionist programs to free the Negro slaves, logically led to only one policy. Since the slaveholders would not voluntarily let the oppressed go, and since the slaves were too tightly controlled to stage their own revolution, those who wished to see the slaves freed would have to fight to free them. In the second half of the twentieth century, however, war was a much different proposition than it had

been a hundred years earlier. Freeing the slaves would lead
to the destruction of much of the world; most of the slaves
themselves would die in the process.

There was another major constraint on action. The Republicans were wedded to conservative fiscal views that
stressed the importance of balancing the budget and cutting taxes. All of Eisenhower's leading cabinet figures, save
Dulles, were businessmen who believed that an unbalanced
federal budget was immoral. Government expenditures
could be reduced significantly, however, only by cutting
the Defense Department budget, which the Republicans
proceeded to do. The cuts made liberation even more
difficult.

In Korea, in July 1953, Ike signed an armistice that restored the status quo ante bellum. General MacArthur,
President Rhee, and many Republicans were furious. They
wanted to fight on until North Korea was liberated, a policy
they thought Ike had endorsed in his "We shall never rest"
statement. But Ike, after considering and rejecting the use
of atomic weapons, decided that the price of victory was
too high, and instead made peace.

In practice, therefore, Eisenhower and Dulles continued
the policy of containment. There was no basic difference
between their foreign policy and that of Truman and Acheson. Their campaign statements frequently haunted them,
but they avoided embarrassment over their lack of action
through their rhetoric. "We can never rest," Ike had
said, but rest they did, except in their speeches, which expressed perfectly the assumptions and desires of millions
of Americans.

Better than anyone else, Dulles described the American
view of Communism. A devout Christian, highly successful
corporate lawyer, something of a prig, and absolutely certain of his own and his nation's goodness, Dulles's unshake-
able beliefs were based on general American ideas. They
differed hardly at all from those of Truman, Acheson,
Main Street in Iowa City, or Madison Avenue in New York
City. All the world wanted to be like America; the common
people everywhere looked to America for leadership; Com-

munism was unmitigated evil imposed by a conspiracy on helpless people, whether it came from the outside as in East Europe or from within as in Asia; there could be no permanent reconciliation with Communism because "this is an irreconcilable conflict."

Dulles's speeches, like Ike's, helped hide the fact that they did nothing about their promise to liberate the enslaved, but perhaps more important to their popularity was their unwillingness to risk American lives, for here too they were expressing the deepest sentiments of their countrymen. On occasion the Republicans rattled the saber and always they filled the air with denunciations of the Communists, but they also shut down the Korean War, cut corporate taxes, and reduced the size of the armed forces. Despite intense pressure and great temptation, they entered no wars. They were willing to supply material, on a limited scale, to others so that they could fight the enemy, but they would not commit American boys to the struggle. Like Truman they did their best to contain Communism; unlike him they did not use American troops to do so. They were unwilling to make peace but they would not go to war. Their speeches provided emotional satisfaction but their actions failed to liberate a single slave. No one had a right to complain that the Republicans had been misleading, however, for the policy had been clearly spelled out in the campaign. The militant talk about liberation was balanced by specific promises to end the war in Korea—without liberating North Korea, much less China—and to balance the budget.

When General Marshall was Secretary of State he had complained that he had no muscle to back up his foreign policy. Truman agreed and did all he could to increase the armed forces. Dulles did not make such complaints. He worked with what was available—which was, to be sure, far more than Marshall had at hand in 1948—for he shared the Republican commitment to fiscal soundness.

The extent of the commitment was best seen in the New Look, a term Eisenhower coined to describe his military policy. It combined domestic, military, and foreign considerations. The New Look rejected the premise of N.S.C. 68 that the United States could spend up to 20 percent of its G.N.P. on arms; it rejected deficit financing; it supported a policy of containment. It came into effect at a time of lessening tension. The Korean War had ended and Stalin had died. The world seemed less dangerous. The New Look was based in large part on the success of the N.S.C. 68 program, for the first two years of the New Look were the high-water mark of relative American military strength in the Cold War. As Samuel Huntington has noted, "The basic military fact of the New Look was the overwhelming American superiority in nuclear weapons and the means of delivering them." Between 1953 and 1955 the United States could have effectively destroyed the Soviet Union with little likelihood of serious reprisal. The fact that America did not do so indicated the basic restraint of the Eisenhower Administration, as opposed to its verbiage.

The New Look became fixed policy during a period of lessened tensions and American military superiority, but it did not depend on either for its continuation. In its eight years of power the Eisenhower Administration went through a series of war scares and it witnessed the development of Soviet long-range bombers, ballistic missiles, and nuclear weapons. Throughout, however, Ike held to the New Look. His Defense Department expenditures remained in the $35-to-$40-billion range.

The key to the New Look was the American ability to build and deliver nuclear weapons. Put more bluntly, Ike's military policy rested on America's capacity to destroy the Soviet Union. Soviet strides in military technology gave them the ability to retaliate but not to defend Russia, which was the major reason Eisenhower could accept sufficiency. The United States did not have to be superior to the Soviet Union to demolish it.

To give up superiority was not easy, however, and it rankled with many Americans, especially in the military. Ike had his greatest difficulties with the Army, for it suffered most from his refusal to increase the Defense Department budget. Three Army Chiefs of Staff resigned in protest, and one of them, Maxwell Taylor, later became the chief adviser on military affairs to Ike's successor. The Army wanted enough flexibility to be able to meet the Communist threat at any level. The trouble with Eisenhower's New Look, the Army Chiefs argued, was that it locked the United States into an all-or-nothing response. Wherever and whenever conflict broke out, the Chiefs wanted to be capable of moving in. To do so, they needed a huge standing army, with specialized divisions, elite groups, a wide variety of weapons, and an enormous transportation capacity.

Eisenhower insisted that the cost of being able to intervene anywhere, immediately, was unbearable. "Let us not forget," the President wrote a friend in August 1956, "that the Armed Services are to defend a 'way of life,' not merely land, property or lives." He wanted to make the Chiefs accept the need for a "balance between minimum requirements in the costly implements of war and the health of our economy. . . ." As he told the American Society of Newspaper Editors on April 16, 1953, "Every gun that is made, every warship launched, every rocket fired signifies, in the final sense, a theft from those who hunger and are not fed, those who are cold and are not clothed." He pointed out that the cost of one destroyer for the Navy was equal to the cost of new, modern homes for eight thousand people.

Still, the Army Chiefs had put their finger on the most obvious limitation of the New Look and massive retaliation. Eisenhower and Dulles tried to make up the deficit by signing up allies, as in World War II, who would do the ground fighting that had to be done. Ike offered one reason when he pointed out that while "it cost $3,515 to maintain an American soldier each year, for a Pakistani the price was $485, for a Greek, $424." That was good economics but poor politics, since the Pakistanis and the Greeks were not anxious to fight America's wars.

The New Look meant that Eisenhower had abandoned his former advocacy of universal military training, with its assumption that the next war would resemble World War

II. More fundamentally, he had abandoned the idea of America fighting any more Korean Wars. Ike's policy emphasized both the importance of tactical nuclear weapons and the role of strategic airpower as a deterrent to aggression. He used technology to mediate between conflicting political goals. Big bombers carrying nuclear weapons were the means through which he reconciled lower military expenditures with a foreign policy of containment.

The New Look shaped foreign policy. Since it was almost his only weapon, Dulles had to flash a nuclear bomb whenever he wanted to threaten the use of force. To make the threat believable, the United States developed smaller atomic weapons that could be used tactically on the battlefield. Dulles then attempted to convince the world that the United States would not hesitate to use them. The fact that the NATO forces were so small made the threat persuasive, for there was no other way to stop the Red Army in Europe. Both Dulles and Ike made this explicit. If the United States were engaged in a major military confrontation, Dulles said, "those weapons would come into use because, as I say, they are becoming more and more conventional and replacing what used to be called conventional weapons." Eisenhower declared, "Where these things are used on strictly military targets . . . I see no reason why they shouldn't be used just exactly as you would use a bullet or anything else."

Dulles called the policy massive retaliation. In a speech in January 1954 he quoted Lenin and Stalin to show that the Soviets planned to overextend the free world and then destroy it with one blow. Dulles held that the United States should counter that strategy by maintaining a great strategic reserve in the United States. The Eisenhower Administration had made a decision to "depend primarily upon a great capacity to retaliate, instantly, by means and at places of our own choosing."

Dulles used massive retaliation as the chief instrument of containment. He called his overall method brinksmanship, which he explained in an article in *Life* magazine. "You have to take chances for peace, just as you must take chances in war. Some say that we were brought to the verge of war. Of course we were brought to the verge of war. The ability to get the verge without getting into the war is the necessary art. . . . If you try to run away from it, if you are scared to go to the brink, you are lost. We've had to look it square in the face. . . . We walked to the brink and we looked it in the face. We took strong action."

Dulles implicitly recognized the limitations on brinksmanship. He never tried to use it for liberation and he used it much more sparingly after the Soviets were able to threaten the United States itself with destruction. It was a tactic to support containment at an acceptable cost, within a limited time span under a specific set of military circumstances, not a strategy for protracted conflict.

In the *Life* article Dulles cited three instances of going to the brink. All were in Asia. The first came in Korea. When Ike took office in January 1953 the truce talks were stalled on the question of prisoner-of-war-repatriation. The Chinese wanted all their men held by the U.N. command returned, while the Americans insisted on voluntary repatriation, which meant that thousands of Chinese and North Koreans would remain in South Korea, for they did not want to return to Communism. Truman and Acheson had first raised the issue. They could have had peace early in 1952 had they accepted the usual practice, firmly established in international law, of returning all prisoners, but they decided to offer a haven to those prisoners who wished to defect. The talks, and the war, continued.

Determined to cut losses and get out, Eisenhower warned that unless the war ended quickly the United States might retaliate "under circumstances of our own choosing." On February 2, in his first State of the Union message, the President said there was no longer "any sense or logic" in restraining Chiang, so the U.S. Seventh Fleet would "no longer be employed to shield Communist China." Chiang then began bombing raids against the China coast. Eisenhower's threats to widen the war accomplished his goal— the Chinese agreed to an armistice.

Dulles then warned Peking (through India) that if peace did not come the United States would bring in atomic weapons. Eleven days later the Chinese agreed to place the question of prisoner repatriation in the hands of international, neutral authorities.

In its first test massive retaliation had won a victory. Ominous portents for the future, however, soon appeared. Dulles's policy was based on a bipolar view of the world, which in his rhetoric was good versus evil or free versus slave but which in practice meant that Moscow and Washington ruled the world. He believed that the United States could make the major decisions for the free world while Russia would make them for the Communists. He refused to accept, or perhaps even recognize, the diversity of the world, for he thought all important issues were related to the Cold War and was impatient with those who argued that the East-West struggle was irrelevant to many world problems. His negative expression of this belief in bipolarity was his denunciation of neutrality, which he characterized as immoral.

The second application of brinksmanship came in Vietnam. In December 1952 the lame-duck Truman Administration approved $60 million for support of the French effort against Ho Chi Minh's Viet Minh. Truman, and later Eisenhower, labeled Ho a Communist agent of Peking and Moscow, characterizing the war in Vietnam as another example of Communist aggression.

When Eisenhower moved into the White House, the State Department presented him with a background paper on Vietnam that succinctly summed up the American position not only on Vietnam but on the entire Third World. In 1949 France had broken up Indochina and granted Laos, Cambodia, and Vietnam "independence within the French Union." All objective observers recognized this as a heavy-handed attempt to buy off the Viet Minh without giving anything of substance in return. Even the U.S. State Department could not totally ignore the obvious sham, but it did its best to dismiss it.

In the background presentation to Eisenhower the State Department said that "certain symbols of the former colonial era remain." These "symbols" included total French control over "foreign and military affairs, foreign trade and exchange, and internal security. France continues to maintain a near monopoly in the economic life" of Vietnam. The State Department told Ike that French control of the reality of power in its former colonies was "disliked by large elements of the native population," but said it was "justified" because the French were bearing the major burden of "defending the area." But the only nonnative troops in Vietnam were French, and even State admitted that the bulk of the population "disliked" French rule. American policy was to encourage an end to colonialism; yet in the face of all this State could still seriously assert that France retained "certain symbols" of power and was "defending the area." Against whom, and for what?

While he served as Supreme Commander at NATO headquarters in Europe, and again in his first year in the White House, Eisenhower continually urged the French to state unequivocally that they would give complete independence to Vietnam upon the conclusion of hostilities. Ike said he made "every kind of presentation" to the French to "put the war on an international footing," that is, to make it clear that this was a struggle between Communism and freedom, not a revolt against colonialism. If France promised independence, and Ho continued to fight, Ike reasoned that the Viet Minh could no longer pretend to be national liberators but would stand revealed as Communist stooges of Moscow. At that point Britain and the United States could enter the conflict to halt "outside" aggression.

Eisenhower was badly confused about the nature of the war, but the French were not. Like Rhee, they were willing enough to talk about the Communist menace in order to receive American aid, but they had no intention of giving up Vietnam. They knew perfectly well that their enemies were in the interior of Vietnam, not in Peking or Moscow, and they were determined to retain the reality of power. If the Americans wanted to fight Communists, that was fine with the French; their concern was with continuing to control Vietnam.

But the war did not go well for the French. By early 1954

the Viet Minh controlled over half the countryside. The French put their best troops into an isolated garrison north of Hanoi, called Dien Bien Phu, and dared the Viet Minh to come after them. They assumed that in open battle the Asians would crumble. The results, however, went the other way, and by April it was the French garrison at Dien Bien Phu that was in trouble. War weariness in France was by then so great, and the French had attached so much prestige to Dien Bien Phu, that it was clear that the fall of the garrison would mean the end of French rule in Vietnam. Eisenhower and Dulles saw such an outcome as a victory for Communist aggression and a failure of containment.

On April 3, 1954, Dulles and Admiral Radford met with eight congressional leaders. The administration wanted support for a congressional resolution authorizing American entry into the war. The Congressmen, including Senator Lyndon B. Johnson of Texas, the Senate majority leader, were aghast. They remembered all too well the difficulties of the Korean War and they were disturbed because Dulles had found no allies to support intervention. Congressional opposition hardened when they discovered that one of the other three Joint Chiefs disagreed with Radford's idea of saving Dien Bien Phu through air strikes.

Eisenhower was as adamant as the Congressional leaders about allies. He was anxious to support the French but only if they promised complete independence and only if Britain joined the United States in intervening. Unless these conditions were met he would not move, but he was worried about what would happen if the French lost. On April 7 he introduced a new political use for an old word when he explained at a press conference that all Southeast Asia was like a row of dominoes. If you knocked over the first one what would happen to the last one was "the certainty that it would go over very quickly."

To make sure the dominoes stood, Ike went shopping for allies. He wanted "the U.S., France, United Kingdom, Thailand, Australia, and New Zealand et al. to begin conferring at once on means of successfully stopping the Communist advances in Southeast Asia." He proposed to use the bulk of the French army already there, while "additional ground forces should come from Asiatic and European troops." America would supply the material, but not the lives. The policy had little appeal to Britain, Australia, New Zealand, et al., but it was consistent with the approach of both Ike's predecessors. The trouble was it had no chance of success. The proposed allies figured that if Americans would not fight in Korea, they would not fight in Vietnam. Even when Eisenhower wrote Churchill and compared the threat in Vietnam to the dangers of "Hirohito, Mussolini and Hitler," the British would not budge.

The Vice-President, Richard M. Nixon, then tried another tack. On April 16 he said that "if to avoid further Communist expansion in Asia and Indochina, we must take the risk now by putting our boys in, I think the Executive has to take the politically unpopular decision and do it." The storm that followed this speech was so fierce that the possibility of using "our boys" in Vietnam immediately disappeared. Ike would never have supported it anyway, and his Army Chief of Staff, Matthew Ridgway, was firmly opposed to rushing into another ground war in Asia.

What to do? The question was crucial because a conference on Vietnam was scheduled to begin in Geneva on April 26. Like Truman in Korea, the Eisenhower Administration was flatly opposed to a negotiated peace at Geneva that would give Ho Chi Minh any part of Vietnam. The United States was paying 75 percent of the cost of the war, an investment too great simply to abandon. But the French position at Dien Bien Phu was deteriorating rapidly. Air Force Chief of Staff Nathan Twining had a solution. He wanted to drop three small atomic bombs on the Viet Minh around Dien Bien Phu "and clean those Commies out of there and the band could play the Marseillaise and the French would come marching out . . . in fine shape." Eisenhower said he would not use atomic bombs for the second time in a decade against Asians, but he did consider a conventional air strike. Dulles flew to London a week before the Geneva conference to get Churchill's approval. Churchill would not approve, and Eisenhower did not act. Brinksmanship had failed.

On May 7, 1954, Dien Bien Phu fell. Still there was no immediate progress in Geneva and the Americans walked out of the conference. At the insistence of the NATO allies, Eisenhower eventually sent his close friend Walter B. Smith as an observer. Dulles himself refused to return to Geneva and the negotiations dragged on. The break came when the French government fell, and in mid-June the Radical-Socialist Pierre Mendès-France assumed the position of Foreign Minister as well as Premier. On the strength of his pledge to end the war or resign by July 20, he had a vote of confidence of 419 to 47. Mendès-France immediately met Chinese Premier Chou En-lai privately at Bern, which infuriated the Americans, and progress toward peace began. Ike, Dulles and Smith were helpless bystanders. On July 20–21, 1954, two pacts were signed: the Geneva Accords and the Geneva Armistice Agreement.

The parties agreed to a truce and to a temporary partition of Vietnam at the seventeenth parallel, with the French withdrawing south of that line. Neither the French in the south of Vietnam nor Ho Chi Minh in the north could join a military alliance or allow foreign military bases on their territory. There would be elections, supervised by a joint commission of India, Canada, and Poland, within two years to unify the country. France would stay in the south to carry out the elections. The United States did not sign either of the pacts, nor did any South Vietnamese government. The Americans did promise that they would support "free elections supervised by the United Nations" and would not use force to upset the agreements. Ho Chi Minh had been on the verge of taking all of Vietnam, but he accepted only the northern half because he needed time to repair the war damage and he was confident that when the elections came he would win a smashing victory. All Western observers agreed with his prediction on how the vote would go.

Desperate to save something from the debacle, in July

1954 Dulles, Radford and Twining, along with others at the Pentagon, worked out an invasion scheme calling for a landing at Haiphong and a march to Hanoi, which American troops would then liberate. Again, General Ridgway opposed, arguing that the adventure would require at least six divisions even if the Chinese did not intervene, and again Eisenhower refused to act.

The New Look had tied Dulles's hands in Vietnam, so after Geneva the Secretary of State moved in two ways to restore some flexibility to American foreign policy. One of the major problems had been the lack of allies for an intervention. Dulles tried to correct this before the next crisis came by signing up the allies in advance. In September 1954 he persuaded Britain, Australia, New Zealand, France, Thailand, Pakistan, and the Philippines to join the Southeast Asian Treaty Organization (SEATO), in which the parties agreed to consult if any signatory felt threatened. They would act together to meet an aggressor if they could unanimously agree on designating him and if the threatened state agreed to action on its territory. Protection for Cambodia, Laos, and South Vietnam was covered in a separate protocol. Thus the United States quickly undermined the Geneva Accords by bringing South Vietnam into an alliance system. The absence of India, Burma, and Indonesia was embarrassing, as was the presence of so many white men. Clearly this was no NATO for Southeast Asia but rather a Western—especially American—effort to regulate the affairs of Asia from the outside. Once again the hoary old Monroe Doctrine had been extended. The United States, as Dulles put it, had "declared that an intrusion [in Southeast Asia] would be dangerous to our peace and security," and America would fight to prevent it.

Not, however, with infantry. Dulles assured a suspicious Senate that the New Look policies would continue, that the American response to aggression would be with bombs, not men. This solved one problem but left another. What if the aggression took the form of internal Communist subversion directed and supported from without? In such an event it would be difficult to get the SEATO signatories to agree to act. Dulles was aware of the danger and assured the Cabinet that in such an event he was ready to act alone. He took a different tack in the Senate Foreign Relations Committee, where he stated that "if there is a revolutionary movement in Vietnam or in Thailand, we would consult together as to what to do about it . . . but we have no undertaking to put it down, all we have is an undertaking to consult." Reassured, the Senate passed the treaty by a vote of 82 to 1.

Dulles's other major post-Geneva move was to unilaterally shore up the government of South Vietnam. In so doing he revealed much about American attitudes toward revolution in the Third World. Dulles grew almost frantic when he thought about the "colored" peoples of the world, for he realized that the struggle for their loyalty was the next battleground of the Cold War and he knew that American military might was often irrelevant in the struggle. Russia had a tremendous initial advantage, since the Third World did not regard the Russians as white exploiters and colonists. Furthermore, the Russian example of how a nation could build its economy through controlled production and consumption rather than by waiting for the slow accumulation of capital through the profits of free enterprise had great appeal to the emerging nations. Finally, the oppressed peoples of the world were not overthrowing their white masters merely in order to substitute local rulers with the same policies. The revolutionaries were just what they said they were, men determined to change the entire social, political, and economic order.

America could neither accept nor adjust to radicalism, either psychologically or economically. Dulles accused the Soviets of being the real imperialists of the modern world, but the Russians were never shocked by, and in fact encouraged, radical action in the Third World. All the Third World peoples had to do to see what America regarded as a proper role for the emerging nations was to look at Latin America, where the Western-owned corporations retained their position, the economy was extractive, the rulers lived in splendor, and the masses of the people remained in poverty.

Given the American habit of defining social change as Communist aggression, given the needs of American business to maintain an extractive economy in the Third World, and given the military desire to retain bases around Russia and China, the United States had to set its face against revolution. "American policy was designed to create maximum change behind the Iron Curtain and to prevent it elsewhere," Norman Graebner has written. "On both counts, this nation placed itself in opposition to the fundamental political and military realities of the age." In 1960 V. K. Krishna Menon of India invited the American delegation to the United Nations to read the Declaration of Independence. "Legitimism cannot be defended," he declared, "and if you object to revolutionary governments, then you simply argue against the whole of progress." But America did object to revolution. In 1958 Senator Fulbright summed up the Truman and Eisenhower approach when he said that the United States "has dealt with princes, potentates, big business, and the entrenched, frequently corrupt, representatives of the past."

Fulbright had accurately described Dulles's post-Geneva policy in South Vietnam. In September 1954 Dulles announced that henceforth American aid would go directly to the South Vietnamese and not through the French. In November American military advisers began training a South Vietnamese Army. The Americans gave power in South Vietnam to Ngo Dinh Diem, who drew his support from the landlords and had good relations with the French plantation owners, and Eisenhower pledged American economic aid to Diem. The President hedged by requiring social and economic reforms from Diem, but from the first it was understood that Diem could do as he wished as long as he remained firmly anti-Communist.

American aid then began to pour into Diem's hands as the United States tried to promote South Vietnam as a model for Third World development. Brinksmanship had failed to prevent the loss of North Vietnam and was of little or no help in dealing with the problems of the underdeveloped nations, so Dulles offered the Diem example as a method of handling what he regarded as the most important problem of the era. Whether it would be a convincing example or not remained to be seen.

If brinksmanship failed to halt or even shape the revolution of rising expectations, it could still be used to protect what was already clearly America's. Dulles faced his third major challenge, and used brinksmanship for the third time, in the Formosa Straits, where he did succeed in achieving his objective.

In January 1953 Eisenhower had "unleashed" Chiang.* The Nationalist Chinese then began a series of bombing raids, in American-built planes, against mainland shipping and ports. The pinprick war was just enough to keep the Chinese enraged without injuring them seriously. In January 1955 the Chinese were ready to strike back. They began by bombing the Tachen Islands, 230 miles north of Formosa and held by a division of Chiang's troops. The Chinese also began to build up strength and mount cannon opposite Quemoy and Matsu, small islands sitting at the mouths of two Chinese harbors and garrisoned by Nationalist divisions. Eisenhower—although not some of his advisers—was willing to write off the Tachens, which were soon evacuated, but he was determined to hold Quemoy and Matsu as he believed they were integral to the defense of Formosa itself. His reasoning, as he explained during a 1958 crisis over the same issue, was that if Quemoy and Matsu fell, Formosa would follow, which would "seriously jeopardize the anti-Communist barrier consisting of the insular and peninsular position in the Western Pacific, e.g., Japan, Republic of Korea, Republic of China, Republic of the Philippines, Thailand and Vietnam." Indonesia, Ma-

---

* In fact, Truman had done so two years earlier, but kept it a secret. Eisenhower made it public for domestic political reasons, to appease the right wing of the Republican Party.

laya, Cambodia, Laos, and Burma "would probably come fully under Communist influence."

To avoid the "catastrophic consequences" of the loss of Quemoy and Matsu, on January 24, 1955, Eisenhower went before Congress to ask for authority to "employ the armed forces of the United States as [the President] deems necessary for the specific purpose of protecting Formosa and the Pescadores against armed attack," the authority to include protection for "related positions," which meant Quemoy and Matsu. Ike feared that if the Chinese moved and he had to go to Congress for authority to act, it would be too late, so he asked for a blank check on which he could draw at will. As the legal adviser of the Department of State who helped draft the resolution remarked, it was a "monumental" step, for "never before in our history had anything been done like that." Nevertheless, there was hardly a debate. The House passed the resolution by 409 to 3, while it went through the Senate by 85 to 3.

A major war scare then ensued. As the Chinese began to bombard Quemoy and Matsu, the Eisenhower Administration seriously considered dropping nuclear weapons on the mainland. At no other time in the Cold War did the United States come so close to launching a preventive war. Had the Chinese actually launched invasions of the islands, it is probable that the United States would have done so. In a speech on March 20 Dulles referred to the Chinese in terms usually reserved for use against nations at war. The Secretary said the Chinese were "an acute and imminent threat, . . . dizzy with success." He compared their "aggressive fanaticism" with Hitler's and said they were "more dangerous and provocative of war" than Hitler. To stop them, he threatened to use "new and powerful weapons of precision, which can utterly destroy military targets without endangering unrelated civilian centers," which meant tactical nuclear bombs. Ike backed him up.

On March 25 the Chief of Naval Operations, Admiral R. B. Carney, briefed correspondents at a private dinner. He said the President was considering acting militarily on an all-out basis "to destroy Red China's military potential and thus end its expansionist tendencies." Dulles told the President that before the problem was solved, "I believe there is at least an even chance that the United States will have to go to war." Dulles thought that small air bursts, with minimal civilian casualties, would do the job quickly and "the revulsion might not be long-lived."

Eisenhower, however, began to doubt that the operation could be limited in time or scope, and he rejected preventive war. He pointed out to reporters that even if successful, such a war would leave China utterly devastated, full of human misery on an unprecedented scale. What, he demanded to know, "would the civilized world do about *that*?" At a press conference on April 28 he said he had a "sixth-sense" feeling that the outlook for peace had brightened, and he revealed that he had been in correspondence with his old wartime friend, Marshal G. K. Zhukov, one of the current Soviet rulers. Chinese pressure on Quemoy and Matsu lessened and the crisis receded. Brinksmanship had held the line.

In the process, however, it had scared the wits out of people around the globe, perhaps even members of the Eisenhower Administration itself, with good reason. The nuclear weapons of 1955 were a thousand times more destructive than the atomic bombs of the forties—one American bomber carried more destructive power than all the explosives set off in all the world's history put together—and everyone was frightened. The small, tactical atomic bombs Dulles was talking about were much larger than those dropped on Japan. Ever since the first American tests of the new fission bomb, Winston Churchill had been urging the United States and the Soviets to meet at the summit to try to resolve their differences. The Americans had consistently rejected his calls for a summit meeting, but by mid-1955, as the Russians began to improve both the size of their bombs and their delivery capabilities, and as the Formosa crisis made the United States face squarely the possibility of a nuclear exchange, Eisenhower and Dulles were more amenable.

Eisenhower's decision to go to the summit meant the end of any American dreams of winning the Cold War by military means. The Russians had come so far in nuclear development that Ike himself warned the nation that nuclear war would destroy the world. There could be no "possibility of victory or defeat," only different degrees of destruction. As James Reston reported in the *New York Times,* "perhaps the most important single fact in world politics today is that Mr. Eisenhower has thrown the immense authority of the American Presidency against risking a military solution of the cold war." Since Ike would not lead the nation into a nuclear war, and since he did not have the troops to fight a limited war, nor could he get them from his allies, and since the Republicans were more determined to balance the budget and enjoy the fruits of capitalism than they were to support a war machine, the only alternative left was peace of some kind with the Russians.

Events broke rapidly in the late spring of 1955, helping to drive Eisenhower and the Russians to the summit. On May 9 West Germany became a formal member of NATO. On May 14 the Soviet Union and the Eastern European nations signed the Warsaw Pact, the Communist military counter to NATO. The next day Russia and America finally solved one of the long-standing problems of World War II by signing the Austrian State Treaty, which gave Austria independence, forbade its union with Germany, and made it a permanent neutral. Both sides had been responsible for various delays. The Russians signed because they wanted to ease tensions and advance to the summit, whereas the Americans accepted it as a reasonable solution for the Austrian problem. Dulles was unhappy. As Ike later recalled, "Well, suddenly the thing was signed one day and [Dulles] came in and he grinned rather ruefully and he said, 'Well, I think we've had it.'"

What Dulles feared was misinterpretation. The fear was justified, for columnists and pundits began to advocate a similar solution for Germany. Actually, far from being a step toward German unity and neutrality, the Austrian treaty was a step toward making German division permanent.

Russia and America in effect agreed that neither of the Germanies would get Austria.

This in turn illustrated one of the most important results of the Second World War, the division of Hitler's Reich into three parts. A united Germany, whether Nazi, Communist, or capitalist, is always a threat to peace—or so the Russians and Americans decided. Both retained a formal commitment to the reunification of Germany, but neither wanted it, as the Austrian Treaty showed.

On May 19, 1955, in an air show, the Soviets displayed impressive quantities of their latest long-range bombers. A week later the new top Russian leaders, Nikita Khrushchev and Nikolai Bulganin, flew to Yugoslavia, where they apologized for Stalin's treatment of Tito and begged Tito's forgiveness. The Soviets were also initiating an economic assistance program for selected Third World countries. Clearly Russia had emerged from the confusion that followed Stalin's death and was on the offensive.

Some ground rules for the Cold War, of spirit if not of substance, were obviously needed. America's NATO allies were adamant about this need, insistently so after NATO war games in June of 1955 showed that if conflict started in Europe (and if the war-game scenario was accurate), 171 atomic bombs would be dropped on West Europe. For the United States to continue to take a stance of unrestrained hostility toward Russia was intolerable. This deeply felt sentiment in Europe plus Eisenhower's personal dedication to peace were the main factors in making the summit meeting at Geneva possible.

The Geneva meeting, the first summit since Potsdam ten years earlier, was not the result of any political settlement. Neither side was willing to back down from previous positions. Dulles made this perfectly clear when he drew up the American demands on Germany. His first goal was unification "under conditions which will neither 'neutralize' nor 'demilitarize' united Germany, nor subtract it from NATO." There was not the slightest chance that the Russians would accept such a proposal. Neither would they ever agree to the only new American offer, Ike's call for an "open skies" agreement, for to them that was only another heavy-handed American attempt to spy on Russia.* Bulganin, who fronted for Khrushchev at Geneva, was no more ready to deal than were the Americans. His position on Germany was to let things stand as they were.

On July 18, 1955, the summit meeting began. It had been called in response to the arms race and it was no surprise that there was no progress toward political settlements. What Dulles had feared most, however, did happen—there emerged a "spirit of Geneva." Before the meeting Dulles had warned Ike to maintain "an austere countenance" when being photographed with Bulganin. He pointed out that any pictures taken of the two leaders smiling "would be distributed throughout the Soviet satellite countries," signifying "that all hope of liberation was lost and that resistance to communist rule was henceforth hopeless." But the pictures were taken and Ike could not restrain his famous grin, and the photographs were distributed.

Dulles had been unable to prevent this symbolic recognition of the failure of Republican promises for liberation of Communist satellites. Geneva did not mean the end of the Cold War but it did put it on a different basis. The West had admitted that it could not win the Cold War, that a thermonuclear stalemate had developed, and that the status quo in Europe and China (where tensions quickly eased) had to be substantially accepted.

Dulles was bitter but helpless. He was especially infuriated because the battleground now shifted to the areas of economic and political influence in the Third World, a battleground on which Russia had great advantages. Dulles warned the NATO Foreign Ministers in December 1955 that the Soviets would thereafter employ "indirect" threats

* The Russians were indignant in their rejection on the "open skies" proposal, but actually Eisenhower was just slightly ahead of technology. The United States began spying on the Russians from the skies anyway, with the C.I.A.'s U-2 airplane, and within a few years both sides had satellites that were constantly spying on each other.

"primarily developed in relation to the Near and Middle East and South Asia." To fight back Dulles needed two things—money and an American willingness to accept radicalism in the emerging nations. He had neither. Republicans who resented giving money to West Europe through the Marshall Plan were hardly likely to approve significant sums for nonwhite revolutionaries.

Beyond diplomatic pressure and threats of all-out war or nuclear holocaust, the United States during the Eisenhower Administration developed another method of achieving its foreign policy objectives, especially in the Third World. As noted earlier, the C.I.A. got its start under Truman, but it really began to operate on a grand scale after 1953, when Allen Dulles, younger brother of the Secretary of State, became the Director of Central Intelligence. Allen Dulles, an O.S.S. agent during the war, worked behind the scenes on covert operations to accomplish the same objectives his brother worked on in public—primarily, the containment of Communism. An idealist himself, Allen Dulles attracted other idealists into the C.I.A. According to the Church Committee of the Senate, which in 1976 undertook a thorough investigation of the C.I.A., "during the 1950s the C.I.A. attracted some of the most able lawyers, academicians, and young, committed activists in the country." The C.I.A. was, indeed, thought to be a "liberal institution . . . that fostered free and independent thinking." To those who joined the C.I.A. it was the "good way" to fight Communism, as opposed to Senator McCarthy's "bad way."

The fifties were the glory years for the C.I.A. Few questions were asked of it, and even fewer answered. Congressional watchdog committees specifically told Allen Dulles they did not want to know about clandestine operations. The President and the public took it for granted that the only way to fight the Russians and their K.G.B. (secret police) was to use dirty tricks about which the less that was known, the better. No questions were asked about cost, either, for who could put a value on advance information that, for example, the Russians were massing in East Germany for a strike across the Elbe River? That generation of American leaders had been through Pearl Harbor and was determined never again to be surprised. Consequently, West Berlin was crawling with C.I.A. agents, who had spies located throughout East Europe, reporting on the movements and activities of the Red Army. The agents, however, could not pull off major covert operations behind the iron curtain, such as toppling the government of Poland or East Germany, because the secret police of the satellite governments were too well organized and too active.

In the Third World, meanwhile, the application of a little force or a little money could have dramatic results. Allen Dulles's first triumph came in 1953 in Iran. Premier Mohammed Mossadegh had, in the view of the Dulles brothers, drawn too close to the Tudeh, Iran's Communist party, and would have to be overthrown before he made a deal with the Russians. Mossadegh had already nationalized Iran's oil fields, to the consternation of the British, who previously had enjoyed a monopoly on Iranian oil production. Mossadegh was also thought to be a threat to Shah Mohammed Riza Pahlavi's retention of his throne.

Allen Dulles decided to save Iran by sending his best agent, Kim Roosevelt (Theodore Roosevelt's grandson) to Teheran, along with General H. Norman Schwarzkopf, an American who had organized the Shah's secret police after World War II. (Organizing and equipping the police force and army of small nations was another method of control often used by the United States in the Cold War.) Roosevelt and Schwarzkopf, spending money as if they did not have to account for it—as they did not—organized demonstrations in the streets of Teheran that overthrew Mossadegh, who went to jail, and brought the young Shah back from exile. The new Premier then divided up Iranian oil production to suit the C.I.A.: the British kept 40 percent, American oil companies got 40 percent, the French got 6 percent and the Dutch 14 percent. It would be years before the Iranians tried again to take control of their own resources, and then it would be the Shah that the C.I.A. saved who would do the taking. Meanwhile, however, the Communist tide had been stopped.

In the New World, too, the C.I.A. scored a victory. In 1951 Jacob Arbenz Guzman had become President of Guatemala. He worked closely with the Communist Party. Arbenz carried out some land reforms and expropriated 225,000 of the United Fruit Companies' holdings. That was bad enough; worse was the threat Arbenz posed to the Panama Canal. Allen Dulles proposed to drive Arbenz from office. After listening to the pros and cons Eisenhower gave him permission to go ahead. C.I.A. agents in Guatemala selected Colonel Carlos Castillo Armas to lead a coup. He set up his base and received his equipment in Honduras. Ike would not commit the United States to any direct military support of the operation, but he did tell the Dulles brothers, "I'm prepared to take any steps [short of sending in troops] that are necessary to see that it succeeds."

But when the invasion bogged down, Eisenhower did agree to allow Allen Dulles to send Castillo Armas a few old World War II bombers. These planes then carried out a bombing mission over Guatemala City. Arbenz lost his nerve, resigned, fled, and Guatemala was "saved." To the C.I.A.'s critics, it had been saved for United Fruit; to its defenders, the C.I.A. had acted decisively to prevent Communism from getting a foothold in the New World.

Driving Latin American Communists from power was much easier than driving the Russians out of East Europe. Secretary of State Dulles had promised liberation and had failed. Neither brinksmanship nor moral persuasion had freed a single slave or prevented North Vietnam from going Communist.

On Christmas Day 1955 the White House sent its usual message to the peoples of Eastern Europe "to recognize the trials under which you are suffering" and to "share your faith that right in the end will bring you again among the free nations of the world." When Khrushchev complained that this "crude interference" was not in accord with the spirit of Geneva, the White House pointed out that the goal of liberation was permanent. The statement said, "The peaceful liberation of the captive peoples is, and, until success is achieved, will continue to be a major goal of United States foreign policy."

A Presidential election year had just begun. As in 1952, captive nations' pronouncements made good campaign material. Unfortunately, some of the captive people did not know how to distinguish between campaign bombast and actual policy. They were about to demand payment on American liberation promises.

9

From Hungary and Suez to Cuba

> In the councils of government, we must guard against the
> acquisition of unwarranted influence, whether sought or un-
> sought, by the military-industrial complex.
>
> DWIGHT D. EISENHOWER,
> Farewell Address

The overwhelming first impression of American foreign
policy from 1956 to 1961 was one of unrelieved failure.
America's inability to do anything at all to aid Hungary's
rebels made a mockery of the Republican calls for liberation. Eisenhower and Dulles were unable to contain the
Russians, who succeeded in their centuries-old dream of
establishing themselves in the Mediterranean and the Middle East. Spectacular Soviet successes in rocketry, beginning
with Sputnik, sent the United States into a deep emotional
depression. Russia seemed to have won the arms race and
in 1959 it was Khrushchev who played at brinksmanship
from a position of strength. After the Suez crisis the French,
British, and Americans could never fully trust each other.
In Southeast Asia Communist guerrillas in South Vietnam
and Laos threatened to upset the delicate balance there in
favor of the Communists. In Latin America the Eisenhower
Administration was helpless in the face of a revolution in
Cuba, which soon allowed the Russians to extend their influence to within ninety miles of the United States.

Surface appearances, however, reveal only surface truths.
Eisenhower's outstanding achievement was to avoid war.
However irresponsible Republican emotional appeals to the
anti-Communist vote may have been, and despite the Russian shift to the offensive in the Cold War, Eisenhower

refused to engage American troops in armed conflict. He was not immune to intervention, nor to provocative rhetoric, nor to nuclear testing, nor to the arms race (within strict limits), but he did set his face against war. It became the Democrats' turn to complain that the United States was not "going forward," that it was not "doing enough," that America was "losing the Cold War."

But despite the Democratic complaints, the United States emerged from the Eisenhower years in a strong position. The American gross national product went up—without inflation. The Western European economy continued to boom. NATO was intact. Anglo-American oil interests in the Middle East were secure. The Latin American economy remained under American domination. American military bases in the Pacific were safe. Chiang remained in control of Formosa. And the United States, although Ike was spending only about two-thirds the amount that the Democrats wanted him to on defense, was militarily superior to the Soviet Union.

Eisenhower had been unable to contain the Communists, much less liberate East Europe, and he remained wedded to the clichés of the Cold War, but he was a man of moderation and caution with a clear view of what it would cost the United States to resist Communist advances everywhere. He thought the American economy could not pay the price, which was the fundamental distinction between Ike and his Democratic successors. Because of Eisenhower's fiscal conservatism, Dulles's hands were tied. The Secretary of State was reduced to vapid fulminations that provided emotional satisfaction but kept the budget balanced.

Eisenhower showed his reluctance to take aggressive action most clearly in response to the events that preceded and accompanied the 1956 Presidential campaign. The Democratic nominee, Adlai Stevenson, accused Ike of not doing enough to stop the Communists. Half of Indochina had become a "new Communist satellite," Stevenson declared, and the United States "emerged from the debacle looking like a 'paper tiger.'" Stevenson was also upset at what he called NATO's decline, wanted the American armed forces strengthened, and charged that Ike had rejected "great opportunities to exploit weaknesses in the Communist ranks." Finally, Stevenson charged that Ike had allowed the Russians to get ahead in the arms race. There was, he warned, a "bomber gap."

Eisenhower would not be stampeded, although the opportunities for action were certainly present. In the Middle East, ignoring ideology, the Russians were extending their influence. Although Dulles had broken with Truman's policy of support for Israel and was trying to improve relations with the Arabs, he was either unable or unwilling to match Communist aid programs for the area. In late 1955 he had a "conniption fit" when he learned that the Egyptians had negotiated an arms deal with the Czechs. Dulles's initial response was to offer the Egyptian leader, Colonel Gamal Abdel Nasser, American aid for the Aswan Dam, a gigantic project designed to harness the power of the lower Nile. Technical experts then studied the project and pronounced it feasible. By February 1956 Nasser was ready to conclude the deal.

Dulles, however, had trouble selling the Aswan Dam in the United States. Pro-Israeli politicians denounced the dam. Southern Congressmen wondered why the United States should build a dam that would allow the Egyptians to raise more cotton. In the Cabinet old-guard Republicans feared the cost of the dam would unbalance the budget. All the opponents agreed that the Egyptians could not possibly provide the technicians nor the industry to use the dam properly. Dulles himself began to back off when in April 1956 Nasser formed a military alliance with Saudi Arabia, Syria, and Yemen and refused to repudiate the Czech arms deal. The Secretary assumed that the Russians could not replace the Americans as backers of the Aswan Dam, an assumption based on the curious notion that the Russians did not have the technological know-how. When Nasser withdrew recognition from Chiang Kai-shek and recognized Communist China in May, Dulles had had enough. He decided to withdraw from the Aswan Dam project, but he did not make the decision public.

Then, on July 19, 1956, at the moment the Egyptian Foreign Minister was arriving in Washington to discuss the project, Dulles announced that America was withdrawing its support from the Aswan Dam. Nasser's immediate response was to seize the Suez Canal, which restored his lost prestige at a stroke and gave him the $25-million annual profit from the canal operation. Now it was the British and French who were furious. They were dependent on the canal for oil, they were certain that the Arabs did not have the skills to run the canal properly, they feared that Nasser would close it to their ships, and their self-esteem had suffered a serious blow. Long, complicated negotiations ensued. They got nowhere. Dulles's main concern was to protect American oil interests in the Middle East, whereas the British and French could be satisfied by nothing less than complete control of the canal. Dulles, fearing Arab reaction, was unwilling to restore the colonial powers, and was in any event—like Ike—strongly opposed to old-style European colonialism.

It was indeed a mess. In a later investigation Senator Fulbright charged that the Aswan Dam project was sound, that its repudiation was a personal decision by Dulles, that Dulles misjudged both Nasser's attitude toward the Soviet Union and the importance of the dam to Egypt, that he confused Egyptian nationalism and neutralism with Communism, and that he never made any serious effort to persuade the Congressional opponents of the project. Dulles had damaged the American position in France, Britain, and NATO, lost a chance to tie Nasser to the West, allowed the Soviet Union to begin preparation for a naval base in the Mediterranean, alienated Israel and her supporters, and failed to gain any more Arab adherents.

The anger of the critics was justified, but it did not take everything into account. The Middle East contained 64 percent of the world's then-known oil reserves. The leading producers were Kuwait, Saudi Arabia, and Iraq. During and after World War II American oil companies, aided by the United States government, had forced concessions from both the British and the Arabs and now had a major interest in Middle Eastern oil. Despite Dulles's bumbling, these interests were secure.

The Suez remained necessary to move the oil. Dulles began a complex series of negotiations designed to help Nasser run the canal without the British or French. The Europeans thereupon decided to take matters into their own hands. In conjunction with Israel, the British and French began plans for an invasion of Egypt. They did not inform the United States.

Another development, in East Europe, complicated everything. At the 20th Party Congress in February 1956 Khrushchev shocked the party by denouncing Stalin for his crimes, confessing that there could be several roads to communism, and indicating that Stalinist restrictions would be loosened. Two months later the Russians dissolved the Cominform. The C.I.A. got a copy of Khrushchev's secret speech and distributed copies of it throughout East Europe and the world. Ferment immediately swept through East Europe. Riots in Poland forced Khrushchev to disband the old Stalinist Politburo in Warsaw and allow Wladyslaw Gomulka, an independent Communist, to take power (October 20, 1956). Poland remained Communist and a member of the Warsaw Pact, but it won substantial independence and set an example for the other satellites.

The excitement spread to Hungary, before the war the most Fascist of the East European states and the one where Stalin's imposition of Communism had been most alien. On October 23 Hungarian students took to the streets to demand that the Stalinist puppets be replaced with Imre Nagy. Workers joined the students and the riot spread. Khrushchev agreed to give power to Nagy, but that was no longer enough. The Hungarians demanded the removal of the Red Army from Hungary and the creation of an anti-Communist political party. By October 28 the Russians had given in and begun to withdraw their tanks from around Budapest.

Liberation was at hand. Eisenhower was careful in his campaign speeches to use only the vaguest of phrases, although the Voice of America and Radio Free Europe did encourage the rebels. So did Dulles, who promised economic aid to those who broke with the Kremlin. At the decisive moment, however, just as it seemed that the European balance of power was about to be drastically altered, the Israeli Army struck Egypt. In a matter of hours it nearly destroyed Nasser's army and took most of the Sinai Peninsula. Britain and France then issued an ultimatum, arranged in advance with the Israelis, warning the combatants to stay away from the Suez Canal. When Nasser rejected the note, the Europeans began bombing Egyptian military targets and prepared to move troops into Suez, on the pretext of keeping the Israelis and Arabs apart.

On October 31, the day after the bombing in Egypt began and less than a week before the U.S. Presidential elections, Nagy announced that Hungary was withdrawing from the Warsaw Pact. The Russians, hoping that events in Egypt and the American Presidential campaign would paralyze the United States, and unwilling in any event to let the Warsaw Pact disintegrate, decided to move. Russian tanks crushed the Hungarian rebels, who fought back with Molotov cocktails. Bitter street fighting left seven thousand Russians and thirty thousand Hungarians dead. Radio pleas from Hungary made the tragedy even more painful: "Any news about help? Quickly, quickly, quickly!" And the last, desperate cry, on a teletype message to the Associated Press: "Help!—Help!—Help—SOS!—SOS!—SOS! They just brought us a rumor that the American troops will be here within one or two hours. . . . We are well and fighting."

There never would be any American troops. Eisenhower did not even consider giving military support to the Hungarians and he would not have done so even had there been no concurrent Middle Eastern crisis. Under no conceivable circumstances would he risk World War III for East Europe. Liberation was a sham; it had always been a sham. All Hungary did was to expose it to the world. However deep Eisenhower's hatred of Communism, his fear of nuclear war was deeper. Even had this not been so, the armed forces of the United States were not capable of driving the Red Army out of Hungary, except through a nuclear holocaust that would have left all Hungary and most of Europe devastated. The Hungarians, and the other Eastern European peoples, learned that there would be no liberation, that they could not look forward to tying themselves to the West, that their traditional policy of playing East against West was finished. They would have to make the best deal they could with the Soviets. The Russian capture and execution of Nagy made the point brutally clear.

In Egypt, meanwhile, the British and French had bungled. They blew their cover story almost immediately. Their advance was so rapid that they could not pretend that their invasion was one by a disinterested third party designed to keep the Israelis and Egyptians apart. Ike was upset at their use of nineteenth-century colonial tactics; he was livid at their failure to inform him of their intentions. The Americans backed a resolution in the U.N. General Assembly urging a truce, then imposed an oil embargo on Britain and France. Khrushchev, meanwhile, rattled his rockets, warning the British and French on November 5 to withdraw before he destroyed them. Although they were only hours away from taking the Suez Canal, the Anglo-French governments agreed to a ceasefire and pullback.

It had been quite a week for lessons. American politicians learned to stop their irresponsible prattling about liberation. The Russians learned just how strong a force nationalism was in East Europe, while the Israelis saw that they would have to make it on their own in their conflict with the Arabs. United States and United Nations pressure soon forced the Israelis to give up their gains in Sinai. The Egyptians learned to look to the Soviet Union for support—encouraged by Nasser, they believed that the Russian ultimatum, not the United States' U.N. actions and oil embargo, had saved them. The British and French learned that they no longer stood on the center of the world stage—they were second-rate powers incapable of independent action.

Dulles seemed to be losing the Third World, but from his point of view things were not that bad. To be sure, the Russians were taking over the great Western military base in Egypt, but the oil-rich countries stayed in the

Anglo-American orbit. To solidify this hold, Dulles and Eisenhower pushed through Congress (January 1957) the Eisenhower Doctrine, which gave the President the right to intervene in the Middle East whenever a legitimate government said it was threatened by Communism and asked for aid. Simultaneously, Ike broke all diplomatic precedents and went to the airport to meet King Saud of Saudi Arabia (the Mayor of New York City had just refused to meet the King, who was violently anti-Israel), and in the talks that followed gave the King extensive military aid in return for an American air base at Dhahran.

In April 1957, when pro-Nasser officers tried to oust King Hussein of Jordan, Ike dispatched the U.S. Sixth Fleet from the French Riviera to the eastern Mediterranean and gave $20 million to Hussein in military aid. There were sardonic references in Britain and France about unilateral action and gunboat diplomacy, but it worked. The three feudal Arab monarchies, Jordan, Saudi Arabia, and Iraq, were now wedded to the United States. A year later, when Russia began to move into Syria, and Iraq moved toward Nasser, thereby threatening its neighbor, Lebanon, Ike rushed troops to that Arab country (July 14, 1958). The Russians may have gained bases in the Mediterranean, but the United States still had the oil.

The intervention in Lebanon illustrated Ike's methods. It was a unilateral action that risked general war in support of a less than democratic government threatened by pro-Nasser Arabs. Eisenhower tried to tie the action into great historic precedents by invoking Greece and the 1947 Truman Doctrine. He emphasized the danger by mentioning the Communist takeovers in Czechoslovakia and China, and he explained that the United States "had no intention of replacing the United Nations in its primary responsibility of maintaining international peace and security." The United States had acted alone merely "because only swift action would suffice."

The rhetoric was grand, the intervention itself less sweeping. The Joint Chiefs wanted American troops to overrun all of Lebanon, but Ike ordered the men to limit themselves to taking the airfield and the capital. If the government could not survive even after American troops had secured the capital, Ike said, "I felt we were backing up a government with so little popular support that we probably should not be there." The British used the occasion to send troops into Jordan to prop up King Hussein and to make sure their oil interests in Iraq were not damaged. The British then asked the Americans to join them in occupying Jordan. Although many administration officials wanted to do so, Ike flatly refused. As always, he wanted to limit the risks and America's commitment.

The Russians, too, were unwilling to take drastic action. Nasser flew to Moscow to beg for aid; Khrushchev turned him down. The Soviet ruler knew that Eisenhower acted to protect Western oil holdings and he knew how vital those holdings were to the West. As long as Ike was willing to hold down the scope of the intervention, Khrushchev would not interfere.

Khrushchev's caution surprised many observers, since the Russians were generally believed to have achieved military superiority. On October 4, 1957, the Soviet Union successfully launched the world's first man-made satellite, Sputnik. Two months earlier they had fired the world's first intercontinental ballistic missile (I.C.B.M.). Americans were frustrated, angry, ashamed, and afraid all at once. As Walter LaFeber puts it, " 'gaps' were suddenly discovered in everything from missile production to the teaching of arithmetic at the preschool level." Eisenhower dispersed Strategic Air Force units and installed medium-range ballistic missiles in Turkey and Italy, but this was hardly enough to assuage the sudden fear. When the Russians began trumpeting about their average increase in their G.N.P. (7 percent, nearly twice the American rate), the pressure on Eisenhower to "get the country moving again" became almost irresistible.

Eisenhower refused to panic, even when in late 1957 the newspapers discovered and published the findings and recommendations of a committee headed by H. Rowan Gaither,

Jr., of the Ford Foundation, which painted an exceedingly dark picture of the future of American security. The Gaither Report, as Ike typically understated it, included "some sobering observations." It found that the Soviet G.N.P. was indeed increasing at a much faster rate than that of the United States, that the Russians were spending as much on their armed forces and heavy industry as the Americans were, that the Soviets had enough fissionable material for fifteen hundred nuclear weapons, with forty-five hundred jet bombers, three hundred long-range submarines, and an extensive air-defense system, that they had been producing ballistic missiles with a seven-hundred-mile range, that by 1959 the Soviets might be able to launch an attack against the United States with one hundred I.C.B.M.'s carrying megaton-sized nuclear warheads, and that if such an attack should come, the civilian population and American bombers would be vulnerable.

The Gaither Report was similar to N.S.C. 68 in its findings, and like N.S.C. 68 it recommended a much-improved defense system. The committee wanted fallout shelters built on a massive scale, an improvement in America's air-defense capability, a vast increase in offensive power, especially missile development, a buildup of conventional forces capable of fighting limited war, and another reorganization of the Pentagon. As a starter the Gaither Report urged an increase in defense spending to $48 billion.

Eisenhower said no. "We could not turn the nation into a garrison state," he explained in his memoirs, adding as an afterthought that the Gaither Report was "useful; it acted as a gadfly. . . ." He kept the Defense budget under $40 billion, quietly rejected the demands for fallout shelters and increased conventional-war capability, and cut one Army division and a number of tactical air wings from active duty. He did speed up the ballistic-missile program, although Congress had to appropriate more funds than the administration requested for the I.C.B.M. and Polaris missile to get those programs into high gear.

Democrats charged that the Republicans were allowing

their Neanderthal fiscal views to endanger the national security, but Ike knew what he was doing. The C.I.A., in one of the great intelligence coups of all time, had in 1956 inaugurated a series of flights over the Soviet Union in specially built high-altitude airplanes called U-2s. The photographs that resulted from the flights revealed, as Eisenhower later put it, "proof that the horrors of the alleged 'bomber gap' and the later 'missile gap' were nothing more than imaginative creations of irresponsibility." The United States still had a substantial lead in strategic weapons.

One of the most important points about the U-2 flights was that Khrushchev knew they were taking place (none of the Russian fighter airplanes could reach the altitude at which the U-2s flew, so they could not knock them down), which meant that Khrushchev knew that Ike knew how false were the Soviet boasts about their strategic superiority. The fact that Eisenhower made no strong statements about Soviet inferiority during the American domestic controversy about the missile gap should have reassured the Soviets and convinced them that Ike really was a man of moderation who was sincerely interested in some sort of *modus vivendi*. The flights, the information they produced, and Eisenhower's rejection of the Gaither Report, all indicated to the Soviets that Eisenhower had accepted the fundamental idea that neither side could win a nuclear war and that both would lose in an arms race.

The events in the year following Sputnik had the effect of establishing ground rules for the Cold War. By staying out of the Lebanon situation the Soviets indicated that they recognized and would not challenge the West's vital interests. By refusing to take the easy way out of the missile gap controversy, Ike indicated that he did not want an arms race and was eager for détente. Through their negative signals both sides showed that they would keep the threshold of conflict low. The years of Eisenhower's second term marked the height of bipolarity, for, as the British, French, Israelis, and Egyptians could testify, what the Big Two wanted they got. Whether they could continue to control their allies, especially France and China,* much less the Third World, was an open question. Indeed, it was not at all clear that Eisenhower and Khrushchev could control the hard-liners in their own countries.

A major test soon came in divided Berlin. Ike's desire for détente was based on a continuation of the status quo, which Khrushchev could not accept everywhere and certainly could not accept in Berlin. West Berlin was a bone in his throat. Each year 300,000 East Germans defected to the West via Berlin, most of them young, talented, educated, and professional people. Since 1949 East Germany had lost three million people through the West Berlin escape hatch. West Berlin also contained the largest combination of espionage agencies ever assembled in one place, 110 miles deep in Communist territory, as well as radio stations that constantly beamed propaganda into East Europe.

Equally important was the West Berlin economic miracle. The Americans had poured $600 billion into the city, which the Bonn government had matched. West Berlin was turning out nearly $2 billion worth of goods per year. It had become the greatest manufacturing city in Germany and its G.N.P. exceeded that of more than half the members of the United Nations. The glittering social, intellectual, and economic life in West Berlin stood in sharp contrast to the drab, depressed life of East Berlin. What made the situation especially intolerable for Khrushchev was the steady flow of American propaganda about Berlin. Americans used the refugees and the economic contrast between the two Berlins as the ultimate proof of the superiority of capitalism over communism.

The situation had, however, existed for over a decade. Why did Khrushchev decide to move against West Berlin in late 1958, during a period of relative calm in the Cold

* Much to the American's displeasure, France was pushing forward the development of its own nuclear weapons; China, in August 1958, inaugurated the second Quemoy crisis.

War? He may have reasoned that since Ike would not build up conventional forces, and since the President would do everything possible to avoid a nuclear exchange, a diplomatic solution was now possible. More immediately, Khrushchev feared the growing rearmament of West Germany. The Americans had sent artillery capable of firing nuclear shells and airplanes that could carry nuclear bombs to West Germany. Konrad Adenauer, the West German leader, was increasing the pace of rearmament. Finally, the Bonn government was on the verge of joining with France, Italy, and the Benelux nations in the Common Market, which would tie West Germany more firmly than ever into the Western bloc. Khrushchev was under intense pressure to do something about the German situation.

On November 10, 1958, Khrushchev declared that the Soviet Union was ready to turn over control of Berlin to East Germany. Then the West would have to negotiate rights of access to West Berlin with the East German government, which none of the Western governments recognized. The West was in Berlin only on the basis of presurrender occupation agreements; if Khrushchev signed a peace treaty with the East Germans, the occupation would have to come to an end. Khrushchev warned that any attack against East Germany would be considered an attack on the Soviet Union. He set a time limit of six months and said that if agreement were not reached by then, the West would have to deal with the East Germans. In later speeches he indicated that the only satisfactory resolution of the Berlin situation was to turn West Berlin into a free city with the British, French, and Americans withdrawing their ten thousand troops. He also wanted the West Berlin economy integrated into that of East Germany and the Soviet Union.

Eisenhower rejected the free-city proposal but he also refused to increase the armed services dramatically as a prelude to taking a hard line over Berlin. In March 1959, as Khrushchev's deadline approached and Democrats urged him to mobilize, Ike told Congress that he did not need additional money for missiles or conventional-warfare forces to deal with the crisis. At a press conference on March 11, with considerable emotion, he dismissed demands that he refrain from carrying out his plans to further reduce the size of the Army. He wanted to know what in heaven's name the United States would do with more ground forces in Europe. Thumping the table, he declared, "We are certainly not going to fight a ground war in Europe," and he pointed out the elementary truth that a few more men or even a few more divisions in Europe would have little effect on the military balance there. He thought the greatest danger in the Berlin crisis was that the Russians would frighten the United States into an arms race that would bankrupt the country. The contrast between what Eisenhower did and what the Democrats wanted (and did a few years later in a similar Berlin crisis) could not have been greater.

Khrushchev, who wanted to reduce his own armed forces and who was no more anxious to exchange nuclear strikes than Ike, began to back down. He denied that he had ever set a time limit, agreed to visit the United States in September of 1959, and arranged with Eisenhower for a summit meeting in Paris, scheduled for May 1960.

During private talks with Khrushchev at Camp David, Maryland, in the fall of 1959, Eisenhower admitted that the situation in Berlin was abnormal and that some modification would be necessary. Ike was prepared to make concessions in order to normalize the situation. Dulles had resigned due to a fatal illness, and Ike became noticeably friendlier to the Russians than any American leader had been since 1945. Eisenhower had managed to avoid a crisis over Berlin by simply denying that a crisis existed, in a sense an awesome display of Presidential power—a "crisis" can exist only when the President says it exists.

In a limited and halting but nevertheless real way, Ike had opted for peace. Throughout his second term he warned of the danger of turning America into a garrison state and of the need to learn to live with the Communists. As a professional soldier of the old school Eisenhower felt his first responsibility was the nation's security, which he realized could never be enhanced by an arms race in the nuclear age. This was Ike's fundamental insight, that the more one spent on atomic weapons, the less secure one became, because as the United States built more weapons, the Russians were bound to follow.

Negotiation with the Russians was a more effective way to enhance the nation's security. Democrats thought the primary reason for Ike's concern was his commitment to a balanced budget, and it was true that he had decided that the cost of the Cold War was more than America could bear, but there was something else. By 1958 Eisenhower realized that he had only two more years on the world stage, that if he were to leave any lasting gift to the world he would have to do it soon. His deepest personal desire was to leave mankind the gift of peace.

Eisenhower and Khrushchev were anxious to solidify the concept of peaceful coexistence, or détente, each for his own reasons, but by 1959 the Cold War had gone on for so long that calling it off was no easy task. Both men had to fend off hard-liners at home, both had troubles with their allies, and both were beset by Third World problems that they could neither understand nor control. Eisenhower had to deal with the Democrats, who were unhampered by orthodox fiscal views and who did want an arms race. In their view government spending would help, not hurt, the economy. The Democrats, led by Senators John F. Kennedy, Lyndon B. Johnson, and Hubert H. Humphrey, were impatient with Eisenhower's conservatism, yearned for a dynamic President, and talked incessantly about America's loss of prestige. They wanted to restore America to world leadership, which in practice meant extending American commitments and increasing American arms. On the other side, Eisenhower was beset by Republicans who wanted to hear more about liberation and getting tough with the Communists, and the President himself had by no means escaped fully from the patterns of thought of the Cold War.

Neither had Khrushchev, who also had hard-liners in Moscow pushing him toward the brink. In addition, Mao had become as much a problem for Khrushchev as Chiang was for Eisenhower. Khrushchev's refusal to support Mao's call for wars of national liberation signified to Mao that the Russians had joined the have powers against the have-nots. There was other evidence, such as Khrushchev's trip to the United States, his willingness to go to the summit again, and the cooling of the Berlin crisis. As the Chinese saw it, the Soviets were selling out both Communism and the Third World. They accused Khrushchev of appeasement. Mao's propaganda increasingly warned of winds blowing from the east instead of the west and of a worldwide revolt of the rural peoples against the urbanites, among whom the Chinese counted the Russians. Mao's radicalism, heightened by his emphasis on racism, appealed strongly to the Third World and made it almost as difficult for the Soviets to influence development in Southeast Asia and Africa as it was for the United States. Mao challenged, directly and successfully, Khrushchev's leadership of the Communist world. Indirectly, he challenged bipolarity. The world was simply too large, with too much diversity, to be controlled by the two superpowers, no matter how closely together they marched.

Khrushchev and Eisenhower, in short, had gone too far toward coexistence for the Cold Warriors in their own countries and for their allies. Khrushchev was in the weaker position at home, since Eisenhower was almost immune to criticism, especially on military matters. When the Air Force and certain Congressmen demanded that one-third of America's heavy bombers be airborne at all times, for example, Ike dismissed the proposal as too costly and not necessary. As one Senator, an Air Force supporter, put it, "How the hell can I argue with 'Ike' Eisenhower on military matters?" Khrushchev did not have such prestige and he found it increasingly difficult to ward off those in the Kremlin who wanted more arms and something done about Berlin. He also had to face the Chinese challenge for Communist leadership.

Khrushchev badly needed a Cold War victory, both for internal political reasons and to compete with China for followers. He may have felt that Ike, who would shortly be leaving office, would be willing to allow him a victory. Whatever his reasoning, Khrushchev announced on May 5, 1960, on the eve of the Paris summit meeting, that a Russian surface-to-air missile (SAM) had knocked down an American U-2 spy plane inside Russia.

The event illustrated more than Khrushchev's flair for the dramatic, for it also showed how entrenched Cold War interests could block any move toward peace. Having finally achieved the ability to knock down the U-2s, the Soviets could have waited for the results of the Paris meeting to actually do it. On the other side, the C.I.A. could have suspended the flights in the period preceding the meeting. Or Khrushchev could have kept quiet about the entire affair, hoping that the C.I.A. had learned a lesson and would cease and desist thereafter. Instead, he deliberately embarrassed the President. Khrushchev boasted about the performance of the SAMs but concealed pilot Francis Gary Powers's survival in order to elicit an American explanation that could be demolished by producing Powers. When Ike fell into the trap, Khrushchev crowed over his discomfort and demanded an apology or a repudiation of Presidential responsibility. He had misjudged the man. Ike stated instead that the United States had the right to spy on the Soviet Union and he took full personal responsibility for the flight. The summit conference was ruined. The best hope for an agreement on Berlin was gone, although Khrushchev did abandon his effort to change the status quo there. He said he would wait for the new President to take office before he brought it up again.

Khrushchev had improved his position at home, and with the Chinese, but not much. Eisenhower had tried but in the end he was unable to bring the Cold War to a close. Despite the U-2 and the wrecked summit meeting, he had improved Russian-American relations. He had failed to liberate any Communist slaves—indeed, he had been forced to acquiesce in the coming of Communism to Indochina and in the establishment of a Russian base in the Mediterranean—but he had avoided war and kept the arms race at a low level. He had tried, insofar as he was capable, to ease the policy of permanent crisis he had inherited from Truman.

Eisenhower's major weakness was that he was an old man, head of an old party, surrounded by old advisers. He dealt with old problems. His image, deliberately promoted by the Republicans, was that of a kindly grandfather. He could not anticipate new problems nor adjust to the winds of change that Mao always talked about, and which were, indeed, blowing across the world.

Cuba illustrated Eisenhower's limited view best, but it also showed the constraints within which any President would have to operate in dealing with Third World revolution. The United States had given verbal support to the colonial revolutions in Africa and Asia in the immediate postwar period, but it found it much more difficult to adjust to the thoroughgoing social and economic revolutions that followed. When African and Asian states achieved their independence, they found themselves in the same position as the Latin Americans. Their economy remained extractive, their principal sources of income were owned or controlled by the West, and their masses continued to live in poverty. They needed to change the nature of their economies. To do that, they needed money. To get money, since neither the United States nor the Russians would loan it on anything like the scale required, they had to nationalize the major foreign holdings, as Nasser had done in Egypt. They also had to have state planning and control in order to use their limited resources most effectively.

The underdeveloped nations, in short, needed to change their entire relationship with the West, which posed a continuing problem for the United States. On the simple economic level, American citizens and corporations lost money when plants, mines, or plantations were expropriated. Most emerging nations did not pay for what they seized, partly out of principle—they had been exploited so long they felt they deserved whatever they took, and more—and partly because they did not have the funds.

Beyond the immediate loss the Americans also lost the opportunity for further profits and an area of potential further investment. Within the United States, whenever an American investment was nationalized there were cries of anguish and Congressional demands for action, which made it extraordinarily difficult for a President to deal effectively with the Third World.

All of America's difficulties in the underdeveloped world came to a head in Cuba. Throughout the nineteenth century, Americans had looked with undisguised longing toward the island. In 1898 they drove the Spanish out and occupied it. After the Cubans wrote a constitution that gave the United States the right to intervene on the island whenever Washington felt it was necessary, the American troops left. Investors stayed behind. Three times after 1902 the United States intervened in Cuba to protect the investments, which by the end of World War II had grown to impressive proportions. Americans owned 80 percent of Cuba's utilities, 40 percent of its sugar, 90 percent of its mining wealth, and occupied the island's key strategic location of Guantanamo Bay. Cuban life was controlled from Washington, for almost the only source of income was sugar, and by manipulating the amount of sugar allowed into the United States, Washington directed the economy. As Ambassador Earl Smith later confessed, "Senator, let me explain to you that the United States . . . was so overwhelmingly influential in Cuba that . . . the American Ambassador was the second most important man in Cuba; sometimes even more important than the [Cuban] President."

Fulgencio Batista was the Cuban dictator. He had come to power as a revolutionary but had adjusted to the realities of leading a small nation in which the United States had a large investment. Postponing land reform and other promised improvements, by the fifties he had become a fairly typical Latin American ruler. His sole support was the Cuban Army, which was equipped by the United States, and his policies were repressive. In January 1959, after a long struggle, Fidel Castro, who had placed himself at the head of the various anti-Batista guerrilla movements, drove Ba-

tista from power. At first the general public in the United
States welcomed Castro, casting him in a romantic mold
and applauding his democratic reforms. Castro helped by
putting leading Cuban liberals in important posts on his
Cabinet. American supporters of Castro expected him to
restore civil liberties, introduce gradual and compensated
land reform, look to the United States for leadership, maintain Havana as the swingingest city in the New World, and
not tamper with the fundamental source of Cuba's poverty,
American ownership of the mines and sugar plantations.

Within the American government, however, Castro did
not receive an enthusiastic welcome. Allen Dulles told Ike
that "Communists and other extreme radicals appear to
have penetrated the Castro movement"; Dulles warned that
the Communists would probably participate in the government. "When I heard this estimate," Eisenhower later said,
"I was provoked that such a conclusion had not been given
earlier." The limitations on American policy then became
apparent. Someone suggested that the United States help
Batista return to power. Eisenhower refused —Batista was
too much the dictator. Since Castro was too close to the
Communists to deserve American support, the administration began working on a third alternative. "Our only hope,"
Ike said, "lay with some kind of non-dictatorial 'third force,'
neither Castroite nor Batistiano." The statement summed
up the entire American relationship to the underdeveloped
world—find a liberal who would not disturb the existing
economic arrangements but who would rule in a democratic manner. It was a self-defeating program, for in Cuba—
and elsewhere—there was little point to having a revolution
if the basic economic structure were not changed, beginning with expropriation of foreign-owned property.

In Cuba, meanwhile, forces in Castro's movement combined with the realities he faced to push him to the left.
His own inclination was toward radicalism anyway, and
there was no possibility of improvement in Cuba as long
as the profits continued to flow back to the United States.
Castro therefore began an extensive land-reform program
and a nationalization of American-owned property, with-

out compensation.* The United States turned down his requests for loans and relations steadily worsened. Cuban liberals began to flee the country; Cuban Communists rose to power under Castro. Khrushchev welcomed Castro as a new force in Latin America, pronounced the Monroe Doctrine dead, and in February 1960 signed a trade agreement to exchange Cuban sugar for Soviet oil and machinery. Four months later the United States eliminated the Cuban sugar quota; in the first days of 1961 Eisenhower formally severed diplomatic relations with Cuba.

The search for a liberal alternative went on. Eisenhower gave the C.I.A. permission to plan an invasion of Cuba and to begin training Cuban exiles to carry it out, with American support. Some of Castro's original liberal Cabinet members participated in the invasion scheme. Preparations were not complete when Ike left office and the decision to go forward with the invasion or not became his successor's problem.

By the time Eisenhower left office he knew that the United States was in deep trouble in Cuba. He also made a point of briefing his successor on the situation in Berlin, Formosa, NATO, and the Middle East. He never mentioned Vietnam in the briefings, however, and the American press and government continued to present Diem as the liberal model on which the Third World could base its revolution.

Eisenhower was not alone in his lack of foresight. The young Democrats who had taken over the party by nominating John F. Kennedy for the Presidency, and who were urging dynamism in foreign relations and a major increase in America's armed forces, as well as a totally new American relationship to the Third World, did not give much thought to the problem in Vietnam either. Kennedy and his advisers, like Ike, were most concerned with finding a liberal

---

* Castro did offer to pay for what he took, on the basis of the value of the property as stated by the owners themselves in response to an early Castro request for a reassessment for taxation purposes. American investors denounced this as a fraud and refused to accept Cuban bonds.

alternative to Castro. During the campaign Kennedy said his policy would be to give American support to "non-Batista democratic anti-Castro forces." The major foreign-policy issue in the Nixon-Kennedy campaign of 1960 was Quemoy and Matsu. Kennedy doubted that the islands were worth defending, although he never suggested anything approaching a reorientation of American policy in regard to China. Nixon insisted that Quemoy and Matsu had to be held. Kennedy also stressed the missile gap, which Nixon denied existed. There were no other significant differences on foreign-policy issues. Kennedy won by a narrow margin.

In January 1961 Eisenhower delivered his farewell address. He was concerned about the internal cost of the Cold War. His ideals were those of small-town America. He was afraid that big government and the regimentation of private life were threatening the old American values. He had no precise idea of what could be done about the dangers, for he knew that both were necessary to carrying on the Cold War, but he did want to warn his countrymen. He pointed out that the "conjunction of an immense military establishment and a large arms industry, . . . new in American experience, exercised a total influence . . . felt in every city, every state house, every office of the federal government. . . . In the councils of government, we must guard against the acquisition of unwarranted influence, whether sought or unsought, by the military-industrial complex."

The Democrats paid no attention. In the campaign, and in his inaugural address, Kennedy emphasized that a new generation was coming to power in America. Hardened by the Cold War, it was prepared to deal with all the tough problems. He promised to replace Eisenhower's tired, bland leadership with new ideas and new approaches. Since these generalities were not reinforced by any specific suggestions, it was difficult to tell what the new directions would be. What was clear was that a forward-looking, offensive spirit had come to America. Action was about to replace inaction. Kennedy promised to get the country moving again. Where to, no one knew precisely.

[10]

Kennedy

Let every nation know, whether it wishes us well or ill, that we shall pay any price, bear any burden, meet any hardship, support any friend, oppose any foes, in order to assure the survival and success of liberty. This much we pledge—and more.

JOHN F. KENNEDY,
Inaugural Address

John Kennedy had a vision. He thought the United States was the last, best hope of mankind. He wanted prosperity and happiness for all the world's people and believed the United States was capable of supplying the leadership necessary to achieve those goals. He surrounded himself with the very best minds America had to offer, appointing men who had the techniques and the brains that would enable the new administration to solve any problem, indeed to go out and find new problems so that they could solve them.

Kennedy and the men around him had been impatient with Eisenhower's leadership. Ike had not been aggressive enough, he tended to compromise, he could not stir the nation to great deeds. Fundamentally, Eisenhower had rejected the idea that there could be a military solution to Cold War problems or that America could shape the world's destiny. He had accepted limitations on America's role. Kennedy did not. Where Eisenhower had been passive, Kennedy would be active. Where Ike had been cautious, J.F.K. would be bold. Kennedy and his aides were especially interested in restoring the prestige and primacy of the Presidency, which they felt had fallen under Eisenhower.

Kennedy's energy was almost boundless. He was interested in every area of the world, anxious to bring the benefits of cost analysis and rational planning to everyone. He was dynamic, good-looking, youthful. He exuded confidence. He got on easily with the intellectuals who flocked to Washington to help the new administration and he was by far the most sophisticated President America had had since the Cold War began. His wit and charm seemed to place him light years ahead of his predecessor.

Republican rhetoric had consisted of unrestrained hostility to the Soviet Union and emphasized permanent war with Communism. It was filled with Cold War clichés. Republican action, however, was restrained and cautious. The Democratic rhetoric, under Kennedy, favored coexistence. Kennedy abandoned the clichés of the Cold War, especially with regard to the Third World, where he claimed to be ready to accept neutralism and even socialism. He was sympathetic to the nonwhite peoples, believed himself to be free of any taint of racism, showed an interest in black Africa unique to American politicians, and in general spoke of an entirely new relationship between America and the Third World. But Democratic actions revealed a dynamic militancy, which traditional Cold Warriors like Acheson and Truman could and did applaud.

The new President deeply believed that the United States was not doing nearly well enough in the Cold War. He said he was "not satisfied as an American with the progress that we are making." Kennedy wanted the people of Latin America and Africa and Asia "to start to look to America, to what the President of the United States is doing, not . . . Khrushchev or the Chinese Communists." Freedom was under the "most severe attack it has ever known." It could be saved only by the United States. And if the United States failed, "then freedom fails." The recurring theme, therefore, was, "I think it's time America started moving again."

If anyone thought Kennedy was merely indulging in campaign rhetoric, he quickly dispelled that idea. In his first State of the Union address, on January 30, 1961, he warned, "Each day the crises multiply. . . . Each day we draw nearer the hour of maximum danger." He felt he had to tell the Congress the truth: "The tide of events has been running out and time has not been our friend." Finally, the grim prophecy: "There will be further setbacks before the tide is turned."

Kennedy wanted the United States to take the initiative. This sounded suspiciously like Dulles's talk about liberation, but Kennedy emphasized that "a total solution is impossible in the nuclear age." He did not expect to "win" in any traditional sense. The military realities precluded victory, while America's view of the nature of the change and of Communism precluded peace. This tended to lock the nation into a policy of containment. Since stalemate was no more satisfactory to Kennedy than it had been to Dulles, however, Kennedy had to hold out a long-range hope. "Without having a nuclear war," he said, "we want to permit what Thomas Jefferson called 'the disease of liberty' to be caught in areas which are now held by the Communists." Sooner or later freedom would triumph. How? Partly by waiting, partly through the example of American vitality. Kennedy told the American people to expect a long, slow process of evolution "away from Communism and toward national independence and freedom."

The Third World provided the key. "The great battleground for the defense and expansion of freedom today," Kennedy said, "is the whole southern half of the globe . . . the lands of the rising people." Kennedy, like the Communists, believed in the inevitable victory of his system in the long run. Again like his enemies, however, he was not averse to speeding up the process. Fittingly, his first great opportunity, and his first crisis, came in a Third World revolutionary nation. For all the President's speeches about willingness to tolerate differences in the world, he was no more ready to accept a Communist regime off the tip of Florida than Eisenhower had been. In late 1960 the C.I.A., with Eisenhower's approval, had begun training anti-Castro Cuban exiles in the arts of guerrilla warfare. The plan was to land the counterrevolutionaries in a remote section of

Cuba, with covert American assistance, so that they could set up a base of operations to overthrow Castro.

In mid-April 1961 the invasion began. Cuban exiles, carried in American ships and covered by American airplanes, waded ashore at the Bay of Pigs. Castro completely crushed them. He proved to be far stronger than the Americans had thought, the Cuban people showed no inclination to revolt against him, and the exiles were unable to find support in the Cuban mountains. Kennedy had played a delicate game, trying to give enough support to make the invasion work but not enough to make the American involvement obvious. He had failed on both counts.

Later, in analyzing the failure, Kennedy muttered that "all my life I've known better than to depend on the experts. How could I have been so stupid, to let them go ahead?" That the fault lay with the C.I.A. and the Joint Chiefs became the standard explanation. The President, young and inexperienced, had depended on their expert judgment and had been let down. He would, thereafter, know better.

That explanation was patent nonsense. The Bay of Pigs was hardly an operation carried out against the President's wishes or in opposition to his policy. He had advocated such activity by exile forces during the 1960 campaign, and the fact was that it fit perfectly into his general approach. The C.I.A. had been wrong in predicting an uprising against Castro, but the prediction was exactly what Kennedy wanted to hear. He, too, believed that Castro had betrayed the Cuban revolution; he, too, believed that the Cuban people were groaning under the oppressor's heel. The President believed there was a liberal alternative between Castro and Batista and that the exile counterrevolutionary group would supply the liberal leadership around which the Cuban people would rally. It was not the experts who got Kennedy into the Bay of Pigs; it was his own view of the world.*

* Afterward, furious at Castro for so thoroughly embarrassing him, J.F.K. ordered Castro assassinated. The C.I.A. tried, but failed to carry out the orders.

Before he gave the final go-ahead Kennedy had consulted with Senator Fulbright. On March 29 the Senator
sent a memorandum to the President. "To give this activity
even covert support," Fulbright warned, "is of a piece with
the hypocrisy and cynicism for which the United States is
constantly denouncing the Soviet Union." The Bay of Pigs,
the Senator said, would compromise America's moral position in the world and make it impossible for Kennedy to
protest treaty violations by the Communists. Kennedy ignored Fulbright, partly because he felt that success would
provide its own justification, more because to back down
on the invasion would compromise America's position.
Kennedy believed, as he later explained, that "his disapproval of the plan would be a show of weakness inconsistent
with his general stance."

One of Kennedy's great fears was to appear weak. And,
like most Cold Warriors, he thought the only way to deal
with the Russians and their associates was from a position
of strength. How much strength became the great question.
The man J.F.K. picked to answer it, Robert S. McNamara,
the Secretary of Defense, maintained that "enough" meant
great superiority. He set out to give America that superiority. McNamara, whose brilliance and ability to use the
new technological tools to solve old problems epitomized
the Kennedy Administration, described the result in some
detail in a 1967 speech to the editors of United Press International. McNamara recalled that when he took office,
the Soviets possessed "a very small operational arsenal of
intercontinental missiles," but they had the ability to "en-
large that arsenal very substantially." The Americans had
"no evidence that the Soviets did in fact plan to fully use
that capability," but the possibility existed that they intended to so expand. McNamara and Kennedy decided that
"we had to insure against" a Soviet buildup by dramatically
increasing American strength. After two years in office J.F.K.
had the Defense budget up to $56 billion; with the coming
of war in Vietnam it would skyrocket even higher. By 1967
America had forty-one Polaris submarines carrying 656
missile launchers and six hundred long-range bombers, 40

percent of which were always in a high state of alert. In I.C.B.M.s, Kennedy and McNamara had increased the American force level by a factor of five. They had inherited two hundred I.C.B.M.s from Eisenhower; by 1967 the United States had one thousand I.C.B.M.s.

The Kennedy-McNamara team had launched the greatest arms race in the history of mankind. It extended far beyond nuclear delivery weapons. The White House and the Pentagon cooperated in vastly increasing America's conventional-war capability and, as a Kennedy favorite, guerrilla-warfare forces. Eisenhower had backed away from involvement in Dien Bien Phu because, unless he wished to inaugurate a nuclear exchange, he did not have the forces required. J.F.K. wanted, and got, an ability to intervene anywhere. The new strategy was called flexible response.

As a reaction to the enormous American buildup, the Russians increased their I.C.B.M. forces. As McNamara put it in 1967, the Soviets had had no intention of engaging in an arms race and might have been satisfied to accept the status quo of 1960, under which America had superiority but not enough to launch a first strike. The Kennedy-McNamara program, however, apparently convinced the Kremlin that America did in fact aim at achieving a first-strike capability, which left the Soviets with no choice. They increased their missile forces, which forced the United States to begin another round of expansion. But, as McNamara confessed, the whole thing had been a terrible mistake. America had been unwilling to take the risk of allowing the Soviets to achieve parity in nuclear delivery systems, but by building more missiles the Americans only increased their own danger. Given the inevitable Soviet response, the more missiles America built, the less secure America was.

McNamara himself recognized this when he admitted that "the blunt fact is that if we had had more accurate information about planned Soviet strategic forces [in 1961], we simply would not have needed to build as large a nuclear arsenal as we have today." The heart of the matter was that J.F.K. and McNamara probably did not aim at achieving a first-strike capability, and even if they had they quickly realized that such a goal was impossible. Therefore, as McNamara concluded, American superiority in I.C.B.M.s by 1967 was "both greater than we had originally planned, and is in fact more than we require."

The political response to the Kennedy buildup was as important as the military reaction. Whereas the Republicans had been content to rest their military policy on the grounds that General Ike knew best, and make general, vague statements to the effect that there was no missile gap, the Democrats made specific statements in insistent tones about American superiority. Coupled with the Bay of Pigs, the new American military policy indicated to the Soviets that they had to deal with an aggressive, outward-looking administration. The "hards" in the Kremlin found their direst prediction fulfilled and they charged Khrushchev with having neglected Soviet military security. Even Khrushchev and his followers, committed to the possibility of détente, had to alter their view, for it seemed to them that the United States was trying to shift the military balance in its favor before reaching a worldwide settlement, part of which would be an agreement to keep military forces at the existing levels. J.F.K. was always talking about arms limitation talks and at the end of his first year in office said his greatest disappointment was the failure to secure a nuclear test-ban treaty. The Russians saw Kennedy's expressed desire for arms limitation as a deliberate propaganda lie, coming as it did concurrently with the American military buildup, and believed it was a cover for the continuation of the status quo throughout the world, especially in Berlin, Vietnam, Korea, and Formosa. Kennedy, the Russians charged, would use superior American arms to block all change.

Kennedy said as much in the summer of 1961, when he met Khrushchev in Vienna. Again and again the President urged the Premier to preserve the existing balance of power in arms and geography. J.F.K. insisted that the entry of additional nations into the Communist camp, or the loss of Formosa or Berlin, would alter the equilibrium and force the United States to react. Khrushchev rejected the concept. Even if he wanted to, he said, he could not stop change, and in any case the Soviet Union could hardly be expected to cooperate in enforcing stability on a world that was predominantly colonial and capitalist. Khrushchev complained that Kennedy "by-passed" the real problem. "We in the U.S.S.R. feel that the revolutionary process should have the right to exist," he explained. The question of "the right to rebel, and the Soviet right to help combat reactionary governments . . . is the question of questions." It was, he said, "at the heart of our relations" with the United States. He was sorry that "Kennedy could not understand this."

To explore the subject further, Khrushchev asked about Formosa. J.F.K. said that withdrawal of American forces from Formosa would impair the American strategic position in Asia and would therefore be resisted. Khrushchev shook his head. That meant that the Chinese Communists would have to fight for Formosa, which was a "sad thing." It forced him to doubt America's sincerity about peaceful coexistence. If he were in the Chinese' shoes, he added, he would already have fought for Formosa. Kennedy urged him to restrain Peking, for America would fight back. However abnormal the Formosan situation, J.F.K. was as determined as Truman and Eisenhower to maintain Chiang and the American military bases on the island.

Kennedy wanted the struggle for the Third World to take place without violence. In his conception the Cold War would turn on whichever side could pour the most money and arms into former colonies and thus buy the greatest support. What he did not recognize was how completely his policy ignored the hopes and needs of the Third World masses. The Alliance for Progress, for example, which Kennedy launched with great fanfare as an alternative to Castro in Latin America, was woefully inadequate to the need. The major revenue-producing properties in Latin America remained in the hands of American corporations, which meant that the profits returned to the United States. In addition, the Alliance for Progress loans carried strings, the most important of which was that the money had to be spent on American-made goods, which cost more than the European or Japanese equivalents. The "question of questions" was exactly what Khrushchev said it was, the nature of change. The United States, like Europe in the nineteenth century and the first four decades of the twentieth, had no intention of allowing any real change in the exploitive relationship that existed in its dealing with Asia, Africa, and especially Latin America.

The American military buildup indicated that the United States would stop, by force if necessary, revolutionary movement in the Third World. It also indicated that the United States was willing to use force to maintain the status quo in Europe. But just as Khrushchev could not forfeit the Soviet Union's right to aid revolutions, neither could he accept the situation in Berlin as permanent. The bone continued to catch in his throat. By the summer of 1961, however, he had to move soon if he wished to do anything about it before the Kennedy-McNamara program gave the United States the capability of matching the Red Army on conventional terms—along with great superiority in strategic weapons.

Kennedy, for his part, seemed open to reasonable accommodation. He was impatient with Third World leaders who continued to squabble with each other over what he considered to be irrational issues. He urged India and Pakistan to get together and jointly solve the problems of Asia; he thought the Arabs and Israelis should settle their differences, forgetting prestige and other nonrational factors. He wanted everyone to be open-minded, prepared to offer and accept alternatives, ready to advance the cause of peace and prosperity. Yet in Berlin he showed that he could be just as stubborn, just as committed to old positions, just as unwilling to consider compromise as the most extreme Arab or Asian nationalist. As if to underscore the point, when Khrushchev started another crisis in Berlin, Kennedy turned to Dean Acheson for advice. Acheson, as always, recommended keeping the powder dry and standing firm. The gist of his stance was, do not negotiate.

Kennedy agreed. All through the summer of 1961

Khrushchev insisted that there had to be some settlement in Berlin before the end of the year. Kennedy's response was cold and firm: Nothing could be changed. Kennedy insisted, "If we don't meet our commitments in Berlin, it will mean the destruction of NATO and a dangerous situation for the whole world. All Europe is at stake in West Berlin."

Khrushchev had raised the issue of Berlin for many reasons; one that played a large role was the American military buildup. The Russians wanted a satisfactory settlement in Germany before the effects of Kennedy's policies were complete. Kennedy, meanwhile, raced ahead. He put a $3.2 billion additional military budget through Congress, tripled the draft calls, extended enlistments, and mobilized 158,000 reserves and national guardsmen. Altogether he increased the size of the armed forces by 300,000 men, sending 40,000 of them to Europe and making six "priority divisions" in the reserves ready for quick mobilization.

The two sides were now on a collision course. Khrushchev could not allow West Berlin to remain as an escape hatch; Kennedy could not accept any change in its status. Walter Ulbricht of East Germany announced that after he signed a peace treaty with the Russians he would close West Berlin's access to the Western world. The President prepared the American people for the worst. In a television address on July 25, 1961, Kennedy showed how determined he was to stay in Berlin by invoking heroic deeds from the past. "I hear it said that West Berlin is militarily untenable," he began. "And so was Bastogne. And so, in fact, was Stalingrad. Any dangerous spot is tenable if men— brave men—will make it so." He again said that if Berlin went, Germany would follow, then all of Western Europe. Berlin was essential to the "entire free world."

Khrushchev regarded the speech as belligerent and called Kennedy's arms policy military hysteria. Kennedy had made no new offers; indeed, he had made no offers at all to adjust the Berlin situation. East Germans continued to escape via Berlin; soon it would be a country without people. Western propaganda continued to embarrass the Communists by loudly proclaiming that the flow of refugees proved the superiority of capitalism. By early August both world leaders had so completely committed themselves that no solution seemed possible. The crisis appeared destined to end in war.

The refugees were the sticking point. Khrushchev and the East Germans could accept the Western spy apparatus in West Berlin, but they could not afford to continue to lose their best human resources to the West nor to give the West such an ideal propaganda advantage. For his part, Kennedy could hardly be expected to shut the doors to West Berlin or to refrain from using the refugee issue for propaganda.

On August 13, 1961, Khrushchev suddenly and dramatically solved the Berlin problem. He built the Wall, presenting America and the West with a *fait accompli* and permanently dividing Berlin. The flow of refugees was shut off and—after an initial reaction of outrage—the tension visibly eased. The Soviet building of the Wall, and the eventual Western acceptance of it, signified the end to all serious attempts to reunify Germany. Khrushchev was willing to live with West Berlin as long as it was isolated and did not drain East Germany. Kennedy was willing to live with the Wall as long as West Berlin stayed in the Western orbit. Khrushchev's Wall was a brilliant stroke.

It was also brutal and unprecedented. Never before in human history had a wall been built around a city to keep people *in*. Immeasurable human tragedy resulted.

The compromise solution in Berlin did not lead to a permanent end to tension. It could not, since Berlin was but one of the unsettled issues remaining from World War II. The American military buildup continued, after being expanded during the crisis. J.F.K. had looked weak to many Cold Warriors in the United States because he had not torn down the Wall. Khrushchev looked weak to the Cold Warriors in the Communist world for building it. Khrushchev was in deeper trouble, however, because the Kennedy Administration insisted on boasting about American military superiority. Kennedy officials and American strategic intellectuals were publicly sketching scenarios in which the United States would strike first. They justified the exercise by expressing their skepticism of Soviet missile credibility.

Khrushchev had to react. He could allow the United States its strategic nuclear superiority, and there was little he could do about it in any case, since the United States could and would outbuild him. But he could not allow the United States to be both superior and boastful about its superiority. He needed a dramatic strategic victory, one that would focus world attention on Soviet military capability and satisfy his own armed services. He found the answer with increased megatonnage. On August 30, 1961, he announced that he was breaking the three-year Russian-American moratorium on nuclear testing with a series of tests that climaxed with the explosion of a fifty-eight-megaton weapon, three thousand times more powerful than the bomb used against Hiroshima and many times more powerful than anything the United States had developed. The big bomb was good for propaganda, but it had little if any military use, as both sides already had bombs larger than they needed.

Khrushchev's series of tests did have the effect, however, of leading to strident demands that Kennedy begin his own series of tests. The President had given top priority to achieving a nuclear test-ban treaty and was despondent when he could not get it. He was furious with Khrushchev for breaking the moratorium, but he refused to be stampeded into a new series of tests. J.F.K. was greatly worried about the fallout problem and he realized that no matter how big Russian bombs grew the United States would remain strategically superior because of American delivery capability. He tried to compromise with a series of underground tests that began in September 1961. It was not enough, however, to satisfy his domestic critics or the atomic scientists or the Pentagon, and in April 1962 J.F.K. ordered a series of American tests (thirty in all) in the atmosphere.

Khrushchev, frustrated in the nuclear field, unable to push the West out of Berlin, incapable of matching the United States in I.C.B.M.s, and increasingly irritated by the

Chinese harping about Soviet weakness, began to look elsewhere for an opportunity to alter the strategic balance. He
found it in Cuba. Since the Bay of Pigs, Russia had increased her aid to Castro and had begun to include military
supplies. Kennedy had warned the Soviets not to give offensive weapons to the Cubans; Khrushchev assured the
President that he had no intention of doing so. But in
August 1962 the Soviet Union began to build medium-
range ballistic missile sites in Cuba.

What did Khrushchev hope to accomplish? He could not
have expected to attain a first-strike capability. The American delivery system was far too vast for the Russians to be
able to destroy it. Nor could Khrushchev have wanted to
expand the arms race, for the Russians would not be able
to match the American productive capacity. Putting missiles
in Cuba would not make Castro any more of a Communist,
but it was possible that Khrushchev thought the missiles
were necessary to protect Cuba from invasion. The American Congress, military, and popular press were all talking
openly of invading Cuba again, and the Russians insisted
after the event that the missiles had been in response to
the invasion talk. If this was his motive, however, Khrushchev badly miscalculated, for the missiles practically invited America to invade.

As with the fifty-eight-megaton bomb, Khrushchev may
have been seeking military parity on the cheap. His
medium-range missiles in Cuba would match America's
I.C.B.M.s. Even this explanation, however, although the
most probable, is unsatisfactory. The Kennedy Administration, once it learned of the presence of the Soviet missiles, never doubted that one way or another it had to get
them out of Cuba, even at the risk of a nuclear war. This
would seem to indicate that in the best judgment of the
Pentagon and the C.I.A. the missiles in Cuba did make a
strategic difference. But the same officials had already decided that American medium-range missiles in Turkey were
obsolete; more important, they believed that if all-out war
came, the United States could be destroyed before the mis-

sile sites in Cuba were operational. Why then did the Cuban sites matter?

The issue in Cuba was prestige. Kennedy had taken from Khrushchev the fiction of the missile gap. The fifty-eight-megaton bomb had not been sufficiently impressive. The hardliners in the Soviet Union and the Chinese continued to pressure Khrushchev to stand up to the United States. The Kennedy Administration continued to boast about American military superiority. As Theodore Sorensen, Kennedy's chief speech writer, later put it, "To be sure, these Cuban missiles alone, in view of all the other mega-tonnage the Soviets were capable of unleashing upon us, did not substantially alter the strategic balance in fact, . . . but that balance would have been substantially altered in appearance; and in matters of national will and world leadership . . . such appearances contribute to reality." The most serious crisis in the history of mankind, in short, turned on a question of appearances. The world came close to total destruction over a matter of prestige.

On October 14, 1962, American U-2s photographed in Cuba a launchpad under construction that, when completed, could fire missiles with a range of one thousand miles. Kennedy was already under pressure from the Republicans, led by New York Senator Kenneth Keating, for failing to stop the Soviet military buildup in Cuba. Congressional elections were less than three weeks away. The pressure to respond was overwhelming. When a high official in the Pentagon suggested that Kennedy do nothing and ignore the missiles since they constituted no additional threat to the United States, the President replied that he had to act. If he did not, he would be impeached.

How to respond became the great question. The President set the general goals: get the missiles out of Cuba; avoid a nuclear exchange; prepare for Russian moves elsewhere, as in Berlin; do not lose face. He appointed a special committee of a dozen or so members, which called itself the Executive Committee (Ex Comm), to give him advice. The leading figure on the Ex Comm was the President's younger brother, Attorney General Robert F. Kennedy. The committee debated a wide range of alternatives, which soon narrowed down to launching a nuclear strike against the missile sites, launching a conventional air strike, followed by an invasion, or initiating a naval blockade that would prevent the Soviets from sending any further material into Cuba. Fear of Russian reprisal soon eliminated the talk of a nuclear strike; support for a conventional attack and an invasion grew. The missiles were a heaven-sent opportunity to get rid of Castro. Invasion forces gathered in Florida and Kennedy had the State Department proceed with a crash program for civil government in Cuba to be established after the occupation of that country.

Robert Kennedy, however, continued to insist on a less belligerent initial response. He refused to countenance a surprise attack, repeating over and over, "My brother is not going to be the Tojo of the 1960s." He wanted to begin the response with a partial naval blockade, one that would keep out Soviet military goods but not force Khrushchev to react immediately. The great advantage of the blockade, as he saw it, was that the pressure could be stepped up if it did not work. Dean Acheson, who was called in for advice, vigorously opposed the blockade and voted for the air strike, as did the Joint Chiefs, but in the end Kennedy chose the blockade as the initial American response.

Having decided on what to do, J.F.K. sent Acheson to Europe to inform the NATO allies. Although somewhat surprised at the extreme American reactions—the Europeans had lived under the shadow of Soviet medium-range missiles for years—de Gaulle, Adenauer, and the others supported the President. So did the Organization of American States. Then at 7:00 P.M., October 22, 1962, Kennedy went on television to break the news to the American people. He explained the situation, then announced that the United States was imposing "a strict quarantine on all offensive military equipment" being shipped into Cuba. He had placed American military forces on full alert and warned Khrushchev that the United States would regard any nuclear missile launched from Cuba against any nation in the Western Hemisphere as an attack by the Soviet Union on the United States, requiring a full retaliatory response upon the Soviet Union. He appealed to Khrushchev to remove the offensive weapons under United Nations supervision.

Kennedy had seized the initiative. It was now up to Khrushchev to respond. His first reaction was belligerent. In a letter received in Washington on October 23 Khrushchev said the Soviet Union would not observe the illegal blockade. "The actions of U.S.A. with regard to Cuba are outright banditry or, if you like, the folly of degenerate imperialism." He accused Kennedy of pushing mankind "to the abyss of a world missile-nuclear war" and asserted that Soviet captains bound for Cuba would not obey the orders of American naval forces. The United States Navy meanwhile deployed five hundred miles off Cuba's coast. Two destroyers stopped and boarded a Panamanian vessel headed for Cuba carrying Russian goods. It contained no military material and was allowed to proceed. Soviet ships continued to steam for Cuba, although those carrying missiles turned back. Work on the missile sites in Cuba continued without interruption, however, and they would soon be operational.

The threat of mutual annihilation remained high. Kennedy stood firm. Finally, at 6:00 P.M. on October 26 Khrushchev sent another message. Fittingly, considering the stakes, it was long and emotional. The Premier wanted the President to realize that "if indeed war should break out, then it would not be in our power to stop it." He said once again that the missiles were in Cuba for defensive purposes only: "We are of sound mind and understand perfectly well that if we attack you, you will respond the same way. But you too will receive the same that you hurl against us. . . . Only lunatics or suicides, who themselves want to perish and to destroy the whole world before they die, could do this." He said he did not want an arms race. "Armaments bring only disasters. When one accumulates them, this damages the economy, and if one puts them to use, then they destroy people on both sides. Consequently, only a madman can believe that armaments are the principal means in the life of society."

Then came the specific proposal. Khrushchev said he would send no more weapons to Cuba and would withdraw or destroy those already there if J.F.K. would withdraw the blockade and promise not to invade Cuba. He urged Kennedy to untie the knot rather than pull it tighter.

The following morning, October 27, the Ex Comm met to consider Khrushchev's proposal. Before they could decide whether or not to accept, a second letter from the Premier arrived. More formal than the first, it raised the price. Khrushchev, perhaps bowing to pressure from his own military, said he would take out the Cuban missiles when J.F.K. removed the American missiles from Turkey. "You are worried over Cuba," Khrushchev stated. "You say that it worries you because it lies at a distance of ninety miles across the sea from the shore of the United States. However, Turkey lies next to us. . . . You have stationed devastating rocket weapons . . . in Turkey literally right next to us."

The Ex Comm was thunderstruck, even though, as Robert Kennedy later put it, "the fact was that the proposal the Russians made was not unreasonable and did not amount to a loss to the United States or to our NATO allies." The President had actually already ordered the missiles out of Turkey, but due to a bureaucratic foul-up and Turkish resistance they were still there. To remove them now, however, under Soviet pressure, he regarded as intolerable. The blow to American prestige would be too great. The possibility of a nuclear exchange continued to hang in the balance.

The Joint Chiefs recommended an air strike the next morning against Cuba. The generals and admirals said they had always been against the blockade as being too weak and now they wanted immediate action. Their position was strengthened when a Soviet SAM knocked down an American U-2 flying over Cuba. At this point a majority on the Ex Comm agreed on the necessity of an air strike the next

morning. The President demurred. He wanted to wait at
least one more day. The State Department drafted a letter
from Kennedy to Khrushchev informing the Premier that
the United States could not remove the missiles from Turkey and that no trade could be made.

Robert Kennedy then stepped forward. He suggested
that the Ex Comm ignore Khrushchev's second letter and
answer the first, the one that offered to trade the missiles
in Cuba for an American promise not to invade the island.
Bitter arguments followed, but the President finally accepted his brother's suggestion. He sent an appropriate
letter to Khrushchev.

Far more important than this famous incident, however,
was an oral promise Robert Kennedy gave to the Soviet
Ambassador to the United States, Anatoly Dobrynin. Although the President would not back down in public on
the Turkish missile sites, he evidently had begun to see the
absurdity of the situation—the United States was on the
verge of bombing a small nation with which it was not at
war, and risking in the process a nuclear exchange with
the Soviet Union, over the issue of obsolete missiles in Turkey that he had already ordered removed. Kennedy discussed the issues with his brother and asked him to talk to
Dobrynin. On Saturday night, October 27, Dobrynin came
to Robert Kennedy's office. The Attorney General first presented the Russian Ambassador with an ultimatum: If the
United States did not have a commitment by the next day
that the missiles would be removed, "we would remove
them." Dobrynin then asked what kind of a deal the United
States was prepared to make. Kennedy summarized the
letter that had just gone to Khrushchev, offering to trade
the missiles for an American promise not to invade Cuba.
Dobrynin turned to the sticking point—what about the
American missiles in Turkey?

Robert Kennedy's answer, as given in his own account
of the crisis, was: "I said that there could be no quid pro
quo or any arrangement made under this kind of threat
or pressure, and that in the last analysis this was a decision
that would have to be made by NATO. However, I said,

President Kennedy had been anxious to remove those missiles from Turkey and Italy for a long period of time. He had ordered their removal some time ago, and it was our judgment that, within a short time after this crisis was over, those missiles would be gone."

The statement was sufficient. The Russians had their promise. The next day Dobrynin informed Robert Kennedy that the missiles in Cuba would be withdrawn.

The world settled back to assess the lessons. Everyone learned something different. The Chinese, for example, told the Third World that the Cuban crisis proved one could not trust the Russians. Europe, led by de Gaulle, learned that in emergencies the United States would act on its own, without NATO consultation, on matters affecting not only American security but world survival. The Russians learned that they could not have military parity with the United States, or even the appearance of it. Kennedy, having been to the brink and having looked into the yawning chasm of world holocaust, learned to be a little softer in his pronouncements, a little less strident in his assertions. His administration took on a more moderate tone, at least with regard to the Soviet Union, and the need for peace and arms reductions replaced boasts about American military power.

At American University on June 10, 1963, Kennedy made a dramatic appeal for peace, which he characterized as "the necessary rational end of rational men." The Partial Test Ban Treaty was signed a few weeks later, prohibiting nuclear tests in the atmosphere. As Herbert S. Dinerstein notes, "the test ban treaty symbolically recognized that the accommodation between the Soviet Union and the United States would be made on the basis of American superiority."

The Chinese were furious. They called Khrushchev foolish for putting the missiles into Cuba and cowardly for removing them. Within the Kremlin opposition to Khrushchev mounted. For all his dramatics he had been unable to deliver enough meaningful victories in the Cold War, while his brinksmanship had frightened nearly everyone. Within a year he was out of power.

The easing of tensions that followed the Cuban missile crisis allowed de Gaulle and other Europeans to begin to think in serious terms about revising their relationship with the United States. De Gaulle wanted to restore European primacy; to do so, he realized, he had to break with NATO. After Cuba, he knew that the United States would not consult with its NATO partners before acting; he was convinced that the United States would not risk its own existence for the sake of protecting Europe; he doubted that the Red Army would ever march across the Elbe. He believed that the time had come for Europe to drop out of the Cold War and assert herself. He therefore prepared a Franco-German friendship treaty, moved to establish better relations with the Warsaw Pact nations, quickened the pace of French nuclear development, and decided to keep Britain out of the Common Market.

On January 14, 1963, de Gaulle announced his program. He vetoed British participation in the Common Market because it would transform the character of the European Economic Community and "finally it would appear as a colossal Atlantic community under American domination and direction." Kennedy had been pushing for a multilateral nuclear force within NATO, which supposedly would give the Europeans some say in the use of nuclear weapons while blocking any West German move to develop their own bombs. The trouble with the proposal was that under no circumstances would the United States give up its ultimate veto on the bombs. De Gaulle, therefore, denounced the plan. "France intends to have her own national defense," he declared. "For us, . . . integration is something which is not imaginable." He concluded about the French nuclear force, "It is entirely understandable that this French enterprise should not seem very satisfactory to certain American quarters. In politics and strategy, as in economics, monopoly naturally appears to him who enjoys it as the best possible system."

De Gaulle then proceeded to withdraw French naval forces from NATO and soon asked NATO headquarters to leave France. His bold bid for European independence was not an immediate success, as West Germany decided to maintain her close ties with the United States, but certainly his general goals had enormous appeal. From Yalta in 1945 to Vienna in 1961 the Soviet Union and the United States had presumed to settle the affairs of Europe without any European leaders at the conference table. Those days were rapidly coming to an end. Europe was unwilling to be burned to a cinder because Russia and America disagreed about an island in the Gulf of Mexico, or to continue to be an investment and market area for American corporations and Russian managers.

The greatest lesson from Cuba was the perils of brinksmanship. Henceforth, Russia and America would strive to keep some control over their disputes, to avoid actions that could lead to escalations, to limit their commitments so that they could limit the other side's response. Struggle would continue, most obviously in the Third World, but preferably at a lower level. American goals remained the same, and Kennedy would continue to pursue them energetically, but he would try to do so with less military force and within the confines of the realization that the Third World had its own hopes and programs. Whether or not he could achieve what remained relatively unlimited goals through limited means remained to be seen.

He had learned. An ability to grow was his most impressive asset and he was surely the honor graduate of the Cuban missile crisis class. "In the final analysis," he said in his American University speech, "our most basic common link is the fact that we all inhabit this planet. We all breathe the same air. We all cherish our children's future. And we are all mortal."

[11]

Vietnam: Paying the Cost of Containment

[McGeorge] Bundy said he had come to accept what he had
learned from Dean Acheson—that, in the final analysis, the
United States was the locomotive at the head of mankind,
and the rest of the world the caboose.

> HENRY F. GRAFF,
> in an interview with
> Bundy

In the patriotic fervor of the Kennedy years, we had asked,
"What can we do for our country?" and our country answered, "Kill V.C."

> PHILIP CAPUTO,
> *A Rumor of War*

Kennedy had forced Khrushchev to back down in Cuba
because the United States had overwhelming superiority
in nuclear weapons, delivery systems, and on the high seas.
Following the crisis the Russians vowed that never again
would they be so humiliated. They began a crash program
to modernize and strengthen their fleet and to build nuclear weapons with I.C.B.M.s to carry them. Kennedy and
McNamara responded by increasing the pace of American
production. The Russians then accelerated their program,
and the arms race got worse.

As a Presidential candidate J.F.K. had been critical of
Eisenhower's defense policy because Ike put too much faith
in the big bombs. J.F.K. wanted to be able to respond to
Communist aggression at any level. Kennedy set out to
build a counterinsurgency force that could stamp out insurrection or revolution in the jungles of Asia or the

mountains of South America. With his counterinsurgency force Kennedy would prove to the world that the so-called wars of national liberation did not work. Through the Green Berets, as the force came to be called, the West would win the battle for the Third World.

Kennedy relied heavily on technology to overcome America's inherent manpower shortages, giving the Green Berets first call on all the Army's latest equipment. The whole concept appealed strongly to the elitist strain in J.F.K., for the Berets consisted of the best young officers and enlisted men in the Army. They received extra training, better equipment, and special privileges. As the military equivalent to the Peace Corps, the Berets would apply American techniques and know-how in guerrilla warfare situations and solve the problems that had baffled the French. As Kennedy told a West Point commencement, he would apply "a wholly new kind of strategy." One of the great appeals of counterinsurgency, especially after the Cuban crisis, was that it avoided direct confrontation with the Soviet Union. The risks of an escalation to nuclear war were small, which would allow America to use her enormous military power for political gains.

In J.F.K.'s view, and in that of his advisers, and in the view of millions of American citizens, the United States would be able to do what other white men had failed to do partly because America's motives were pure, partly because America had mastered the lessons of guerrilla warfare. The United States would not try to overwhelm the enemy or fight a strictly conventional war, as the French had done in Vietnam. Instead the Berets would give advice to local troops while American civil agencies would help the governments to institute political reforms that would separate the guerrillas from the people. Kennedy's counterinsurgency would show the people that there was a liberal middle ground between colonialism and Communism. Like Dulles, Kennedy never doubted that when Asians or Africans or South Americans realized that a liberal alternative existed they would reject Communism.

Kennedy read Mao Tse-tung and Che Guevara on guerrilla warfare and ordered the Army's generals to do the same. He put all his influence into the development of a dedicated, high-quality elite corps of specialists, capable of training local troops in guerrilla warfare, equipped to perform a wide range of civilian as well as military tasks, able to live in the jungle behind enemy lines. J.F.K. personally supervised the selection of new equipment. He gave the Green Berets lighter field radios and more helicopters. When all was ready he sent them out to save the world.

The great opportunity came in South Vietnam. It had numerous advantages. Diem was more a low-grade despot than a ruthless dictator. He was relatively honest and a sincere nationalist. He had introduced a a land-reform program that, on paper at least, was a model for others to follow. The Americans were already in Vietnam, with military and economic advisers. Finally, Vietnam was an ideal battleground for the Green Berets. Small-unit actions in the jungle or rice paddies suited them perfectly, as did the emphasis on winning the hearts and minds of the people through medical and technical aid. From J.F.K.'s point of view Vietnam was an almost perfect place to get involved. There he could show his interest in the Third World, demonstrate conclusively that America lived up to her commitments (the 1954 SEATO Treaty had extended protection to South Vietnam if it were attacked from without), and play the exciting new game of counterinsurgency.

The only major difficulty was the fuzzy legal situation. South Vietnam was a sovereign nation only because Diem said it was. Under the terms of the 1954 Geneva Agreements, which the United States had not signed but which it promised not to upset by force, South Vietnam was not a nation but a territory, to be administered by the French until elections were held. The 1954 agreements had also stipulated that neither Ho in North Vietnam nor Diem in South Vietnam should allow the introduction of foreign troops into their territories. The United States redefined the Geneva Agreements, deliberately creating the fiction that Geneva had set up two Vietnams, North and South. The Secretary of State, Dean Rusk, made the redefinition

complete in 1963 when he claimed that "the other side was
fully committed—fully committed—in the original Geneva
settlement of 1954 to the arrangements which provided for
South Vietnam as an independent entity."

The second major problem was the nature of the struggle. After Dulles wrote the SEATO Treaty and extended
protection to South Vietnam he assured the Senate that
under no circumstances would the United States be required to put down an internal uprising or get involved in
a civil war. Assuming that South Vietnam was a sovereign
nation, the question then became one of ascertaining whether
the opposition to the government came from within or
without. The question was almost impossible to answer.
After 1956 the North Vietnamese had concentrated on
reconstruction in their own territory, and on building socialism there. After Diem refused to hold the elections in
1956, meanwhile, the Viet Minh in the South grew restive.
Beginning in 1957 they carried on a systematic campaign
to assassinate village chiefs and thus destroy Diem's hold
on the countryside. They suffered from political persecution, as did all Diem's opponents, for Diem was incapable
of distinguishing between Communist and anti-Communist
resistance to his government. In early 1960 eighteen national figures, including ten former ministers in the Diem
government, issued a public manifesto protesting Diem's
nepotism and the "continuous arrests that fill the jails and
prisons to the rafters." They called for free elections. Diem
threw them all into jail.

In March 1960 full-scale revolt began. Diem labeled his
opponents Viet Cong, or Vietnamese Communists. The
V.C. established the National Liberation Front (N.L.F.) as
its political arm. The struggle intensified, even though the
V.C. received little support from Ho in the North. Some
two thousand men did go south in 1960, but nearly all were
old Viet Minh who had lived there before 1954. The great
bulk of the V.C. were recruited in South Vietnam and
captured most of their arms and equipment from Diem's
army. In September 1960 the Communist Party of North
Vietnam finally bestowed its formal blessing on the N.L.F.

and called for the liberation of South Vietnam from American imperialism.

Under the circumstances it was exceedingly difficult to prove that South Vietnam was the victim of "outside" aggression. The American Secretary of State, however, had no doubts that North Vietnam was committing aggression, nor did he doubt what was at stake. Rusk's views had changed not at all since 1950, when he decided that the Chinese Communists were "not Chinese." As he saw it, the war in Vietnam was sponsored by Hanoi, which in turn was acting as the agent of Peking. If the United States allowed the Viet Cong to win in South Vietnam, the Chinese would quickly gobble up the rest of Asia. Again and again Rusk warned his countrymen of the dangers of a Far Eastern Munich, thereby equating Ho Chi Minh with Hitler and raising the dreaded specter of appeasement.

Rusk warned of the dangers of another Munich so often, however, and the idea of Ho being the Asian Hitler was so silly that the Secretary became almost an embarrassment to the administration. Nevertheless he persisted. In their memoirs J.F.K.'s aides had great fun at Rusk's expense, pointing to the slowness and shallowness of his mind, his supercilious personality, and the rigidity of his views. Arthur Schlesinger and Theodore Sorensen presented Rusk as a figure out of the past, a man still caught in the clichés of the late forties, a Secretary of State whose prime aim was to encircle Communist China just as Acheson had encircled Russia. They were amused by his emphasis on military force and argued that Rusk never understood the new sophistication of the Kennedy foreign policy. What Schlesinger and Sorensen ignored was that Kennedy had picked Rusk for the job—after a strong recommendation from Acheson—and that Rusk had never hidden his beliefs.

In any case, Rusk was hardly alone in recommending the American involvement in Vietnam, nor was the decision to save Diem an aberration or the result of a conspiracy. Everything in the Kennedy record pointed to increased aid to Diem, and nearly everyone in the Kennedy Administration supported the decision. The Joint Chiefs went along,

[handwritten margin note: Rusk compared Ho to Hitler, No more Munichs]

but they did not push Kennedy into Vietnam, nor did American corporations with Asian interests, nor did the Asia-firsters in the Republican Party.

General William Westmoreland, who commanded the American military effort in South Vietnam from 1964 to 1968, later said that before he left for Vietnam he discussed the situation there with every top official in the White House, the State Department, and the Pentagon. All agreed that the United States had to stand up to the aggressors from the north, using whatever means were necessary. He could not recall a single dissenter. There was also universal agreement on the need to prove to the Chinese that wars of national liberation did not work and to show the Third World that America stood by her commitments. These views were held most strongly by J.F.K.'s personal advisers, led by Walt Rostow and McGeorge Bundy. Westmoreland emphasized that America did not get into Vietnam, or stay there, because of a military conspiracy, or a military-industrial complex conspiracy, or any other conspiracy. America fought in Vietnam as a direct result of a world view from which no one in power dissented and as a logical culmination of the policy of containment.

Vietnam was the liberals' war. It was based on the same premises that Truman and Acheson had used. The United States, as Sorensen put it, "could supply better training, support and direction, better communications, transportation and intelligence, better weapons, equipment and logistics" to halt Communist aggression. With American skills and Vietnamese soldiers ("South Vietnam will supply the necessary men," J.F.K. said), freedom would prevail.

In early 1961 Kennedy began sending his advisers to South Vietnam to report to him on what was needed and to teach Diem how to get the job done. The first to head a mission was the dynamic Texas politician, Vice-President Lyndon Baines Johnson. He returned in May 1961, determined to save the Alamo from the encircling enemy. "The basic decision in Southeast Asia is here," he declared. "We must decide whether to help these countries to the best of our ability or throw in the towel in the area and pull back

LBJ wanted in!

our defenses to San Francisco and a 'Fortress America' concept." L.B.J. never explained how the fall of Diem could drive the United States from its major Asian bases in the Philippines, Formosa, Okinawa, and Japan, not to mention Guam, Midway, and Hawaii.

The Kennedy team, like that of Truman and Acheson, felt that America could not afford to back down anywhere. As Johnson put it in his report, if America did not stand behind Diem, "we would say to the world that we don't live up to our treaties and don't stand by our friends," which were almost the same words Kennedy was using with respect to the concurrent Berlin crisis. The Kennedy Administration also assumed that if America set her mind to it there was no limit to what the nation could do, which made Johnson's conclusions inevitable: "I recommend that we move forward promptly with a major effort to help these countries defend themselves." American combat troops would not be needed and indeed it would be a mistake to send them because it would revive anti-colonial emotions throughout Asia. Johnson thought the South Vietnamese themselves could do the fighting, aided by American training and equipment.

Shortly after Johnson's trip Professor Eugene Staley, an economist from Stanford University, went to Saigon to advise Diem. Staley made a number of suggestions, the most important of which was that Diem institute a strategic hamlet program. The idea was that by bringing the peasants together it would be easier to protect them from the V.C. and prevent the V.C. from recruiting, raising taxes, or hiding in the villages among them. In practice, however, the strategic hamlets amounted to concentration camps. Diem's troops forced villagers to leave land their families had lived on for generations and thereby turned thousands of Vietnamese against the government. The war continued to go badly. Although the V.C. were concentrated in the least populated districts, they controlled nearly half the countryside.

In October 1961 J.F.K. sent another mission to Saigon, headed by Rostow and Maxwell Taylor. Rostow was a Rhodes scholar, an M.I.T. professor, and an internationally famous economic historian. Taylor was a war hero, former Superintendent of the U.S. Military Academy, and one of the leading critics of Eisenhower's reliance on massive deterrence. Between them, the professor and the soldier made a team that represented the best and the brightest in America. Whatever judgments and recommendations they made, J.F.K. had to regard as authoritative.

The Rostow-Taylor mission reported that South Vietnam had enough vitality to justify a major United States effort. Taylor said the major difficulty was that the South Vietnamese doubted that the Americans really would help them and he therefore recommended an increased American intervention. He wanted the South Vietnamese Army (ARVN) to take the offensive, with American troops supplying the airlift and reconnaissance. Taylor also urged Kennedy to send a combat unit of ten thousand men to South Vietnam. Rostow thought that Diem, if pressed by the United States to reform, would be satisfactory. Both Rostow and Taylor agreed that the key to victory was stopping infiltration from the north. If it continued, they could see no end to the war. Rostow argued forcibly for a policy of retaliation against the north by bombing, graduated to match the intensity of Hanoi's support for the V.C. Kennedy accepted the main conclusions (although he refused to bomb North Vietnam) and increased the shipment of troops and equipment to Diem. When Eisenhower left office there were a few hundred American advisers in South Vietnam; at the time of the Rostow-Taylor mission there were 1,364; by the end of the following year, 1962, there were nearly 10,000, and by November 1963 there were 15,000. Equipment, especially helicopters, came in at a faster rate.

The American commitment to Diem was so strong, as David Halberstam reported in the *New York Times*, that Saigon "became more convinced than ever that it had its ally in a corner, that it could do anything it wanted, that continued support would be guaranteed because of the Communist threat and that after the commitment was made, the United States could not suddenly admit it had made a vast mistake." The entire emphasis of the Rostow-Taylor report had been on a military response, and Kennedy concentrated on sending military hardware to Saigon. The American Ambassador did try to put pressure on Diem to institute political and economic reforms, but Diem ignored him. When the V.C. liberated a village, they immediately told the peasants that the land was now theirs; when ARVN took a village they brought the landlords along with them, and the landlords collected back rents, often covering the past five years.

As a consequence, the war seemed to be going well. McNamara visited Vietnam in June 1962 and reported, "Every quantitative measurement we have shows we're winning this war." In March of 1963 Rusk declared that the struggle against the V.C. had "turned an important corner" and was nearly over. A month later he said there was "a steady movement in South Vietnam toward a constitutional system resting upon popular consent." The American generals on the spot made similar statements. The Buddhist uprisings against Diem in May of 1963, brought on by religious persecution, dampened the official optimism, but even the Buddhist display of dissatisfaction with Diem only caused embarrassment, not a reevaluation of policy. Kennedy continued to increase the size of the American military contingent and in one of his last press conferences declared, "Our goal is a stable government there, carrying on a struggle to maintain its national independence. We believe strongly in that. . . . In my opinion, for us to withdraw from that effort would mean a collapse not only of South Vietnam but Southeast Asia. So we are going to stay there."

Kennedy's statement was a concise summary of the continuity of policy. Vietnam was Greece and South Korea all over again. The C.I.A. was soon involved in plots in Saigon to overthrow Diem and bring an efficient, honest government to power—in short, as in Cuba, to find a liberal alternative. Diem did not fit the role. A Catholic aristocrat, he had little support in his own army and no real ties with the non-Catholic majority of his people. His repressions

DIEM

were too blatant, his strategic hamlet and land-reform programs had too obviously failed. He had to go. In November 1963 ARVN, acting with the knowledge and approval of the C.I.A., although not at its prompting, overthrew and then killed Diem and his brother. A military regime that could hope to fight the war somewhat more efficiently, but that otherwise had neither program nor policy, took over.

With Diem eliminated, the N.L.F. contacted the generals in Saigon and proposed negotiations "to reach a cease-fire and solve important problems of the nation . . . with a view to reaching free general elections . . . to form a national coalition government composed of representatives of all forces, parties, tendencies, and strata of the South Vietnamese people." Important elements of the ARVN officer corps were willing to flirt with the idea of a coalition government and a neutral South Vietnam, but the Americans in Saigon and in Washington refused to have anything to do with the idea. Three weeks after Diem's death Kennedy himself was assassinated and Lyndon B. Johnson became President.

In Vietnam, as elsewhere, Johnson continued Kennedy's policies. In a 1964 New Year's Day message to South Vietnam, Johnson strengthened the hands of the hardliners in ARVN by declaring that "neutralization of South Vietnam would only be another name for a Communist take-over. The United States will continue to furnish you and your people with the fullest measure of support in this bitter fight. We shall maintain in Vietnam American personnel and material as needed to assist you in achieving victory." In July 1964 Moscow, Hanoi, and Paris joined together to issue a call for an international conference in Geneva to deal with an outbreak of fighting in Laos and with the war in Vietnam. China, the N.L.F., and Cambodia supported the call for a conference, as did the U.N. Secretary General, U Thant of Burma. Johnson replied, "We do not believe in conferences called to ratify terror," and the next day announced that the American military advisers to South Vietnam would be increased by 30 percent, from sixteen thousand to twenty-one thousand.

The American government continued to believe that it could win the war by applying a limited amount of force, primarily through ARVN. Throughout the summer of 1964 American officials continued to issue optimistic statements. Faith in the Kennedy-McNamara program of flexible response, counterinsurgency techniques, and the new theories of limited war remained high. Years later, when almost everyone was unhappy with the war, the American military and their supporters would charge that the failure in South Vietnam resulted from an inadequate application of force. America could have won the war, some generals and admirals claimed, had it put in more men sooner. The fact that North Vietnam could match American escalation step by step, and did, made the logic questionable, and in any case the claim only showed that the critics suffered from the same myopic view that got America into trouble in the first place—that the struggle in South Vietnam was a military one.

The real point was that at each step along the path the White House, the American military, the intelligence community, and the State Department, all believed that enough was being done. Ten thousand more troops, or a hundred thousand more, or five hundred more helicopters, or three more bombing targets, would do the trick. The restraints on American action in Vietnam were self-imposed, and such factors as the public's unwillingness to pay a high cost for the war or fear of Chinese intervention played a role in limiting the use of force. But by far the most important reason for the gradualism was the deep belief within the Kennedy and Johnson administrations that enough was being done. All the old myths, such as the idea that Communism could never inspire genuine support or the notion that Asians could not stand up to Western military techniques, led to a consistent underestimation of the enemy.

Barry Goldwater, Republican candidate for the Presidency in 1964, was one of the few politicians who disagreed. He thought that more, much more, had to be done, and soon. Goldwater said he was prepared to go to the Joint Chiefs and tell them to win, using whatever measures were necessary, including nuclear weapons. He also wanted to carry the war to North Vietnam, starting with bombing raids.

Johnson gleefully took up the challenge. In the 1964 campaign he ran on a platform promising major social reforms at home and peace abroad. He presented himself as the reasonable, prudent man who could be trusted to win in Vietnam while keeping the war limited. Johnson scornfully rejected Goldwater's bellicose suggestions. Bombing North Vietnam, the President said, would widen the war and lead to committing American troops to the battle. He was especially insistent about the last point: "We are not going to send American boys nine or ten thousand miles away from home to do what Asian boys ought to be doing for themselves."

In the by now familiar pattern of American Presidential campaigns in the Cold War, Goldwater was accusing Johnson of not being tough enough with the Communists. Johnson had to show that he could be firm as well as patient, hard as well as reasonable. He therefore seized the opportunity that came on August 2 and 3, 1964, when he received reports that American destroyers had been attacked by North Vietnamese torpedo boats in the Gulf of Tonkin. At the time few doubted that the attacks had actually taken place, although the *New York Times* and others suggested that the U.S. Navy had provoked the attacks by escorting South Vietnamese commando raids into North Vietnam. Later, in 1968, Senator Fulbright's Senate hearings convinced millions that the entire Tonkin Gulf affair was a fraud. In any case, Johnson, without an investigation, charged North Vietnam with committing "open aggression on the high seas."

The result was the Gulf of Tonkin Resolution. Like Eisenhower in the Middle East, Johnson wanted and got a blank check that would allow him to expand the war as he saw fit without consulting Congress. The President asked Congress for authority to use "all necessary measures" to "repel any armed attack" against American forces. In addition, Congress gave the President the power to "prevent further aggression" and take "all necessary steps" to protect any nation covered by SEATO that might request aid "in defense of its freedom." The Resolution sailed through the House on August 7, 1964, by a vote of 416 to 0. In the Senate Fulbright steered the Resolution through. He insisted that the Congress had to trust the President and turned back an amendment to the Resolution that would have explicitly denied to the President authority to widen the war. The election was only three months away and Fulbright did not want to embarrass Johnson. The Senate then voted 88 to 2 in favor of the Resolution (Wayne Morse and Ernest Gruening were the dissenters).

Hanoi, meanwhile, had sent out peace feelers. Perhaps encouraged by Johnson's charges that Goldwater was reckless, perhaps frightened by the Gulf of Tonkin Resolution, Ho Chi Minh secretly offered to negotiate. Neither Johnson nor his advisers nor the ARVN generals in Saigon were remotely prepared to accept a compromise solution to the war, however, for it would have meant a coalition government in South Vietnam with close ties to Hanoi. Elections almost surely would have eliminated the ARVN generals altogether. The new Saigon government would then reunite with the north and order the American troops out of Vietnam. These prospects were much too painful to contemplate and Johnson certainly did not want to make it possible for Goldwater to charge him with appeasement, or the loss of Vietnam. L.B.J. refused to negotiate, the war went on, and the American voters overwhelmingly voted for Johnson over Goldwater.

The key to victory remained hidden. Indeed, as the war turned increasingly against Saigon the real question was whether the South Vietnamese government could hang on, much less prevail. The American military advisers before 1960 had trained ARVN to fight a conventional war, under the theory that if Hanoi decided to move against Saigon it would launch a North Korean–type assault. This was subsequently cited as a major factor in ARVN's difficulties, but it only hid the deeper malaise. The officer corps had no real connection with the troops. Half were Catholics, many from North Vietnam. Corruption was rampant. The desertion rate was the highest in the world. The truth was that in the face of a conventional assault, ARVN probaby would have scattered even more than it did when faced with guerrilla warfare. There was simply no will to fight, for there was nothing to fight for.

ARVN's failure made Johnson's problem acute. He had to either negotiate or introduce American combat troops to retrieve the situation. If he continued Kennedy's policy of all-out material support plus Green Beret advisers, the Saigon government would collapse and the V.C. would take control of all South Vietnam.

The main debate in Washington after the Gulf of Tonkin and the election, then, was whether to escalate American involvement in the war or to negotiate. Either option was open. Hanoi had indicated in various ways its willingness to talk, but few American officials were interested. L.B.J., Rusk, and the Kennedy aides who had stayed with Johnson consistently refused to negotiate. In the words of David Kraslow and Stuart Loory, "In 1964 the dominant view in official Washington was that the United States could not entertain the idea of talks or negotiations until after it applied more military pressure on the enemy. As a former White House aide later described the mood of that period, 'The very word "negotiations" was anathema in the Administration.'" Rostow, Taylor, and others argued that the military imbalance would have to be redressed before negotiations could be considered, which really meant that they wanted and expected victory. As Rostow explained the policy, in a statement almost anyone in the Administration could have made, "It is on this spot that we have to break the liberation war—Chinese type. If we don't break it here we shall have to face it again in Thailand, Venezuela, elsewhere. Vietnam is a clear testing ground for our policy in the world."

Johnson's great problem, after he rejected negotiation, was how to win the war without sending in American ground troops. The Air Force had the answer. Undaunted by the failure of interdiction bombing in North Korea, strategic–

air-power advocates told the President they could stop Hanoi's aggression in a month. When a civilian aide asked the generals what would happen if Hanoi did not quit in a month, they answered that then another two weeks would do the trick. More specifically, Secretary of Defense McNamara, who also advocated taking the air war to North Vietnam, believed it would improve the morale of the South Vietnamese forces, reduce the flow and increase the cost of infiltration of men and equipment from North to South Vietnam, and hurt morale in North Vietnam. The net result would be to "affect their will in such a way as to move Hanoi to a satisfactory settlement." The third point was sometimes described as "ouch warfare." Sooner or later Ho Chi Minh would decide that his potential gain was not worth the cost, say "ouch," and quit. Another advantage to bombing was its peculiarly American flavor—the United States would win the war by expending money and material, of which it had an abundance, and avoid manpower losses.

In late 1964 Johnson decided to initiate a bombing campaign against North Vietnam. The Air Force and Navy made the necessary preparations. But to bomb a country with whom the United States was not at war, that had committed no aggressive actions against the United States, and against whom no one in Washington intended to declare war, was a serious step. Johnson decided to make one last move to be certain the air campaign was really necessary to save the situation in the south. In late January he sent a delegation headed by McGeorge Bundy, his special assistant for national-security affairs and a Kennedy confidant, to Saigon to investigate.

On February 7, 1965, V.C. troops broke through the defense perimeter around the American air base at Pleiku in South Vietnam and mortared the flight line and some American military barracks. Eight American soldiers were killed, six helicopters and a transport plane were destroyed. Bundy went to the scene to inspect the damage. As a White House official later recalled, "a man from the ivory tower was suddenly confronted with the grim horror of reality. Mac got mad and immediately urged a retaliatory strike."

The Ambassador to South Vietnam, Maxwell Taylor, and the American military commander, General William Westmoreland, joined Bundy in recommending instant retaliation. Within twelve hours what was called a retaliatory raid began. The first major escalation had started.

On his way back to Washington Bundy prepared a memorandum urging a steady program of bombing the north. He argued that within three months of the start of the bombing Hanoi would give up and seek peace. Bombing, he asserted, was the way to avoid the unpleasant decision to send combat troops. In Washington planning went forward for a program of regular bombing of the north.

On March 2, 1965, American bombers hit an ammunition dump ten miles inside North Vietnam and a harbor fifty-five miles north of the demilitarized zone. The raids were the first launched without any alleged specific provocation by the North Vietnamese. Others quickly followed. Johnson himself picked the targets at luncheon meetings every Tuesday with McNamara, Rusk, and Rostow. Representatives of the Joint Chiefs and the C.I.A. were sometimes present. They set limits based on a check list of four items: (1) the military advantage of striking the proposed target; (2) the risk to American aircraft; (3) the danger of widening the war by forcing other countries into the fighting; (4) the danger of heavy civilian casualties. The third point was the most important, for it was imperative to keep Russia out of the conflict, and Soviet ships were usually docked at Haiphong harbor, which was therefore not bombed. The last limitation, on civilian casualties, became less important as time went on.

Simultaneously with the bombing offensive in the north, American airmen drastically stepped up their activity in South Vietnam. Indeed, according to Bernard Fall, "what changed the character of the Viet-Nam war was *not* the decision to bomb North Viet-Nam; *not* the decision to use American ground troops in South Viet-Nam; but the decision to wage unlimited aerial warfare inside the country at the price of literally pounding the place to bits." The sheer magnitude of the American effort boggled the mind.

First the headlines proclaimed that America had dropped more bombs on tiny Vietnam than in the entire Pacific theater in World War II. By 1967 it was more bombs than in the European theater. Then more than in the whole of World War II. Finally, by 1970, more bombs had been dropped on Vietnam than on all targets in the whole of human history. Napalm poured into the villages while weed killers defoliated the countryside. Never had any nation relied so completely on industrial production and material superiority to wage a war.

Yet it did not work. Hanoi did not quit or lose its morale, the infiltration of men and supplies continued (indeed increased), the V.C. still fought, and the political situation in Saigon got worse. Johnson had rejected negotiation and given the Air Force its opportunity. The Air Force had failed. New decisions had to be made.

Despite the bombing offensive the option to negotiate remained and Johnson came under heavy pressure from the NATO allies and the neutral nations to talk to Hanoi. L.B.J. gave his answer in a speech on April 7, 1965, at Johns Hopkins University. He promised to launch a massive economic rehabilitation program in Southeast Asia once the conflict ended, a sort of Marshall Plan for the area, and he claimed that he would go anywhere to discuss peace with anyone. But far more important than the olive branch the President waved was the sword he flourished. The central lesson of the twentieth century, he proclaimed, was that "the appetite of aggression is never satisfied." There would be no appeasement in South Vietnam as long as he was President. "We will not be defeated. We will not grow tired. We will not withdraw, either openly or under the cloak of a meaningless agreement." The next day American bombers launched a particularly severe series of air raids on North Vietnam, and fifteen thousand additional American troops started for South Vietnam.

The Air Force continued to strike North Vietnam, without success, and two months later, on June 8, 1965, L.B.J. announced that he was authorizing U.S. troops, formerly confined to patrolling, to search out the enemy and engage in combat. Three days later Saigon's last civilian government fell and Air Vice-Marshal Nguyen Cao Ky, who had fought for the French against the Viet Minh, became Premier. Ky soon announced that "support for neutralism" would henceforth be punishable by death. Despite the hard line in Washington and Saigon, however, the war was going badly. The V.C. had destroyed the railway system in South Vietnam. Acts of terrorism increased in the cities and more territory fell into Communist hands. Hanoi, meanwhile, working from its position of increasing strength, again attempted to open discussions by explicitly stating that approval in principle of American withdrawal, rather than withdrawal itself, was all that was needed to get the negotiations started.

In a major policy speech on July 28 L.B.J. repeated the untenable but customary claim that "there has been no answer from the other side" to America's search for peace. He, therefore, was compelled to send an additional 50,000 men to South Vietnam, bringing the total commitment to 125,000 men. It was clear that the American forces would actively engage in ground combat. America had decided to win in Vietnam by overwhelming the enemy. Johnson had already, on July 10, declared that there would be no limit on the number of troops sent to General Westmoreland.

From MacArthur onward, every responsible American military officer who had commented on the subject had warned against American involvement in a land war in Asia, yet the nation was now fully involved in one. Time and again L.B.J. had declared during the 1964 Presidential campaign that he did not want American boys dying in South Vietnam, doing what Asian boys ought to be doing for themselves, yet now the American boys were dying there. The State Department had repeated over and over that the United States should never allow the Communists to claim that America was fighting a white man's war against Asians, yet that was exactly what had happened. Kennedy and his aides had repeatedly pointed out that counterinsurgency was primarily a political task and that no guerrilla war could be won without an appropriate political response, yet 90 percent or more of the material America was sending to South Vietnam was military, and U.S. troops were the only force that stood between a dictatorship and total collapse.

Why had the Americans not heeded their own warnings? Because they were cocky, overconfident, sure of themselves, certain that they could win at a bearable cost, and that in the process they would turn back the Communist tide in Asia. They expected to accomplish in Vietnam, in short, what L.B.J. had pulled off in the Dominican Republic.

From 1916 to 1940 the U.S. Marines had controlled the Dominican Republic, where American corporations had large investments in plantations that provided fresh fruits and vegetables to American markets during the winter. President Roosevelt eliminated an overt American presence in 1940 when Rafael Trujillo won a rigged presidential election and established a ruthless, efficient dictatorship. Roosevelt characterized Trujillo as "an s.o.b., but our s.o.b." In May 1961 Trujillo was assassinated.

With Trujillo gone, Kennedy saw three possibilities. In "descending order of preference," they were: "A decent democratic regime, a continuation of the Trujillo regime, or a Castro regime. We ought to aim at the first, but we really can't renounce the second until we are sure that we can avoid the third." This typified Kennedy's—and America's—approach to the Third World. Kennedy wanted a democracy, but if the revolutionary government had socialistic elements in it or there was a threat that the country would go Communist, he would accept a dictator and see what could be done later on about restoring civil liberties. Above all he was determined to keep out the Soviets and retain American economic and political influence.

Kennedy did not have to make a choice between a Castro and a Trujillo, for on December 20, 1962, following a series of transitory provisional governments, the Dominican people elected Juan Bosch as their president. Bosch was a leftist, non-Communist visionary and writer who had spent

years as an anti-Trujillo exile and who seemed to represent
the liberal alternative Kennedy was searching for. But Bosch
was no match for the Dominican military and their conservative partners. Ten months after his election the military overthrew him in a coup. Donald Reid Cabral took
over, but even though he was a member of the Dominican
oligarchy, he could not command the wholehearted support of the military and had almost no following among
the masses. By early April 1965 the Republic was ready to
explode again, even though the United States had sent $5
million to Reid Cabral.

On April 24 young Boschist officers in the army launched
a coup that drove Reid Cabral from office, but they were
unable to restore order. Angry masses poured into the
streets of Santo Domingo. A junta of the regular military,
described in Washington as the Loyalists, decided to take
power for themselves. The rebels armed thousands of civilians and fighting began. The American Ambassador,
W. Tapley Bennett, warned that a sudden Communist takeover was one likely result of the civil war.

Johnson immediately decided that the revolt was part of
a larger conspiracy, probably masterminded by Castro, and
that the challenge to American interests in the Dominican
Republic was a challenge to American interests throughout
Latin America. He decided to intervene. On April 28 L.B.J.
sent in the Marines, to be followed by the Army's 82nd
Airborne Division. His initial rationale was to protect the
lives of American citizens in Santo Domingo, but on April
30 he announced a quite different reason: "People trained
outside the Dominican Republic are seeking to gain control." The American Embassy in Santo Domingo issued a
documented list of fifty-eight "identified and prominent
Communist and Castroite leaders" in the rebel forces, a list
that was obviously, even outrageously, false—it came from
one initially prepared years earlier by Trujillo himself.
Bosch's assessment was more widely accepted: "This was a
democratic revolution smashed by the leading democracy
in the world."

L.B.J. had acted unilaterally, partly because of the need

for speed, partly because of his opinion of his partners in the Alliance for Progress. "The O.A.S.," he remarked, "couldn't pour piss out of a boot if the instructions were written on the heel." Once the Marines had restored some order and prevented Bosch from taking office, however, it was necessary to deal with the O.A.S. Johnson was able to persuade the Latin Americans to join him in the Dominican Republic and by May 28 an O.A.S. peacekeeping force had reinforced and taken control from the U.S. troops. The search for a middle ground in the government went on. Eventually, in September, a government was formed and in June 1966 moderate rightist Joaquin Balaguer defeated Bosch in a Presidential election.

Johnson had won. The intervention had been limited in time, number of troops involved, cost, and lives lost. American Marines and paratroopers had prevented the rise of either a Castro or a Trujillo in the Dominican Republic, American corporations retained their plantations, and the O.A.S. had been mollified.

At the height of the crisis Johnson had been besieged by liberal critics. The *New York Times* editorialized: "Little awareness has been shown by the United States that the Dominican people—not just a handful of Communists— were fighting and dying for social justice and constitutionalism." Robert Kennedy protested that L.B.J. had failed to notify the O.A.S. before acting. Johnson ignored the critics and his eventual success proved justification enough. He may have concluded that he could do the same in Vietnam and that success there would also silence the critics.

Vietnam provided the setting for Lyndon Johnson's agony, indeed for the agony of an entire nation. From 1965 on, Vietnam brought up all the old questions about America's position in the world, questions that had lain dormant since Senator Taft had first raised them in response to the Truman Doctrine. America had been called upon to pay up on an insurance policy written in 1947 for Europe and extended from 1950 to 1954 to Asia. The price proved to be higher—far higher—than anyone had expected. Eventually the almost universal commitment within the United States to the policy of containment began to give way. Senators, intellectuals, businessmen, and millions of citizens launched a massive attack on some of the fundamental premises of American foreign policy during the Cold War, especially the definition of America's vital interests and the domino theory. The tendency had been to define the nation's vital interests as any area in which the United States had political, economic, or military influence, which meant that America's vital interests were always moving outward. There had been little serious oposition to this trend until Vietnam. By 1968, for the first time since the late forties, the State Department had to defend the definition of vital interests.

In Vietnam the American people had been forced to face up to the true cost of containment. In 1965 most Americans agreed that it was necessary to hem in China and Russia militarily, that America had vital interests in Western Europe, Japan, Latin America, and certain sections of the Middle East, that the United States would have to do whatever was required to prevent any of these areas from going Communist, and that to protect these areas it was necessary to defend the regions around them. This was the original escalation—the escalation of what America considered its vital interests. It was also assumed that America's needs included worldwide stability and order, which in practice meant the preservation of the status quo. These had been the broad general aims of all the Cold War Presidents and although there had been differences in degree, Truman and Eisenhower and Kennedy had been prepared to take the risks and pay the cost involved in maintaining them. It was L.B.J.'s bad luck that he got stuck with Vietnam.

At bottom, Vietnam differed from the Dominican Republic intervention only in the cost. The Vietnamese intervention was not, in L.B.J.'s view, the misapplication of an otherwise sound policy but rather one possible outcome that had always been implicit in the policy of containment. On every possible occasion the President emphasized that he was only following in the footsteps of Truman, Eisenhower, and Kennedy, and he never saw any good reason to question the basic assumptions.

Others did. As the American commitment mounted, from $10 billion to $20 billion to $30 billion a year, from 150,000 to 300,000 to 500,000 and more men, as the casualties mounted, as the bombs rained down on the women and children of both North and South Vietnam, Johnson's critics began to wonder not just about Vietnam but about containment itself. Riots in America's cities, air and water pollution, the persistence of racism, the revolt of young people against the draft—all added to the force of the questioning. The college students of the fifties had not questioned the policy of containment for many reasons, but the most important was probably that, after the Korean War, containment did not entail the slaughter of thousands of civilians, the death of thousands of young American men, the squandering of billions of dollars. In the late sixties, as the war in Vietnam went on and on and on, students and others began not only to ask about the war in Vietnam, but more significantly, to ask what kind of a society could support such a war. This led to an examination of all aspects of American life. As a result some students came to believe that they lived in an evil, repressive society that exploited not only foreigners but Americans as well.

The campus revolt, however, was not as immediately significant as the broader questions raised by older men who had a stake in the society and a commitment to preserving it. Many came to believe that containment, and the specific expression of that policy in Vietnam, was not saving America but destroying it. They returned to an older vision of America, best expressed by Lincoln at Gettysburg, which saw America's mission as one of setting an example for the world. "America can exert its greatest influence in the outer world by demonstrating at home that the largest and most complex modern society can solve the problems of modernity," Walter Lippmann wrote. "Then, what all the world is struggling with will be shown to be soluble. Example, and not intervention and firepower, has been the historic instrument of American influence on mankind, and never has it been more necessary and more urgent to realize this truth once more." Senator Fulbright added, "The world has no need, in this age of nationalism and nuclear weapons, for a new imperial power, but there is a great need of moral leadership—by which I mean the leadership of decent example." But for Johnson it was in America's self-interest—and it was her duty—to use military force to stop the spread of Communism, whether in the Dominican Republic or in Vietnam.

L.B.J.'s foreign-policy advisers, almost to a man Kennedy appointees, agreed. Secretary Rusk took the lead. In private as well as in public Rusk argued that China was actively promoting and supporting the war in Vietnam, which in his view did not differ in any significant way from Hitler's aggression in Europe. "In his always articulate, sometimes eloquent, formulations," as Townsend Hoopes, Under Secretary of the Air Force, put it, "Asia seemed to be Europe, China was either Stalinist Russia or Hitler Germany, and S.E.A.T.O. was either N.A.T.O. or the Grand Alliance of World War II." Johnson echoed Rusk's theme. "The backstage Johnson," Philip Geyelin reported, "was quite capable of telling one of the Senate's more serious students of foreign affairs that 'if we don't stop the Reds in South Vietnam, tomorrow they will be in Hawaii, and next week they will be in San Francisco.' "

There was an obvious difficulty with the approach, a difficulty inherent in the policy of containment. If the threat were really as pervasive as Johnson and Rusk said it was, if the stakes were actually as cosmic as they claimed, it made little sense to fight the tail of the snake and leave the head alone. The only possible justification for the death of fifty thousand American soldiers and twenty times or more that many Vietnamese, was to win, which meant cutting off the head of the snake in Peking. But no one dared risk taking the war to China, or even to Hanoi (except in the air). The Vietnam War differed from the Korean War in many ways, but one of the most important was that the administration never attempted to liberate North Vietnam. Yet unless Hanoi itself were occupied by American troops, the North

Vietnamese and the V.C. could carry on the war for a very long time. Bombing could not harm their source of strategic materials, since the source was in China and even more in Russia, and the U.S. Air Force could not seriously disrupt a line of communications that depended in large part on trails and men on bicycles. Nor could the United States impose an unacceptable toll on the enemy's manpower or material resources on the battlefield, for whenever the V.C. wished to cut their losses they could withdraw into the jungle or across the Cambodian or Laotian borders and avoid further combat.

The war could not be won. The influx of American combat troops meant that it would not be lost. Hanoi would not negotiate until the bombing ended, nor until America promised to withdraw her troops, nor on the basis of elections held under the auspices of the Saigon government. America would not negotiate until Hanoi "stopped her aggression" by withdrawing her troops and material support for the V.C., nor would America withdraw until she was assured that the Saigon government would remain in power. Since who ruled in Saigon was what the war was all about, and since neither side would surrender, America was committed to a seemingly permanent war in the East.

The Kennedy liberals, meanwhile, turned against L.B.J., although as much because they were offended by his style as because they disagreed with the policy. The Senate doves began holding frequent meetings to complain about the President. At the meetings, as in their public statements, they tended to personalize the issues. At one of the private sessions, Senator Eugene McCarthy of Minnesota was reported to have said, "We've got a wild man in the White House, and we are going to have to treat him as such," and Senator Albert Gore of Tennessee called Johnson "a desperate man who was likely to get us into war with China, and we have got to prevent it."

Much of the criticism missed the point. Johnson was flamboyant, he did overreact to events, and he was as guilty of personalizing everything as the doves were, but his policies were simply a logical outgrowth of those pursued by his predecessors, as he himself pointed out on every possible occasion.

By 1967, however, style seemed to be the issue. The doves called L.B.J. a monster. He called them "chickenshit." "I'm the only President you have," he was fond of declaring, with the implication that any criticism was unpatriotic. "Why don't you get on the team?" he would demand of the few critics who got into the White House to see him. In November of 1966 L.B.J. told assembled officers at the Officers' Club in Camranh Bay, "Come home with the coonskin on the wall." Dean Rusk kept on talking about Munich and appeasement, a theme Johnson picked up, thereby linking the doves with Chamberlain and the Administration with Churchill. Fulbright's private rejoinder was, "We go ahead treating this little piss-ant country as though we were up against Russia and China put together."

The opposition mounted, but Johnson was probably right in asserting that its strength was overstated. America had never fought a war without some internal dissension and it would be impossible to prove that the doves' dissatisfaction with Vietnam was deeper or more vocal than the Whig dissatisfaction with the Mexican War or the Copperheads' opposition to Lincoln, or even than the opposition F.D.R. had faced before Pearl Harbor. There was not, in any case, a straightforward dove position. All Johnson's critics on the Left agreed on the need to halt the bombing of the north, but beyond that they could not rally behind a program. Some wanted to get out of Vietnam altogether, admitting defeat, but continuing the general policy of containment. Their criticism was tactical—America had overextended herself. Other doves wanted to struggle on in South Vietnam—they remained wedded to an all-out containment and objected only to the bombing of the north. A growing number wanted not only to get out of Vietnam but to go further and reexamine the entire containment policy. The deep divisions within the opposition allowed Johnson to hold to his course.

As the public criticism mounted, L.B.J. fought back with predictions that victory was just around the corner. Rostow was in the vanguard of the effort. He fed the press carefully selected figures from the American computers in Vietnam that proved the Administration was on the high road to victory. The "weapons loss ratio" was 4.7 to 1 in favor of the Americans, as opposed to the unfavorable 1 to 2 ratio in 1963. Enemy desertions were up from 20,000 in 1966 to 35,000 in 1967. ARVN desertions were down from 160,000 to 75,000. The V.C. were incapable of mounting any large-scale attacks. The number of people under Saigon's control had jumped from eight million to twelve million, or nearly 75 percent of the south's population.

The overwhelming application of American power, the Johnson Administration insisted, was having a cumulative effect that would, in time, bring Hanoi and the V.C. to their knees. The enemy's losses in the south were little short of catastrophic, yet Hanoi was not sending more troops from North Vietnam to the south to make up the losses because the bombing campaign in the north tied down enormous numbers of workers and troops. Captured documents indicated that V.C. morale was low. There was light at the end of the tunnel. America was winning the war of attrition.

When Rostow's brave analysis failed to silence the critics, L.B.J. tried a harder sell. He brought General Westmoreland back to the States to explain how and when the victory would be won. At the National Press Club Westy declared, "I am absolutely certain that whereas in 1965 the enemy was winning, today he is certainly losing." On national television the General predicted victory within two years; Johnson, meanwhile, to give the one last shove needed to force Ho Chi Minh to surrender, again expanded the bombing. In mid-November 1967 the heaviest attacks yet against the Hanoi-Haiphong complex began.

Through it all ran a single thread—military victory was possible and necessary. Although the administration presented the war as limited in scope and purpose, in fact the only satisfactory outcome for America was the maintenance in power of the Saigon regime, which meant the total frustration of Hanoi and the V.C. America was committed, as

Townsend Hoopes put it, "to the preservation and anchoring of a narrowly based government in the South, which could not survive without a large-scale U.S. military presence, whose constitution ruled out all political participation by the main adversary, and which was diligently throwing in jail even those non-Communists who advocated opening a dialogue with the National Liberation Front."

It could not have been otherwise. Containment meant containment. Any compromise solution would have led to an N.L.F. participation in the politics of South Vietnam, which would have carried with it the very great risk of an eventual Communist victory, which would have meant that the Communists had not been contained, which would have meant that all the sacrifices had been made in vain. Hoopes sums it up nicely: "In short, President Johnson and his close advisers had so defined our national purposes and so conducted the war that a compromise political settlement would be tantamount to a resounding defeat for U.S. policy and prestige. Accordingly, it could not be faced. Military victory was the only way out." Throughout 1967, and into 1968, the administration insisted that victory was possible.

Then came Tet. The Communist offensive in February 1968, launched with brutal swiftness and surprise on the religious holiday of Tet, showed in a direct if painful fashion that everything Rostow and Westmoreland had said and everything the computers had reported was wrong. The V.C. drove the Americans and ARVN out of parts of the countryside and into the cities, thereby making a shambles out of the pacification program, and even took some of the cities. In Saigon a V.C. suicide squad actually took temporary possession of the American Embassy grounds. The Americans, it turned out, did not control the situation. They were not winning. The enemy retained enormous strength and vitality.

The American response to Tet illustrated much about the American view of the war and of the American attitude toward the people of Vietnam. As one example, the V.C. took control of the ancient cultural capital of Hue. David Douglas Duncan, a famous combat photographer with long experience in war, was appalled by the American method of freeing the city. "The Americans pounded the Citadel and surrounding city almost to dust with air strikes, napalm runs, artillery and naval gunfire, and the direct cannon fire from tanks and recoilless rifles—a total effort to root out and kill every enemy soldier. The mind reels at the carnage, cost, and ruthlessness of it all."

The administration tried to pretend that Tet represented a last-gasp effort by the enemy, but the interpretation found few adherents. Senator McCarthy, meanwhile, challenged the President in the Presidential primary campaign in New Hampshire and almost defeated him. The junior Senator from New York, Robert Kennedy, then announced that he was entering the campaign. McNamara had left the Cabinet after failing to persuade L.B.J. to stop the bombing, but to Johnson's great surprise the new Secretary of Defense, Clark Clifford, widely considered to be a hawk, also wanted to stop the bombing. Faced by the crisis in confidence in his administration, informed by the polls that he faced almost certain defeat in the upcoming Wisconsin primary, deserted by all but a small handful of the most extreme hawks within his own administration, shocked by a request from Westmoreland for 200,000 additional troops for Vietnam (which would have required calling up the reserves and expanding the draft), Johnson finally decided to change his military policy. On Sunday evening, March 31, 1968, Johnson announced on national television that he was stopping the bombing in North Vietnam, except for the area immediately north of the demilitarized zone. To everyone's astonishment, he then withdrew from the Presidential race.

It was a humiliating end. Certainly L.B.J. had been the most powerful man in the world, and quite possibly he had the strongest will, yet a relative handful of V.C. had resisted and overcome his power and broken his will. The man who had done more for Black Americans than any President since Lincoln found himself accused of fighting a racist war with racist methods. A truly tragic figure, L.B.J. had over-reached himself. He had wanted to bring democracy and prosperity to Southeast Asia but he had brought only death

and destruction. By early 1968 he had learned the painful
lessons that the power to destroy is not the power to control,
and that he had reached and passed the limits of his own
power. As he retired to his beloved hill country of central
Texas, two questions remained. How long would it take his
country to also recognize that it had reached and passed
the limits of its power? How long before the United States
retired from Southeast Asia?

[12]

Nixon and the Debacle in Vietnam

Give us six months, and if we haven't ended the war by then, you can come back and tear down the White House fence.
> HENRY KISSINGER to a group of
> Quakers, March 1969

Let me speak to you honestly, frankly, openheartedly. You are a liar.
> LE DUC THO to
> Henry Kissinger, 1972

I'm not going to be the first President to lose a war.
> LYNDON BAINES JOHNSON, 1967
> RICHARD MILHOUS NIXON, 1972

In the summer of 1968 the Republicans nominated Richard Nixon for the Presidency. The Democrats chose Hubert Humphrey, L.B.J.'s Vice-President, and adopted a platform that pledged to continue Johnson's policies in Vietnam. As one of the original and most ferocious of the Cold Warriors, Nixon hardly offered an alternative to the doves. There was, therefore, no opportunity to vote "yes" or "no" on the Vietnam War in the 1968 election, a fact that contributed heavily to the extreme bitterness of that Presidential campaign. The third-party ticket in that year, the one that did offer an alternative to the two old parties, was headed by George Wallace of Alabama and adopted as its foreign policy a program designed to "bomb North Vietnam back into the stone age." Thus the doves, representing nearly half the population, were left without a candidate for President in 1968.

Precisely because their numbers were so great, however, the doves did have an influence, because both Nixon and Humphrey had to go after their votes. Nixon did so when he announced that he had a "secret plan to end the war." When reporters asked for some details, Nixon responded that he could not reveal his plan. Why not, he never said— and, amazingly, was never asked persistently enough to force an answer. Humphrey, meanwhile, hinted that he was secretly a dove, but could not reveal his true position until safely elected, because after all he was Johnson's Vice-President. Johnson, too, had to appease the doves, because the polls clearly indicated that a move toward peace in Vietnam was essential if Humphrey, trailing badly, were to have any chance of victory at all.

Earlier, in May of 1968, preliminary peace talks between the United States and North Vietnam had gotten under way in Paris. Between that time and the campaign the two sides argued about the shape of the table around which the final peace conference would meet. The real issue was whether the V.C. and Saigon would be represented. Both L.B.J. and Ho Chi Minh were more interested in making propaganda than progress toward peace, at least until the results of the election were known. Throughout the campaign there was no progress in Paris. So L.B.J. needed to find some other way of reaching out to the doves (who were much more numerous in the Democratic Party than in the Republican). He did so on October 31, five days before the election, when he announced a cessation of "all air, naval and artillery bombardment of North Vietnam."

Calling off the bombing gave the Humphrey campaign a great boost. He had started in September nearly 20 percentage points behind Nixon in the polls. Before the bombing halt, he had been closing steadily; after October 31, he came on with a rush. The result was one of the closest of all American elections: Nixon won with 43.4 percent of the vote to Humphrey's 42.7 percent (Wallace got 13.5 percent). Many observers believed that if the campaign had gone on another week, or if L.B.J. had called off the bombing a week earlier, Humphrey would have won.

With his narrow victory Richard Nixon earned the right to decide American policy in the Vietnam War. He had numerous options. He surely recalled how Ike had added to his popularity by ending the Korean War six months after taking office. He could do the same in Vietnam by simply bringing the boys home. Or he could continue L.B.J.'s policy of all-out war in the south, hands off the north. Or he might decide to turn the war over to the Vietnamese, making them do the fighting with American equipment. Or he could extend the bombing campaign to the north, devastate Hanoi, mine Haiphong harbor, and invade with ground troops. Or, the final option, he could use nuclear weapons. Given the nature of the campaign, Nixon might have adopted any one of the above options or a variation thereof, saying that it was his "secret plan to end the war." And, except for the last option, he could have worked up significant, even majority, support for any one of them.

The trouble with the first option, to simply end the war, was that Hanoi would not cooperate. In Korea in 1953 Ike had gotten the Chinese to accept a truce after threatening to use atomic weapons if they did not. But in 1969 Nixon was not dealing with the Chinese; he had to deal with Ho Chi Minh, who was more stubborn than L.B.J. and who would *not* agree to a compromise peace, as the Chinese had done in Korea.* Ho wanted all of Vietnam. For him (as for Johnson and Nixon) the issue was: Who will rule in Saigon? ARVN officers wedded to the United States, or Ho Chi Minh and the Communists? On that question, there could be no compromise. That did not prevent Nixon from pulling out, but it did mean that a complete American withdrawal would be followed by a Communist victory.

* Another reason the Chinese were willing to call it quits in 1953, as the North Vietnamese were not in 1969, was that the South Koreans had built an army capable of defending the nation, while ARVN had made little progress despite arms shipments from the United States nearly four times as great as those that went to Korea.

The second option, continuing Johnson's policies, had nothing to recommend it. All the Kennedy-Johnson assumptions about Vietnam and the nature of the war there had been proven wrong and expensive. Something new had to be tried.

The third possibility, turning the war over to the Vietnamese, had the most appeal. It avoided defeat. It kept alive some hope of an ultimate victory. It would relieve the pressure from the peace groups in the United States and mollify many of the doves. And it left open the fourth option, to step up military action against Hanoi and otherwise escalate the war.

The final option, to use nuclear weapons, although discussed seriously from time to time among high civil and military officials, was never very tempting. Aside from the moral opprobrium it would bring on the United States, and the intense internal opposition it would arouse, the use of the big bomb made little military sense. If the United States dropped one on Hanoi, the chances were good that the Chinese or the Russians, or both, would retaliate by dropping one on Saigon. What would happen next was anyone's guess, but no one, including Nixon, wanted to find out.

So it came down to the program Nixon called Vietnamization. Ten months after taking office he announced that his secret plan to end the war was in fact a plan to keep it going, but with lower American casualties. He proposed to withdraw American combat troops, unit by unit, while continuing to give air and naval support to ARVN and rearming ARVN with the best military hardware America had to offer.

American policy had come full circle. Three decades earlier, when Franklin Roosevelt began his third term as President, he had declared that the United States would serve as the great arsenal of democracy. American boys ought not be fighting in Europe, he said, doing what European boys ought to be doing for themselves (L.B.J. had said the same thing about American and Asian boys). Instead, the Americans would supply the tools of war so that others could contain the Axis aggressors. In 1969 Nixon proposed to contain the Communist aggressors by extending lend-lease to South Vietnam.

It proved to be a disastrous choice, one of the worst decisions ever made by a Cold War President. Some of the direct results were: a prolongation of the war by five years, at immense cost in lives and treasure; double-digit inflation, previously unknown in the United States; more bitterness, division, and dissension among the American people; the flouting of the Constitution by the President as he secretly extended the war to Laos and Cambodia, with tragic results for the people of both countries; and the eventual loss of the war. The best that could be said of Vietnamization was that it bought Nixon some time and helped him avoid having to answer, in his 1972 reelection campaign, the question, "Who lost Vietnam?"

Of course, Nixon had high hopes for his policy when he started out. His brilliant National Security Adviser, Dr. Henry Kissinger of Harvard University, had convinced him that there was a path to peace with honor in Vietnam and that it led through Moscow and Peking. If the two Communist superpowers would only refrain from supplying arms to the North Vietnamese, Kissinger argued, Hanoi would have to agree to a compromise peace. Kissinger, an unsurpassed expert at public relations, presented this plan as a masterpiece of subtle diplomacy and managed to make journalists and broadcasters (and Nixon) believe that he had invented a whole new foreign policy ploy, which he called "linkage." The United States would withhold favors from the Russians until they behaved in Southeast Asia by cutting off the arms flow to Hanoi. Peace would follow.

There were all sorts of problems with linkage, the first being that it was hardly new, that it was in fact exactly the policy every Administration since Roosevelt's had followed (when Truman withheld a loan from Stalin in 1945, it was with the hope that this would make the Russians behave in East Europe) without success. Dean Rusk had already tried it with regard to Vietnam. Linkage ignored the obvious fact that if the United States stopped supplying Saigon, there would also be an immediate peace, and that in any event the Russians and Chinese were sending into North Vietnam only a fraction of the military hardware the United States was shipping into the south.

Linkage assumed that world politics revolved around the constant struggle for supremacy between the great powers. Like Dulles and Acheson and Rusk, Kissinger regarded North Vietnam, South Vietnam, Cambodia, and Laos as pawns to be moved around the board by the great powers. He insisted on viewing the war as a highly complex game in which the moves were made from Washington, Moscow, and Peking. He could not believe that Hanoi had its own aims and objectives, more or less unconnected to Russia's or China's.

Linkage fed Kissinger's megalomania. Nearly every American Secretary of State has had a giant ego—perhaps the job couldn't be done without it—but none surpassed the amazing Dr. Kissinger in this regard. His self-confidence knew no bounds. Thus Kissinger wanted to make peace, not just for his generation, nor just for his children's generation, but for his children's children. This impossible dream drove Kissinger to seek the broadest possible agreement with Russia. Everything was linked—the industrial nations' oil shortage, the Vietnam War, wheat sales to Russia, China's military capacity, etc. Kissinger sought nothing less than an all-encompassing agreement that would bring worldwide, permanent peace. Through linkage, Kissinger would out-Metternich Metternich.

The first step would be an arms-control agreement with the U.S.S.R. From it would flow a more general détente, trade with Russia, lowered tensions in the Middle East, and peace in Vietnam with President Nguyen Van Thieu still in power. For these reasons and because the Strategic Arms Limitation Talks (SALT) were inherently the single most important issue facing the United States and the U.S.S.R., who between them were spending uncountable sums of money on more and more unbelievably destructive weapons, Kissinger put a mighty effort into arms control. The Johnson Administration had started the talks but had given them such a low priority that Nixon and Kissinger were, in effect, starting anew.

They came to SALT with some sobering realizations, chief of which was that the days of American unchallenged superiority were finished. The United States had 1,054 intercontinental ballistic missiles (I.C.B.M.s), 656 submarine-launched missiles, and 540 long-range bombers, a force sufficient to kill each Russian fifty times over. The Russians, however, had built, in a crash program, 1,200 I.C.B.M.s, 200 submarine-launched missiles, and 200 big bombers. As Morton Halperin, one of Kissinger's assistants, noted in a staff study, "It was impossible to escape the conclusion that no conceivable American strategic program would give you the kind of superiority that you had in the 1950s."

Halperin's conclusion was hard to take and hardly taken. Nixon did announce that sufficiency, rather than superiority, would be the new American strategic goal, Kissinger did acknowledge that "an attempt to gain a unilateral advantage in the strategic field must be self-defeating," and the Americans did place a high priority on SALT. Nevertheless, Nixon still hoped to keep the American lead in strategic weapons, and he succeeded.

One of Nixon's first acts as President was to send the nuclear nonproliferation treaty (which prevented the "have-nots" from getting nuclear weapons), negotiated by the Johnson Administration, to the Senate for approval. The day after that approval came—supposedly clearing the way for meaningful SALT talks—Nixon announced a new antiballistic-missile (A.B.M.) program. His purpose was to create "bargaining chips" for SALT. In other words, like bombing in Vietnam to insure peace, Nixon was building new weapons so that the United States would not have to build new weapons. The President also endorsed the Multiple Independently Targeted Reentry Vehicle (MIRV), which could give each I.C.B.M. three to ten separately targeted nuclear warheads. Most military experts considered MIRV to be a quantum leap comparable to the switch from conventional to nuclear weaponry. Despite his talk about "sufficiency," Nixon still pushed on, determined to keep

the United States in first place. He would not allow the
American negotiators at SALT to bring up the subject of
MIRVs; he wanted the United States to develop, perfect,
and deploy the MIRVs before he would consider a freeze
on them.

The SALT I agreement that was finally signed in 1972
froze I.C.B.M. deployment but not MIRV, which was about
as meaningful as freezing the cavalry of the European nations in 1938 but not the tanks. Throughout the period of
the Nixon Administration the Pentagon added three new
warheads per day to the MIRV arsenal, a policy the Gerald
Ford Administration continued. By 1973, according to the
State Department, the United States had six thousand warheads to the Russians' twenty-five hundred. By 1977 the
United States had ten thousand warheads, the Russians
four thousand. It was a strange way to control the arms
race. As Laurence Martin, Director of War Studies at the
University of London, noted, "So far the SALT exercise
has done more to accelerate than to restrain strategic arms
procurement on both sides."

Still, Kissinger had to fight for the ratification of the
interim agreement that SALT I produced. Senators charged
that he was allowing the Russians superiority, an absurd
position to take. Kissinger finally got the interim agreement
through the Senate, thereby completing the first step in
linkage. The next move was to bring Peking in on the game.

Since 1949 the United States had had no relations with
the People's Republic of China, pretending all the while
that the Nationalist Chinese on Taiwan, not the Communists in Peking, represented the "real" China. As a policy,
nonrecognition had little to recommend it (aside from its
value on the domestic political scene); certainly it had not
made China any less Communist. When Nixon and Kissinger took office, China was not an issue they had to face.
Democrats were afraid to raise the subject for fear of being
labeled soft on Communism, and Republicans—led by Nixon
himself—claimed to feel an intense loyalty to the Nationalist
Chinese. Neither the public, the press, nor the Congress

had the slightest hint that the new President might re-examine the old policy, with which he had been intimately associated throughout his career.

Suddenly, in July 1971, Nixon announced that he was going to visit China at the invitation of China's leaders. Henry Kissinger had arranged the trip during a series of secret meetings with Chou En-lai, China's second in command. The trip would take place in February 1972. There had been no public pressure to change the China policy, and no public debate had taken place on the subject for years. Why had it been done? Who stood to gain what from it? Commentators speculated that perhaps Nixon and Kissinger wanted to use the opening to China as a way to squeeze both Moscow and Hanoi.

It appeared that Nixon saw vast possibilities for the United States in a Sino-Soviet split. He specifically believed that he could so manage the split as to force both Communist powers to abandon North Vietnam, which in turn would let the United States safely exit from Vietnam. The way to get China and Russia to cooperate, Nixon reasoned, was to keep them guessing about actual United States intentions. Nixon's active pursuit of détente could not help but make China worry about a possible U.S.-U.S.S.R. alliance against China. Nixon's opening to China, meanwhile, made Russia's leaders fearful of a U.S.-China alliance directed against them. There were many nuances to Nixon's policy, but always a consistent aim: to get Moscow and Peking to force Hanoi to allow the United States to extract itself from South Vietnam and to refrain from toppling Thieu until a "decent interval" had gone by (presumably until Nixon left the White House in 1977).

But whatever their fears and worries about Nixon's moves, neither Moscow nor Peking changed their Vietnam policy. They continued to send supplies to their beleaguered fellow Communists, especially antiaircraft artillery. Neither Communist nation helped Nixon in any way with his Vietnam problem.

Nixon wanted to make history, and recognition of China, especially by Nixon himself, would most assuredly be historic. It was the right thing to do, he believed, and he was the right man to do it, his anti-Communist credentials being what they were. In 1978 Nixon said he believed no other American politician could have gotten away with it. The move was good politics. The right wing might (and to some extent did) complain, but it had no one but Nixon to cling to. The left wing could only applaud. The boldness and drama of the new policy, the basic common sense in recognizing China, and the magnificent television coverage of the trip itself, with Nixon always at the center, could not help but win him millions of votes. Just the sight of Nixon shaking hands with Chou or chatting with Mao Tse-tung gave him stature.

Nixon had taken a historic and sensational step. In a joint communiqué, issued from Shanghai, the governments of China and the United States agreed to take further steps toward normalization of relations between themselves, and further agreed that Formosa was a part of China. The next move came six years later, when in December 1978 President Jimmy Carter announced that the United States was establishing full diplomatic relations with China while simultaneously ending its mutual defense treaty with the Nationalist Chinese on Formosa. In the eighties the two countries began to establish trade relations.

The Nixon-Kissinger policy of détente and linkage had some successes in other parts of the world. An essential part of détente was wrapping up some of the old problems left over from World War II. One such was divided Berlin, the city where so much of the Cold War drama had taken place. In September 1971 the winners in World War II—Britain, the United States, the U.S.S.R., and France—signed the Berlin Accord, which was also endorsed by both Germanys. It provided for improved communications between sectors of the divided city. It became part of a comprehensive Berlin Agreement signed in June 1972 in Berlin, which also provided for an American recognition of East Germany. Formal diplomatic relations between the United States and East Germany were established in 1974. This meant that the United States had abandoned its three-decades-old policy of seeking a reunited Germany.

At Helsinki, Finland, meanwhile, accords were signed in 1972 that recognized the boundaries of the various Russian satellites in East Europe and committed all signatories (including the Russians) to the defense of human rights (there was no enforcement machinery). In essence, when America signed the Helsinki Accords it accepted the outcome of World War II in East Europe. Harry Truman's old policy of demanding 85 percent was abandoned. America no longer challenged Soviet hegemony in the area.

In the Pacific, too, Nixon was able to eliminate a problem left over from the war, the status of Okinawa. America had been in command on the island since 1945; under the terms of an arrangement made in November 1969 between Nixon and Japanese Premier Eisaku Sato, Okinawa reverted to Japanese sovereignty in 1972. The United States did retain its extensive military facilities but agreed to remove its nuclear weapons from the island.

The various settlements gave the Japanese what they wanted in the Pacific, the Communists what they wanted in East Berlin, East Germany, and East Europe. America backed down from demands for democracy and free enterprise in the areas overrun by the Red Army. This retreat reflected, in turn, the coming of a new era in the world's history. The enormous American preponderance of power of 1945 was gone. This was on a relative scale, of course, as America's destructive power in 1975 was far greater than it had been in 1945, but in comparison to the rest of the world it was much less. So too with the American economy, which in the seventies was booming as never before, but which was also dependent on foreign sources as never before. In 1972, for the first time in the twentieth century, the United States had a deficit in its international trade accounts. Once a major exporter of raw materials, America had become an importer of copper, lead, zinc, and most of all oil. Meanwhile, the United States was also importing manufactured goods at record rates (in 1970, 61 percent of American imports were manufactured goods, only 31 percent raw materials—including oil—and foodstuffs). Fortunately, American agriculture remained the most productive in the world, and in 1972 and again in 1979 the United States was able to make a major dent in its balance of payments situation by selling massive quantities of wheat to the Russians. The exports were subsidized by the U.S. government. The wheat deal was perhaps the most direct payoff Nixon got from détente.

A way still had to be found out of Vietnam. The basic difference between the Johnson and Nixon administrations was that Johnson believed in military victory, whereas Nixon knew that the United States could not win the war, at least not at a price the nation would accept. Nixon realized that for economic reasons (the war was simply costing too much) and for the sake of domestic peace and tranquillity he had to cut back on the American commitment to Vietnam, which meant in turn accepting an outcome short of victory. The best Nixon could hope for, and this was his aim, was a gradual United States withdrawal, complemented by a huge improvement in ARVN's fighting qualities. Then, at best, South Vietnam could maintain its own independence, rather like South Korea; at worst, there would be a decent interval between American withdrawal and Communist victory.

To buy the time needed to build up ARVN, Nixon had to moderate the domestic dissatisfaction with the war. Less than two months after he took office the North Vietnamese added to that dissatisfaction by launching (February 23, 1969) a general offensive in which the 541,500 American troops in Vietnam (the peak level in the war) took heavy casualties. Television newscasters announced that the American combat death toll in the Vietnam War had passed that of the Korean War, with more than forty thousand dead.

Nixon responded to the offensive by moving in two directions simultaneously. On the tough side, to let the North Vietnamese know he could not be pushed around, Nixon launched his secret war against the North Vietnamese supply routes in Cambodia. The "secret," obviously, was well known to the Cambodians and Vietnamese, but Nixon managed to keep it from the American public (and Congress) through four years of intensive bombing. It was a bold, risky policy, with much at stake. Unfortunately, the return on investment was low. At their best, America's B-52s caused a 10 percent falloff in movement of men and supplies from North to South Vietnam via Cambodia. As in Korea, interdiction could not work against an enemy who moved his goods on human backs, along foot or bike trails.

In addition to the bombing of Cambodia, Nixon sharply increased the level of bombing in South Vietnam. But he offered not only an iron fist to Hanoi—there was a velvet glove also. On June 8, 1969, after meeting with President Thieu of South Vietnam on Midway Island, Nixon announced the first United States troop withdrawals from Vietnam. By August 1, he said, twenty-five thousand American soldiers would be returned to the United States. Further reductions would follow, as ARVN's fighting quality improved.

It was a historic turning point. Johnson's policy of escalation in Vietnam had been reversed. It was the first important American strategic retreat in Asia since MacArthur fell back from the Yalu in 1950. That it was an act forced on Nixon by public opinion made it no less significant. And it was a great help in appeasing the doves. So, too, was Nixon's promise to end the draft and institute an all-volunteer army. The first step came in November 1969 with the creation of a lottery system to determine who would get drafted, which made the selective-service process fairer to all classes and groups, and let a young man know where he stood with the draft.

The all-volunteer army was excellent politics, because the antiwar movement, as a political event, was essentially a student movement, and an all-volunteer army seriously weakened the political impact of the doves by robbing them of their major support, male college students. So, while constantly proclaiming that he would not allow policy to be dictated in the streets, Nixon allowed just that to happen, giving the protesting students exactly what they had been demanding: no more conscription. Nixon believed that there was not enough idealism in the antiwar movement to sustain it once college students were no longer threatened with the draft, and he was right. Except for a brief period following the Cambodian invasion of May 1970, Nixon had less trouble with street demonstrations than did his predecessor.*

Meanwhile, Nixon was supplying ARVN on a wholly unprecedented scale, to such an extent that when the final surrender came in 1975, ARVN was the fourth-ranking military power in the world.† Nixon warned Hanoi that the speed of American withdrawal from Vietnam would depend on progress in the Paris peace negotiations, and upon the levels of enemy activity, which meant that he was taking the position that while he was sending more weapons into South Vietnam, Hanoi should send less.

That was the administration's public posture. Privately, Kissinger had started, in August 1969, a series of secret negotiating sessions in Paris with Le Duc Tho, a member of Hanoi's Politburo. In these sessions Kissinger sought to bring about an armistice that would lead to the return of the American P.O.W.s, President Thieu's remaining in power in Saigon (at least for a decent interval), and a cease-fire. In return, the United States would withdraw all its troops from Vietnam and would recognize Communist possession of large sections of the South Vietnamese countryside. From Hanoi's point of view the offer was an attempt to buy the Communists off with half a loaf just when they had the whole loaf in their grasp. From Thieu's point of view it was

* It should be added that Attorney General John Mitchell came down very hard on all antiwar groups. He had the F.B.I. infiltrate, then disrupt or sabotage or destroy, numerous student groups; he hauled others into court on trumped-up charges that were never sustained by a jury anywhere but that did have the effect of keeping such organizations as the Vietnam Veterans Against the War tied up in court, spending all their energy and time and money defending themselves. These, and numerous other actions taken by Mitchell, were an important factor in limiting the effectiveness of antiwar groups.

† In 1979 the Vietnamese used these weapons to overrun Cambodia in two weeks.

a sellout, handing over parts of his country to the enemy just so the Americans could extract themselves without too much loss of face. From Kissinger's point of view it was a reasonable compromise, and he put his tremendous energies and unbounded enthusiasm into the task of bringing it off. It took him four years, but he finally made it. In the process his patience was sorely tested. Le Duc Tho would return time and again to the tiniest point, which had been settled over and over in previous sessions. Kissinger would sigh deeply, then take it up once again.

While Kissinger prepared to divide South Vietnam between the contending parties, the war went on. Nixon had to justify it to an increasingly restive Congress and public. He used a series of different justifications. He said he had inherited the war and was fighting on only to extract American troops safely, or he argued that an American defeat in Vietnam would seriously affect American interests elsewhere. At times he referred to America's treaty commitments and the overwhelming need to prove to friend and foe alike that America stood by her word.

Nixon also warned the American people that if they quit and the Viet Cong won, there would be a terrible bloodbath in Saigon, with all America's supporters losing their heads, and the blame would rest with the United States. In his foreign-policy message to Congress in January 1970 Nixon declared, "When we assumed the burden of helping South Vietnam, millions of South Vietnamese men and women placed their trust in us. To abandon them would risk a massacre that would shock and dismay every one in the world who values human life." Most of all, Nixon justified the continuation of the war by raising the issue of the P.O.W.s held by Hanoi. We will fight on until we get them back, he cried again and again, and it was a rallying cry with enough emotional content to convince most Americans that the war must go on.

The P.O.W. issue could not, however, win the war for Thieu. Vietnamization meant, first of all, vastly increased military aid for the Government of South Vietnam (G.V.N.). Backed by the sudden, massive inflow of money and arms,

Thieu ordered a general mobilization. By inducting all men between eighteen and thirty-eight into the service, Thieu expanded the G.V.N. armed forces from 700,000 to 1,100,000, which meant that over half the able-bodied male population of South Vietnam was in uniform. As Frances FitzGerald points out in her award-winning *Fire in the Lake,* counting the militia, the civil service, and the 110,000-man police force, "the United States was arming and, in one way or another, supporting most of the male population of Vietnam—and for the duration of the war."

Coupled with the "search and destroy" policy of American combat troops, the sudden expansion of ARVN produced a temporary but real military advantage for the U.S.-G.V.N. side. FitzGerald describes the results: "Now all, or most, of the Vietnamese were swept up into the American war machine. 'Vietnamization' preempted the manpower base of the country and brought it into a state of dependency on the American economy. And the results were spectacular. The major roads were open to traffic; the cities flourished on American money and goods; those peasant families that remained in the fertile areas of the Delta grew rich on bumper crops of 'miracle' rice. The country was more 'pacified' than it had ever been before."

From the American (and Thieu's) point of view Vietnamization seemed to be working. By 1972, 50 percent of the population lived in cities (Saigon's population alone had jumped from 300,000 to 3,000,000 in ten years), where the refugees from the countryside became dependent upon the Americans. South Vietnam had the population distribution of an industrialized state, but it had no industry, except for the war and the Americans. Vietnamese refugees made their living either in the ARVN (where they were paid by the Americans) or by working directly for the Americans— on construction jobs, unloading (and stealing) at the docks, as shoeshine boys or pimps, as cleaning women or prostitutes. In the cities the refugees were safe, certainly better off than they had been when living in the "free-fire zones," and they were fed by the American government—but they had no real economy.

From 1961 onward, American Presidents never tired of proclaiming that the United States was making such huge sacrifices in Southeast Asia only for the good of the people of the region. The United States had no territorial objectives, nor did it wish to replace the French as the colonial masters of the Vietnamese. It was true that the United States took no wealth out of Vietnam; in fact, it poured money in. "And yet," FitzGerald points out, "it has produced much the same effects as the most exploitative of colonial regimes. The reason is that the overwhelming proportion of American funds has gone not into agricultural or industrial development but into the creation of services for the Americans—the greatest service being the Saigon government's army. As a whole, American wealth has gone into creating and supporting a group of people—refugees, soldiers, prostitutes, secretaries, translators, maids, and shoeshine boys—who do not engage in any form of production."

The G.V.N. was a government without a country. The people were dependent on it—or rather on the Americans—but they felt no loyalty to it. South Vietnam, once a major world exporter of rice, now produced almost nothing. The G.V.N. had guns and money. The other side had a cause. Viet Cong and North Vietnamese morale went up and down over the decade of active American involvement, as would be true in any army in such a long war, but even at its lowest point Communist morale was so much higher than ARVN's that no comparison was possible. The Americans talked incessantly about "pacification" and "winning the hearts and minds of the people," while Nixon dropped new record tonnages of bombs on their heads. Those who escaped the bombing offensive went to the cities to become unwilling conscripts in ARVN or resentful servants to the Americans. In the army they would not fight, for the good reason that they had nothing to fight for. Meanwhile the V.C. and the North Vietnamese held on against the world's most powerful air force, thereby providing—in Fitzgerald's words—"an example of courage and endurance that measures with any in modern history."

Throughout 1969 and into 1970 the Americans regularly

released figures to prove that Vietnamization was working. ARVN, according to the Pentagon, could "hack it." Body counts were higher than ever; ARVN had more troops, more and better leaders and equipment. Then, on April 30, 1970, Nixon made a surprise announcement that a large force of U.S. troops, supported by major air strikes and backed by a huge ARVN force, had invaded Cambodia. Nixon said the purpose was to gain time for the American withdrawal. The invasion of Cambodia resulted in the death of a few Communist troops but otherwise had only negative results. It hardly even slowed the flow of supplies to the V.C. and North Vietnamese in the south. It turned Cambodia into a battleground and eventually prompted a successful Communist insurgency there, thereby making the domino theory come true.

The Cambodian invasion extended the list of nations the United States was pledged to defend, despite Nixon's solemn promise that he was not making any pledges to the Lon Nol military regime, which had recently (March 18, 1970) overthrown the government of Prince Norodom Sihanouk, a neutralist who had tried to keep the war away from Cambodia. The invasion temporarily revived the antiwar movement at home, especially after four students were shot dead on May 4 by the Ohio National Guard at Kent State University, and it gave Henry Kissinger an opportunity to display his academic brilliance as he explained to the Senate why the invasion of Cambodia was not an invasion of Cambodia.*

The American people, however, were not willing to see their boys fighting in yet another country. It was not just

---

* According to Kissinger, the Cambodian government did not know—and did not want to know—what was going on in its border areas. The Cambodian government had not actually invited the American troops into the country, but it had not resisted either. The territory the Americans invaded was hardly "neutral," filled as it was with Communist troops, and the Cambodians did not exercise sovereignty there. We were not making war on the Cambodian government. Therefore the invasion of Cambodia was not an invasion of Cambodia.

the students at Kent State and elsewhere who protested; even the Congress of the United States passed a bill forcing Nixon to remove American ground and air forces from Cambodia by July 1970. Nixon continued to bomb Cambodia while continuing to deceive the public and the Congress about it.* He did have to pull the troops out, announcing as he did so that the operation had been a great success. In fact, he had put himself in the position of having another government to defend that could not possibly defend itself, and he had left ARVN with a new responsibility that it could not meet.

In announcing the invasion, Nixon had said, "If, when the chips are down, the world's most powerful nation . . . acts like a pitiful, helpless giant, the forces of totalitarianism and anarchy will threaten free nations and free institutions throughout the world." The almost totally negative results of the great risk he had taken in expanding the war showed in fact that the United States, in a guerrilla war in Asia, was nearly helpless.

A new force in the making of American foreign policy, meanwhile, was beginning to exert itself. Throughout the Cold War and the Vietnam War the Congress had been a cipher. It had ignored its Constitutional duties on the grounds that in the modern age the President had to be free to act immediately against aggressors. From the mid-forties onward Congress legislated for the domestic front while the President acted on the foreign front. The system was mutually satisfactory as long as America was winning. But the absence of victory in Vietnam, the drawn-out nature of the struggle there, caused a change. Congress began to assert its authority. Democracies, as Lincoln and Wilson and Roo-

---

* Henry Kissinger had no problem justifying the deception. If the secret had been known, he later told a Senate committee, it would have led to demonstrations in the streets, thereby jeopardizing the Administration's plans for peace. This was at least consistent with Nixon's position that the United States was expanding the war to make peace.

sevelt knew, cannot fight long wars, because long wars inevitably become unpopular wars. That unpopularity will first show up in Congress, the branch of government closest to the people.

Like the people, Congress was frustrated by the war, and like them, it hardly knew what to do about it. The instinct to trust the President when the nation is at war is very strong; Nixon always counted on the prestige of his office in carrying through his policy. Some argued that there was nothing Congress could do, because the President is Commander in Chief of the armed forces and thus held all the power.

Under the American Constitution, however, the ultimate power resides not in the White House, but in Congress. At the starkest level, Congress can impeach and remove from office the President, but the President cannot remove Congress or individual Congressmen. On questions of foreign policy only Congress can declare war or appropriate the money necessary to fight it. Here the trouble was more a practical one than one of Constitutional theory. The United States was already *at* war with North Vietnam. On December 31, 1970, Congress repealed the Gulf of Tonkin Resolution, but Nixon simply ignored this action, saying the Resolution was not necessary to justify the continuation of the war. As to money, few Congressmen were willing to risk their careers by voting against the Defense Department budget under ordinary circumstances, much less when American boys were engaged in combat and had to have arms, ammunition, and other equipment to protect themselves.

Congress did find an ingenious way to use the appropriation power to exert its will, without stripping the fighting men of their means of defense. It declared that none of the money it was appropriating for military purposes could be used to widen the war, and specifically forbade the use of American ground troops in Cambodia or Laos. This restriction prevented Nixon from sending American troops into Laos on February 8, 1971, when ARVN launched a major invasion of Laos. Because Congress had failed to restrict his use of the Air Force, however, Nixon did have American bombers and helicopters fly mission after mission to protect the ARVN invaders. Despite the air cover, Hanoi's forces sent ARVN reeling. It suffered 50 percent losses in the forty-five-day operation. It was a major embarrassment. As FitzGerald noted, it convinced the South Vietnamese that Vietnamization "meant increased Vietnamese deaths in pursuit of the American policy objective to extract the American troops from Vietnam without peace negotiations."

On March 30, 1972, Hanoi launched a major offensive across the demilitarized zone. Two weeks later Nixon responded by resuming the intensive bombing of the north, hitting Haiphong and Hanoi on April 16 for the first time since 1968. He also mined Haiphong harbor. Besides giving the Pentagon a chance to prove it could do what it said it could do (in the event, it couldn't—even though the military had claimed for years that such an escalation of the war would be decisive), the action reassured any doubters who feared that Nixon had suddenly gone soft on Communism. To his delight, Nixon got away with something Johnson had always feared to try. Despite the loss of a ship in Haiphong harbor, the Russians acted as if nothing had happened, and a month later Nixon visited Moscow for a summit meeting. Kissinger credited linkage and detente for this success; others attributed it to Russia's need for America's wheat and corn. Peking's reaction was limited to verbal denunciations.

Nixon had gotten away with a major escalation of the war, but by no means did that solve all his problems. He was up for reelection in 1972 and he was determined to win by the biggest landslide ever. To obtain that goal he had to have some semblance of peace in Vietnam, but he also had to have Thieu still in power in Saigon, or he would become "the first President to lose a war." Nixon decided to force Le Duc Tho to accept a compromise peace that would leave the Communists in control of much of South Vietnam's countryside (but not the cities, especially Saigon), by further escalating the war. While Kissinger took a hard line in his continuing secret talks with Le Duc Tho, Nixon stepped up the military offensive against North Vietnam, Cambodia, and Laos.

It was primarily an air offensive, because by the spring of 1972 Nixon had reduced the American ground-troop level in Vietnam to 70,000, far below the 540,000 that had been there when he took office four years earlier. American combat deaths were down from three hundred per week to one per day. Vietnamization was working, from Nixon's point of view, if only Hanoi would sign a peace agreement.

The Kissinger–Le Duc Tho talks were dragged out and terribly complex. Incredibly small points were haggled over while each side blamed the other for insincerity. There was some shifting of positions. What stood out, however, was a real consistency. Throughout, Hanoi was willing to allow the Americans to get out, and to turn over the P.O.W.s when they did. From that point on Hanoi insisted that what happened in Vietnam was none of America's business, which meant Le Duc Tho would sign no binding contract as to Hanoi's behavior in the future. Washington consistently argued that Hanoi had to abandon the use of force in settling the problem of a divided Vietnam. Such an agreement, of course, would have insured Thieu's position for some years to come, given that he controlled the army, the police, the civil service, and most importantly, the ballot boxes in South Vietnam.

Eventually, Le Duc Tho indicated his willingness to sign an agreement. His motives remain unclear. Perhaps he realized that once the Americans were gone, Nixon and Kissinger would find it difficult to influence events. Perhaps he responded to a bribe; Nixon evidently promised a massive program of reconstruction for North Vietnam once the shooting stopped. In any event, on October 26, 1972, just in time for the election, a triumphant Kissinger announced that "peace is at hand," and Nixon claimed that his policies had brought "peace with honor." The Democratic candidate, Senator George McGovern, who had rotten luck throughout his inept campaign, lost the only issue he still had going for him. Despite McGovern's last-minute plea to the American people, "Don't let this man fool you again," more than 60 percent of the voters chose Nixon, who scored the greatest victory in modern American electoral history.

Immediately after the election, astonishingly, the talks broke down again. At Nixon's insistence Kissinger had raised the price just when Le Duc Tho was ready to sign. Nixon demanded an ironclad guarantee that Thieu would remain in power. In part, this was a response to Thieu's intransigence. Thieu knew that he was being sold out, that an American withdrawal would sooner or later lead to his downfall, no matter how many promises Le Duc Tho made, and so Thieu threatened to ignore any cease-fire agreement that Kissinger might sign. Kissinger made extravagant promises to Thieu and Le Duc Tho about American military support in the event of a Communist offensive and about American reconstruction funds that would be available to both sides after peace came. Nixon meanwhile began the Christmas bombing campaign against Hanoi. It quickly made Hanoi the most heavily bombed city in the history of warfare.

Nixon's publicly stated reason for the air offensive was to force Hanoi to release the American P.O.W.'s, but the campaign itself led to the loss of at least fifteen B-52s and eleven fighter-bombers (Hanoi claimed much higher American losses), increasing by ninety-three the number of P.O.W.'s held by Hanoi. The losses, meanwhile, were more than the U.S. Air Force could stand. The generals had never liked the idea of sending costly B-52s over Hanoi, a city heavily defended against air attack, thanks to the Russians. As the losses mounted, the generals wanted out. Nixon must also have been aware of the worldwide opposition to the bombing, and Kissinger may have convinced him that the October agreement was the best the United States could get. Perhaps most important, despite Nixon's personal triumph in the election, the Democrats still controlled Congress and were finally ready to assert themselves. Nixon knew that the new Congress, coming into office in January 1973, was going to cut off all funds for bombing. Nixon therefore called off the bombers and agreed to sign a cease-fire agreement. On January 23, 1973, all active American participation in the war in Vietnam ended.

Nixon claimed that the Christmas bombing had done the trick, but two of his own officials gave that story the lie when they were interviewed by Marvin and Bernard Kalb. "Peanuts," said one official when asked what difference the Christmas bombing had made. "That enormous bombing made little critical difference. What the B-52s did was to get the margin in January pretty much back to where it was in October." Another official explained, "Look, we were in an embarrassing situation. Could we suddenly say we'll sign in January what we wouldn't in October? We had to do something. So the bombing began, to try to create the image of a defeated enemy crawling back to the peace table to accept terms demanded by the United States."

For the next two years Kissinger bragged that he had managed to achieve the impossible. "It took me four years to negotiate peace in Vietnam," he told the Arabs and the Israelis, indicating that although he was indeed a miracle man, even he could not bring an immediate peace to the Middle East. Nixon, meanwhile, spoke and acted as if the United States had won a decisive victory under his command.

The claims had a hollow ring, because fighting continued in South Vietnam while it increased in Cambodia. The huge American Air Force in Asia concentrated on Cambodia in a series of heavy assaults. Congress reacted by cutting off funds for such bombing. On June 27, 1973, Nixon vetoed the bill cutting the funds. Two days later he assured Congress that all United States military activity in Cambodia would cease by August 15, and on July 1 he signed a bill ending all American combat activities in Indochina by August 15. Most observers believed that he caved in only because of his weakened political position due to Watergate.

The cease-fire in Vietnam, meanwhile, broke down before the ink was dry on the agreements. Nixon rushed more arms to Thieu ($3.2 billion in 1973), who already had the fourth largest military force in the world. Indeed, all four sides to the final cease-fire agreement (Saigon, Hanoi, the V.C., and the United States) so painfully negotiated over such a long period of time, violated it in every imaginable way, as everyone had suspected beforehand they would. All that had really been agreed to was that the United States would pull its fighting men out of Vietnam, and that Hanoi would give back the American P.O.W.s.

Over the next two years the battle raged, with relatively little shifting in positions. Congress refused to appropriate additional funds for Thieu's army, despite increasingly strident pleas from Kissinger, Nixon, and eventually President Ford. The final collapse of the Thieu regime began in January 1975, when Phuoc Binh, capital of Phuoc Long Province, fell to the Communists. Thieu decided to shorten his lines—until this time he had been trying to hold onto as much territory as possible—but the attempted retrenchment to more defensible lines proved to be a disastrous mistake. Once ARVN started retreating, it never stopped. Panic among the troops spread to the civilian refugees, who soon clogged the roads. Hue fell on March 26, Da Nang on March 31. On April 22 ARVN withdrew from Xuan Loc, forty miles east of Saigon. A week later the V.C. captured the huge air base at Bien Hoa, fifteen miles from Saigon.

On April 21 President Thieu delivered an emotional speech on Vietnamese radio and television. He accused the United States of breaking its promises of support and blamed the debacle on American cuts in military aid. He then resigned and got out of the country, most of his relatives and friends going with him. On April 28 President Ford ordered the emergency helicopter evacuation of all Americans remaining in South Vietnam. In a dreadful scene, U.S. Marines kept panic-stricken Vietnamese (who had fought alongside the Americans and had much to fear from the Communists) away from the helicopters as the Americans and a select few Vietnamese were evacuated. On April 30, 1975, the remnants of the South Vietnamese government announced its unconditional surrender to the Communists. Saigon was renamed Ho Chi Minh City, and Vietnam was again united into one country. That same month the Lon Nol regime in Phnom Penh fell to the Khmer Rouge. America's most disastrous foreign-policy adventure, the intervention into the Indochinese war, had come to an end.

Nixon's dire predictions about all the dominoes that were going to fall to monolithic Communism proved to be wrong. Within a year Communist Vietnam was at war with Communist Cambodia; by 1978 it was at war with China. But any doves who believed that the Communists of Southeast Asia were democrats and agrarian reformers who only wanted to redistribute the land were in for a great shock, as the Khmer Rouge instituted in Cambodia one of the most repressive regimes in the world's history; it was so bad, in fact, that Senator McGovern—one of the original doves—advocated military action by the United Nations in order to do something about what was going on in Cambodia. In Vietnam, meanwhile, thousands upon thousands tried desperately to get out, by any means possible. For all the faults of the Diem/Ky/Thieu regimes in Saigon, the city was a veritable paradise of free speech and assembly while they were in charge, as compared to what was happening under the Communists. As Nixon noted with some satisfaction in 1978, no one was trying to break into Communist Vietnam.

So the Americans were finally out of Indochina. Except in Hong Kong and South Korea, in fact, the white man was now out of mainland Asia, the Americans being the last to leave. The process begun by the Japanese one generation earlier, when they had proclaimed that Asia should be run by Asians, was nearly complete. America's long relationship with Asia, begun with the acquisition of the Philippines three-quarters of a century earlier, had reached a divide. America had been involved in war in Asia for twenty-two of the thirty-four years between 1941 and 1975. Over 120,000 American boys had died in combat there (41,000 in World War II, 33,000 in Korea, 46,000 in Vietnam, and

530,000 were wounded (130,000 in World War II, 100,000 in Korea, 300,000 in Vietnam).*

And what did America have to show for all the treasure spent, all the lives lost, all the bodies crippled for life? Nothing, unless it was the lesson that Vietnam taught, whatever it may be. Few undertook to find out. President Ford set the tone of the inquiry when he called for amnesia, not analysis. "The lessons of the past in Vietnam," Ford declared in 1975, "have already been learned—learned by Presidents, learned by Congress, learned by the American people—and we should have our focus on the future." He never said what the lessons were, but the American people responded gratefully to his invitation to forget the whole nightmare.

It seemed that one likely legacy was an increased Congressional role in the making of foreign policy. One of the major themes in the American rise to globalism after 1938 had been the immense growth in the power of the Presidency, especially in foreign affairs. To get the country out of Vietnam, to retreat to a policy of realism, Congress had been forced to assert itself. How long it would continue to do so remained to be seen; in the nature of the American political system, Congressmen are much more concerned with domestic than with foreign affairs, unless the United States is at war.

Congress did pass, in 1972, the War Powers Act, which requires the President to give an accounting of his actions within thirty days of committing troops to a foreign war. After that time Congress has to approve the Presidential action.

It was an awkward way for Congress to assert its Constitutional right and duty to declare war. The last time the President consulted Congress over war powers was in 1964, when Johnson sent the Gulf of Tonkin Resolution through

---

* The ratio of combat deaths to wounds was much lower in Vietnam than in previous wars, thanks to helicopter evacuation of the wounded and to magnificent progress in field medical techniques.

the legislature in a breeze. Congress had played absolutely no role in the major decisions of the Nixon White House: Vietnamization, the air and later the ground offensives against Cambodia and Laos, the China trip, détente, linkage, the mining of Haiphong harbor, the Christmas bombing, or the cease-fire agreement. The War Powers Act, by starting with the assumption that the President had to be free to move quickly in a crisis, gave the game away. Once the President, acting in strict accord with the law, had troops committed, could anyone believe that the Congress would force him to pull out?

By wrapping himself in the flag and appealing to the patriotism—and the jingoism—of the public, the President could keep his war going. That the public still yearned, even after Nixon, for strong leadership, that it would still respond enthusiastically to American saber rattling, became clear in May 1975, when President Ford sent the Marines into Cambodia to rescue a captured merchant vessel. The affair revealed that the quickest path to popularity for a President remained a *successful* military adventure. In such situations, hopes for a less active, more cautious and realistic, less expansive foreign policy, were slim.

America and the Middle East
Since 1945

The United States is committed to defend Israel's existence, but not Israel's conquests.

HENRY KISSINGER, 1970

Since 1945 the eastern end of the Mediterranean, where Western civilization began, has been a theater of intense activity. Both the United States and the Soviet Union have tried to impose on the scene their own Cold War mentality and habits—movement and response, bluff and counterbluff—as each superpower has attempted to gain a temporary advantage. The Turks, Arabs, Iranians, Jews and others who live in the region have tried, with fair success, to play one side against the other, but essentially the Cold War has been irrelevant to them. They have taken advantage of the American and Russian obsession with each other, but they have never felt that Communism versus anti-Communism was their problem or that it in any way defined their choices. Consequently, there has been a bewildering shift in alliances over the past generation, with both the Americans and the Russians enjoying brilliant successes, then suffering devastating setbacks.

War, as always, has been the supreme arbitrator. There have been five major Middle Eastern conflicts since World War II, in 1948, 1956, 1967, 1973, and 1982–84, with endemic border warfare in between the big wars. The United States, the Soviet Union, Britain, France, and Czechoslovakia have all sent massive shipments of arms to the area, and fighting men to participate in the struggles.

The stakes are enormous. The Arab world is important

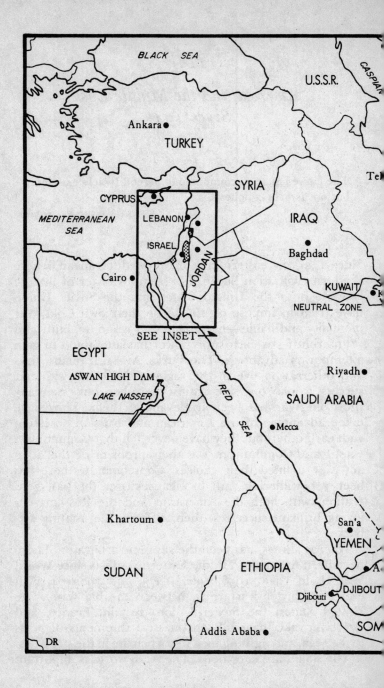

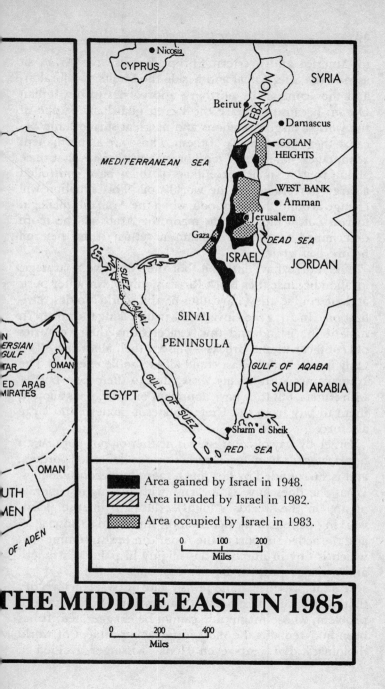

Nicosia
CYPRUS

SYRIA

LEBANON

Beirut ●

● Damascus

GOLAN
HEIGHTS

MEDITERRANEAN SEA

WEST BANK
● Amman

● Jerusalem

Gaza

DEAD SEA

ISRAEL

JORDAN

SUEZ CANAL

SINAI

PENINSULA

GULF OF AQABA

SAUDI ARABIA

EGYPT

GULF OF SUEZ

Sharm el Sheik

RED SEA

N
PERSIAN
GULF

TAR

OMAN

ED ARAB
MIRATES

OMAN

UTH
MEN

OF ADEN

Area gained by Israel in 1948.

Area invaded by Israel in 1982.

Area occupied by Israel in 1983.

0   100   200
Miles

THE MIDDLE EAST IN 1985

0   200   400
Miles

to America and Western Europe because the Arabs sit astride the Suez Canal and beside the Straits of Gibraltar, and they control the northern approaches to the Indian Ocean; because they are the sacred guardians of one of the world's largest religions and its great shrines; and because there are so many of them. Those are all permanent advantages. The Arabs' temporary advantage is that since about 1960 a small percentage of them have controlled a large percentage of the world's oil. This situation will change around the year 2000, when the Arab oil will begin to run out, a fact that has made the Arabs all the more determined to get the maximum return from their oil before it is gone.

The Turks have little oil, but they do have a strategic location because they block Russia's only warm-water port, and of course they have one of the world's oldest civilizations. In 1972 they invaded Cyprus, taking the northern half of the island and thus exacerbating their centuries old conflict with the Greeks—who are their allies in NATO. Only in the Middle East could allies also be enemies! The Iranians are strategically weak, due to their long border with Russia, but they have abundant oil, which has allowed them to buy from the United States a modern and large air force.

Israel, by way of contrast, has neither oil nor population nor strategic advantage, is without easily defended borders, and is surrounded by her much more numerous enemies. What she does have is an army with the highest morale of any in the world, a highly educated, intense, hard-working people, a moral claim on the world's conscience, and the active support of the American Jewish community, which is tiny in numbers but mighty in political strength and a major prop of Israel's economy.

It is the presence of the Jewish state of Israel on territory that was once Palestine that causes the Middle Eastern problem, whose magnitude cannot be exaggerated. It has been and remains the most intractable problem of world diplomacy. For years even Henry Kissinger avoided it, because, as he said, it was impossible to solve and he hated to fail. From 1948 on, most Arabs have refused to agree that the state of Israel had a right to exist, while the Israelis have insisted (especially since 1967) that the Palestinian refugees have no right to a national state of their own. When national existence is at stake, no compromise is possible. That the Israelis and Arabs will someday have to become good neighbors seems as impossible to them as it does obvious to the rest of the world.

Robert Stookey has written, "The land of Palestine belongs of right to a people uniquely favored of God, the vehicle of His revelation respecting the salvation of mankind, charged with a permanent mission for the enlightenment of humanity and the establishment of justice, long the object of repression and injustice, whose enemies are presently sustained by a world superpower for its own imperial interests."

Part of the Palestine problem is that both Israelis and Arabs believe that the above sentence is describing them. In short, the Middle East sets true believer against true believer with survival as the issue. No wonder, then, that solutions are hard to find, or that the warfare has been so bloody and costly and, worst of all, continuous. No wonder, too, that hatreds run so deep.

For American policymakers the Middle East has often been a headache, sometimes a nightmare, as each President has tried, in his own way, to pursue an even-handed policy, if only because he needed both Arab oil and Jewish campaign contributions. By the 1970s the United States also needed Arab goodwill and investment. Complicating everything was the American anti-Communist crusade, which made it difficult for the Secretaries of State to deal realistically with the essential problem of national homelands for both Israelis and Palestinians. Nor were the Secretaries altogether wrong to see Communism as a threat to the Middle East, for the Russians certainly were constantly meddling in the area, just like the Americans. Both sides poured arms into the hands of their friends, to such an extent that in 1973 the Israelis, Egyptians, and Syrians fought the second biggest tank battle in history.*

Neither of the superpowers has had much interest in ideological purity. At various times the Russians have supported the most reactionary of the richest Arab rulers, while the United States has given aid to the most radical of the poorest Arab governments. American and Russian involvement is done on a day-to-day, or at best month-to-month, basis, because neither side has a well-thought-out program for the region. They cannot have one, because they have no solution to the problem of national homelands. So each plays it by ear, with resulting policy shifts that often appear to be not only sudden but incomprehensible. One looks in vain for consistency, except that both sides insist that the other has no right to intervene in the Middle East (except when war breaks out, when each demands that the other exert its influence to stop the fighting).

The process began immediately after World War II, when American policy collided with Russian expansion. Stalin had violated his agreement to pull his troops out of Iran six months from the end of hostilities. The Russians promoted separatist revolts in Azerbaijan and Kurdistan; on March (16, 1946, Truman sent a protest note to the Soviets demanding "immediate" withdrawal, in what was the first expression of his not-yet-announced policy of containment. Soon thereafter the Russians did withdraw. In Turkey, meanwhile, the Russians had been applying pressure to allow joint Soviet-Turkish control of the Dardanelles, and to provide the Soviets with naval and land bases in the strait. Truman warned Stalin on April 6, 1946, that the United

---

* Kursk, a battle fought on the Russo-German front in 1943, was first, while the 1944 Battle of the Bulge used to be second. Counting the Syrian front, there were sixty-three hundred tanks committed in 1973, nearly twice the total number of tanks commanded by General Eisenhower in Europe in 1945. Losses in 1973 were horrendous. The Arabs lost eighteen hundred tanks, the Israelis more than five hundred.

States would aid the United Nations with military power to protect the Turks from Russian "coercion or penetration." On August 21 and October 11, 1946, Truman sent further strong protest notes to Stalin, rejecting Russian demands for a foothold in the Dardanelles, and he sent the U.S. Sixth Fleet to the eastern Mediterranean as a show of force. Late in 1946 Russian pressure on Turkey eased. In 1947 the United States, in response to Communist guerrilla pressure on the Greek government, adopted Truman's Doctrine of Containment as its Cold War policy (see chapter 5). Thus early was the pattern of Russian threat followed by American counterthreat established in the eastern Mediterranean.

That pattern has been most pronounced in the Arab-Israeli struggle, which also goes back to World War II. Like so many of the problems of the modern world, Hitler created this one. Zionism, a movement born in Russia, advocated that Jews return to their homeland in Palestine after two thousand years of wandering, in order to establish their own nation. Zionism became a driving force among world Jewry only in response to the Nazi Final Solution. Most of those European Jews who survived the holocaust had no desire to return to the old country; they wanted to go to Palestine, where a sizable Jewish population had already been built up in the first forty years of the century. Britain had a mandate to govern Palestine. Anxious to placate the Arabs, because of their large oil interests, the British tried to prevent further Jewish immigration into Palestine, while the Jews tried to drive the British out through terroristic tactics, of which the blowing up of a wing of the King David Hotel in Jerusalem (a feat engineered by Menachem Begin, later to become Israeli Prime Minister) was the most famous. Exhausted, the British turned the problem over to the United Nations, where the Soviets and Americans banded together to force a solution on the Arabs. That solution was the partition of Palestine to create a Jewish state along the Mediterranean coast, with almost indefensible borders. On May 14, 1948, Israel proclaimed its independence. The United States was the first country to recognize the new state, Russia a close second. Israel looked to Russia, not to the United States, for the arms she needed to defend herself.

The Arabs invaded, and in the first few weeks the Israelis retreated before the combined might of the Egyptian, Jordanian, Lebanese, Syrian and Iraqi armies. The Israelis asked the United Nations for help, and once again the United States and the Soviet Union worked together to bring about a four-week truce. During this time the Israelis procured quantities of heavy arms from Communist Czechoslovakia. When the shooting started again it was the Israelis who drove their enemies from the field. The United States forced a cease-fire resolution through the United Nations but it was generally ignored and Israel continued to conquer Arab territory, including western Galilee and parts of the Negev Desert. The Egyptians, their best army surrounded, sued for peace. In what would become a familiar role, American statesman Dr. Ralph Bunche stepped forward in January 1949 to arrange the disengagement of forces. After tortuous negotiations, Bunche arranged for armistice agreements among all the parties.

Israel was born, thanks in no small part to Russian military support and American negotiating skill. Her boundaries already extended those assigned her by the U.N. partition, and included thousands of unhappy Palestinian Arabs. There were, in addition, other Palestinians who had fled or who had been forced out by the fighting, thus beginning the problem of the Palestinian refugee. Another pattern in American relations with Israel began at this time, as President Truman put exceedingly strong pressure on Prime Minister David Ben-Gurion for concessions on both the refugee and boundary issues, only to meet with an indignantly negative response, backed by the veiled threat that the American Jewish community would turn against Truman if he persisted.

Endemic warfare along the borders, especially in and near the Gaza Strip, followed. In 1956 the Israelis joined in a conspiracy with Britain and France to launch a surprise attack against Egypt. Israel enjoyed great success, taking all of the Sinai Peninsula. But Ike would not allow it, nor would Khrushchev. Working together in the United Nations they forced the British, French, and Israelis to withdraw.

Their motives were mixed. The British and French had tried to convince Eisenhower that Gamal Abdel Nasser, the leader of Arab socialism and unity, could be toppled. Ike thought it unlikely. Furthermore, he wanted to retain good relations with the oil-rich Arab states, especially the Saudis, who were unwilling to fight the Israelis themselves but supported those who did. So Ike stepped forward as the defender of Egypt, but he got precious little thanks for it. Instead, Nasser praised the Russians, who were building the Aswan High Dam for him and who were so delighted to have a foot on the ground in the Middle East that they abandoned their decade-old policy of support for Israel.

As Nasser continued to spread propaganda for Arab unity and socialism while taking more aid from the Soviet Union and allowing more Russians into his country, Eisenhower and Dulles feared that the Russians would move into the Middle East "vacuum" (the phrase always infuriated the Arabs) and had to be forestalled. Attempted coups and countercoups in Syria, Jordan, and Iraq by pro- and anti-Nasserites increased American anxiety. So on January 5, 1957, Ike asked Congress for authority to use American armed forces in the Middle East "if the President determines the necessity . . . to assist any nation . . . requesting assistance against armed aggression from any country controlled by international communism." The next year Ike used the authority granted him in the so-called Eisenhower Doctrine when on July 15, 1958, he sent the Marines into Lebanon to support President Camille Chamoun. They did no fighting, because no fighting was going on, and Ike pulled them out in October. What they had accomplished was as much a mystery as why they had been sent in in the first place.

The great event of the ensuing years was the Arab takeover of their oil resources. Before World War II the British had held the lion's share of Middle East oil. During and after the war American oil companies forced the British to share the riches with them. But the postwar Arab governments, along with Iran, began demanding more for their precious, limited, and only important natural resource. Premier Mossadegh in Iran was the first to attempt a full-scale nationalization of the oil fields (1951), and he was toppled (1953) by the C.I.A. In 1959 the producing states—Venezuela, Iran, Saudi Arabia, Kuwait, and Iraq—together formed the Organization of Petroleum Exporting Countries (OPEC). OPEC's first objective was to halt a worldwide slump in the price of crude oil. The United States was still an exporter of oil in 1959, and there was such a glut on the market that it took ten years to raise the price of oil back to its pre-1959 levels. In the meantime each of the producing states had nationalized its oil fields, whether by agreement with the British and American oil companies or by the simple exercise of their sovereign power.

Nasser, meanwhile, as other Arabs got rich, was unable to bring about any miracles in Egypt. Despite his commitment to socialism and Arab unity, neither really existed as the Egyptian people remained mired in nearly the worst poverty in the world, despite Soviet aid. His United Arab Republic was falling apart. By 1967 Nasser needed a dramatic victory to restore his sagging fortunes. He had an opportunity because ever since the 1956 war the Russians had been supplying Egypt, Syria, and Iraq with advanced weapons, while following a strongly anti-Israel policy. The Arabs greatly outnumbered the Israelis and were now better armed. By 1967 the Russians were encouraging the Arabs to attack Israel, although they made it clear there would be no open Soviet backing for the Arabs, who could not expect help if their military adventure failed. Still, with thousands of Russian technicians and their families in Egypt, working on the Aswan High Dam or with the Egyptian military, Nasser assumed the Russians had to support him.

In May 1967, goaded by the Russians and by Arab extremists, Nasser demanded the removal of the U.N. Emergency Force, which had stood between the Egyptians and Israelis since 1956. Secretary General U Thant, noting that he could hardly keep U.N. troops in place in opposition to the host government, promptly pulled the U.N.E.F. out of the Sinai. This seems to have surprised both Nasser and the Russians. The Soviets now changed their position, urging caution on Nasser, as they feared the outbreak of a war that they could not control and that might lead to a United States–U.S.S.R. confrontation. But Nasser could not back down at this juncture; Egyptian troops took possession of Sharm al-Shaikh, overlooking the Strait of Tiran, and closed Israel's access to the Gulf of Aqaba and thus to the port of Elath.

The United States was preoccupied with Vietnam at this time, becoming more dependent on Arab oil, and above all anxious to avoid another war, particularly one in the Middle East, with possible repercussions too frightening to think about. But it could not simply abandon Israel to Nasser and the Russians. President Johnson tried to organize international attempts to run the Egyptian blockade, but the Western European nations, fearing Arab oil embargoes, would not cooperate. Israel believed the American efforts were half-hearted at best and decided to take matters into her own hands, before she was slowly strangled.

At this juncture General de Gaulle gave Israel's Foreign Minister, Abba Eban, some perceptive advice. "Don't make war," de Gaulle declared. "You will be considered the aggressor by the world and by me. You will cause the Soviet Union to penetrate more deeply into the Middle East, and Israel will suffer the consequences. You will create a Palestinian nationalism, and you will never get rid of it." De Gaulle's last prophecy proved to be especially accurate. The Russians and Americans were meanwhile urging Egypt and Israel, respectively, not to strike the first blow.

But on the morning of June 5, 1967, the Israeli Air Force struck. By flying over the Mediterranean rather than over the Sinai, the planes avoided Egyptian radar and consequently achieved complete tactical surprise. They demolished most of Egypt's planes and left its airfields inoperative, then turned and repeated the operation against the Jordanian, Syrian, and Iraqi air forces. It was a dazzling demonstration of the superiority of the Israeli flyers and gave them control of the air. Nasser sank ships to block the Suez Canal. Soviet Premier Aleksei Kosygin got on the Hot Line that morning to inform President Johnson that the Soviet Union would not intervene unless the United States did. Israeli tanks and infantry columns were already marching into the Sinai, seizing the Golan Heights, and capturing from Jordan the West Bank and Jerusalem. L.B.J. told Kosygin that America was ready to demand a cease fire, which the U.N. Security Council did the next day, June 6. Meanwhile, Johnson had put the U.S. Sixth Fleet in the Mediterranean on full alert and had sent two aircraft carriers toward Egypt.

Inadvertently, L.B.J. had given Nasser a perfect excuse for the miserable showing of the Egyptian armed forces. Although the Soviets had the American Sixth Fleet under tight surveillance, and thus knew perfectly well that no American combat aircraft had been launched on either June 5 or 6, Nasser falsely charged that American planes from the Sixth Fleet and British planes from Cyprus had participated in the initial waves of attack. He was widely believed in the Arab world. By the morning of June 7 Egypt, Algeria, Iraq, Sudan, Syria, and Yemen had broken relations with the United States and Britain. But Nasser was unable to bring the moderate Arab states along with him—relations were preserved between the United States and Jordan, Libya, Morocco, Kuwait, Tunisia, and Saudi Arabia. The Arab petroleum ministers did proclaim an embargo of oil shipments to Israel's backers, especially Britain and the United States, but it had little effect.

Israel, meanwhile, had won a stunning victory. When she accepted a cease-fire on June 10 (giving the conflict its name, the Six Day War), Israel had conquered all of Egypt's Sinai Peninsula and the Gaza Strip, driven twelve miles into Syria, seizing the Golan Heights, and taken all of Jerusalem plus the West Bank of the Jordan River.

For both Russia and the United States the results of the Six Day War were melancholy. Russian arms had been blasted by French arms (the French Mirage was the backbone of the Israeli Air Force), and the huge buildup of Russian tanks in the Arab world had come to naught—indeed, those tanks not destroyed were now part of Israel's captured booty. The Arabs, generally, were furious with the Russians for not helping them more directly during their time of troubles. The Americans had tried to deter war and had failed. Now Suez was blocked, the Arabs had placed an embargo on oil, the Soviet Union was more entrenched than ever in the Middle East (because, much as they hated it, the Arabs were more dependent than ever on Russia for rebuilding their armed forces), and half the Arab states had broken diplomatic relations with the United States.

Worst of all, Israel now occupied territory that was indisputably Arab* (Sinai has been an integral part of Egypt for more than five thousand years), and the Palestinian refugee problem had grown from an irritant to a cancer. There were tens of thousands of new refugees, who spilled over into Jordan, Lebanon, Egypt, and Syria, and other thousands of Palestinians now living under armed Israeli occupation. The immediate consequence was the expansion of the Palestine Liberation Organization (P.L.O.) and a dramatic increase in the scope and number of terrorist acts carried out by the desperate Palestinians. Israel had won, but in the process it had added enormously to its problems and put off into the indefinite future the day when it could live at peace with its Arab neighbors. Nevertheless, the Israelis believed that territory was security, and they refused to pull back to the June 4, 1967, borders.

France, meanwhile, acceding to demands by the oil-holding Arabs, announced that it was imposing an embargo on all arms sales to the Middle East. De Gaulle even blocked delivery to Israel of fifty Mirages on order and already paid for. The Russians rushed new aircraft to Syria and Egypt. Under the circumstances L.B.J. was under intense pressure, because for the first time an American President had to choose between supplying Israel with weapons on a large

---

* Before 1967 Israel occupied only territory once a part of the British Palestine Mandate.

scale* or taking the domestic political consequences of seeing
Israel lose her military superiority. Johnson decided he had
to support Israel, and the United States became her chief
supplier of sophisticated weaponry with the 1968 sale of
fifty Phantom F-4s (supersonic jet fighter-bombers).

The Arabs, badly defeated, began a slow retreat. In July
1967 they rejected a draft resolution prepared by the United
States and the Soviet Union for the U.N. General Assembly.
The resolution called upon Israel to withdraw from all
territories occupied after June 4 and urged all parties to
acknowledge the right of each to maintain, in peace and
security, an independent national state. The Arabs refused
to recognize Israel's status as a sovereign state, but they did
tacitly abandon the call for the extinction of the Zionists
and committed themselves to diplomatic efforts to solve the
problem. In August they lifted the embargo on oil shipments to America and Britain. In October Egyptian missiles
sank an Israeli destroyer and Israeli artillery fire destroyed
Egypt's two principal oil refineries. Both sides by then had
had enough and requested action by the U.N. Security
Council to bring about a meaningful cease-fire.

The result was the famous Security Council Resolution
242, drafted by Lord Caradon of Great Britain and adopted
on November 22, 1967. An evenhanded document, 242
attempted to reconcile the vital interests of the opposing
sides. For Israel it promised peace with her neighbors, secure and recognized boundaries, and free navigation of
regional waterways. For the Arabs it promised Jewish evacuation of the conquered territories and a national homeland for the Palestinians. Both the Arabs and the Israelis
accepted 242, but Israel with the understanding that firm,
guaranteed peace treaties must be signed before there would
be any withdrawal, while the Arabs insisted that 242 meant
full Israeli withdrawal must precede any other diplomatic
move.

Thus the two main results of the Six Day War, which

* The United States had sold surface-to-air antiaircraft missiles
to Israel in 1962, Patton tanks in 1965, and A-4 Skyhawks in 1966.

most Israelis and Americans interpreted as a great victory for Israel, were Israeli occupation of Arab national territory and the creation of a fully developed, and fanatic, Palestinian nationalism. The Arabs could not rest until they had their territory back, and the Palestinians would not rest until they had their own national state.

A third result of the war—military over-confidence—allowed the Israelis to feel that they could safely ignore these threats. They began to think of themselves as invincible. So did other observers, including the C.I.A. These impressions were strengthened in 1970 when Nixon began selling arms to Israel on a wholly unprecedented scale. A fourth result was to drive the most moderate of the Arab states solidly into the anti-Israel column, because of the occupied territory, the Palestinian problem, and because Israel now had possession of the old city of Jerusalem, as holy to the Muslims as to the Jews and Christians. Most Arabs agreed that the Israelis could have peace, or they could have territory, but they could not have both.

In September 1970 Nasser died. His successor, Anwar el-Sadat, was painfully aware that Egypt was held in contempt or pity by much of the world. This included the Russians, who were supplying him with military hardware and financial support, but who treated him indifferently at best, with contempt at worst. Because of the huge military budget, what little money the Russians did provide was hardly enough to stave off national bankruptcy in the poverty-stricken land (Israel was also approaching bankruptcy due to military expenses). Furthermore, Sadat doubted that the Russians would ever be able to move the Israelis out of Sinai, while the Americans might be able to force them back. Also, it was obvious that the United States did a far better job of supplying its friends than Russia did. But the United States could hardly be expected to come to Egypt's aid when Soviet soldiers and technicians were swarming over the country.

So in 1972 Sadat presented the United States with one of its greatest victories in the Cold War: Without informing Secretary Kissinger in advance of his intentions or extracting anything from Washington in return, he expelled the twenty thousand Russians from Egypt. It was a foreign policy setback to the Russians of the first magnitude. Nothing remotely like it had happened previously. At a stroke Russian influence in the Middle East was cut back, her presence dramatically reduced. But because there had been no preparation, and because Kissinger (and Nixon and the C.I.A. and the Israelis) continued to believe that Sadat would not dare take up arms to rectify the situation in the Sinai, the United States did nothing to follow up on Sadat's bold initiative. Kissinger made no serious attempt to force Israel to compromise; indeed he looked the other way as Israelis began building permanent settlements in the occupied territories. Sadat, meanwhile, knew that with every passing day the Israeli occupation of Arab lands would come to seem more acceptable, even normal. Soon the world would accept it as a fact. He could not abandon his homeland. Again and again Sadat warned that war must come if the Israelis did not withdraw. Again and again he was ignored.

The Israeli Army, in the meantime, had overextended itself. By occupying all of the Sinai up to the east bank of the Suez, it had gone far to the west of the natural defensive line on the high ground running north and south through the middle of the Sinai. Further, the presence of Israeli soldiers along the Suez was a standing affront to the Egyptians.

Sadat had set 1971 as the "year of decision." It came and went, with no action. Egypt looked more pathetic than ever. In 1972 Sadat kicked out the Russians. In March 1973 Sadat sent his security adviser, Hafez Ismail, to Washington. Kissinger later told Prime Minister Golda Meir, "What did I do in those conversations? I talked with Ismail about the weather . . . just so we wouldn't get to the subject. I played with him. . . . Ismail told me several times that the present situation could not continue. He asked me whether the United States did not understand that if there weren't some agreement then there would be war. . . . There wasn't even a slight smile on my face, but in my heart I laughed and laughed. A war? Egypt? I regarded it as empty talk, a boast empty of content."

So empty, in fact, that the United States seemed to go out of its way to insult Ismail. Although Nixon promised him that the United States would use its influence with Israel, a few days after he left Washington the United States announced that it was supplying Israel with forty-eight additional Phantom jets.

Sadat gave up on a political approach. The only way to get back Egyptian territory was to drive the Israelis from it. Since the Americans would not take him seriously, Sadat swallowed his pride and turned to the Russians, after first arranging with Syria for a coordinated attack on Israel, and with King Faisal of Saudi Arabia for a simultaneous imposition of an oil embargo, which would presumably have the effect of paralyzing the United States. When the Kremlin heard Sadat's plan, the Russian leaders decided in turn to swallow their pride and supply the Egyptians and Syrians with enough hardware—especially missiles and tanks—to launch an attack.

On October 6, 1973, during the Jewish religious holiday of Yom Kippur, the Egyptian and Syrian armies struck with tanks, missiles, and planes. The Israelis were caught by surprise. On the Syrian front they were driven off the Golan Heights; along the Suez the Egyptians destroyed the much-vaunted Bar-Lev defense line, which the Israelis had thought impregnable, then drove several miles deep inside the Sinai and entrenched.

These stunning victories, coming as a surprise to everyone except possibly Sadat, marked a historic turning point in world history. It is, perhaps, only a slight exaggeration to say that the Arabs had finally woken from their centuries-long slumber and were now ready to take their place as active participants in the affairs of the modern world. Israel may not have been quite on the verge of extinction, but her national existence was threatened as it had never been before, and her leaders knew that without outside assistance she was doomed. Only the United States could provide the necessary help in the form of new planes, tanks, and missiles.

Thus began one of the most controversial events in Dr. Kissinger's controversial career. Because of the role he chose to play, and because of the way in which he played it, he was vilified by both sides at various times, cursed, hanged in effigy, accused of having neither morals nor common sense, denounced as a man who was incapable of responding to the misery of millions of Palestinians, and perhaps worst of all, charged with not caring a fig for his own Jewish people. Even before he got involved, Kissinger knew that such accusations were the most likely outcome of any interference on his part. As noted, he hated to fail and had for that reason avoided the Middle East for years. Yet now he jumped in with both feet, because the situation left him no alternative.

The first requirement was to save Israel from a complete military disaster. A second was to avoid, if at all possible, an oil embargo, which would be much more effective in 1973 than in 1967, because in the intervening six years the United States had switched from being a net exporter of oil to a net importer. A third requirement was to find some formula, such as 242, to bring peace to the Middle East. Kissinger failed to solve the problem of how to help Israel without goading the Arabs into an oil embargo, and he was unable to bring peace to the area, but what Kissinger did manage to accomplish was impressive enough.

Kissinger was the first to recognize that the Israeli loss of tanks and planes during the early hours of the fighting, coupled with the now demonstrated fact that Egyptian and Syrian soldiers could fight and kill, shifted the strategic balance away from Israel. His first step was the traditional proposal of a cease-fire in place, but Israel would not accept it because she was losing and Sadat would not accept because he was not winning enough. Recovering from their surprise, the Israelis began to hold their own, but to retake lost ground they needed new weapons. They began making frantic demands on Kissinger for supplies, especially after October 10, when the Russians launched a large-scale airlift of supplies to Syria and Egypt, replacing the arms lost in battle. The Russian objective was to support a cease-fire after the Arabs had won the maximum advantage from their surprise attack and before Israel had time to mount an effective counteroffensive.

Kissinger was under heavy pressure. The American public and the Congress regarded Israel as the victim of aggression (which ignored the obvious fact that the Arabs were only trying to recover territory conquered by Israel in 1967). The Soviets, by shipping arms after promising restraint, had directly challenged the United States in a crucial spot on the globe. The Israeli Ambassador to the United States punctuated his demands for help with explicit threats to mobilize American Jews against Kissinger.

The Secretary of State gave in to the pressure, perhaps most of all because of his determination that Russian guns should never be allowed to prevail over American guns. On October 13 Kissinger got Nixon to order an all-out airlift by American military aircraft direct to Israel. In the end American deliveries substantially exceeded those of Moscow to the Arabs, proving that America's military capacity in time of crisis was superior to that of the Russians'. On October 15, with the American equipment, the Israelis began their counterattack, crossed Suez at two points, and encircled the Egyptian Third Army while driving the Syrians back from the Golan Heights.

The shift in the tide of battle brought the Russians back onto the scene, this time as promoters of a cease-fire in place. Kissinger agreed. He did not want to let the Israelis win a big victory and certainly did not want to humiliate Sadat. In addition, he now had to deal with his worst nightmare become reality: The Arab oil states, led by Faisal of Saudi Arabia, had imposed an effective embargo on oil shipments to the United States and to Israel's friends in Europe.

The Great Oil Embargo of 1973 was as important an event in the awakening of the Arabs as the Egyptian/Syrian victory in the first week of the Yom Kippur War. From Kissinger and Nixon on down, Americans had assumed that the Arabs could never stick together, that any attempt at coordinated action would break down into petty bickering in a matter of days, and that therefore Arab threats about making political use of oil were not to be taken seriously. This was a great mistake, because in 1973 the Arabs did impose an embargo and made it stick. Americans discovered, to their collective chagrin, that they needed the Arabs more than the Arabs needed them.

Kissinger's first step, in what he called step-by-step diplomacy, was to get the shooting stopped and the talking started. He therefore joined with the Russians on October 22 to put through the Security Council Resolution 338, which called for a cease-fire in place and the implementation of Resolution 242.

Israel ignored it. General Moshe Dayan, Israel's Minister of Defense, kept the pressure on the surrounded Egyptian Third Army, because, as he later told the *New York Times,* he wanted to capture thirty thousand Egyptian soldiers, "and Sadat would have had to admit it to his people. We might only have held them for a day and let them walk out without their arms, but it would have changed the whole Egyptian attitude about whether they had won or lost the war." Kissinger, fully aware of Dayan's intentions, was furious. There could be no productive talks if the Egyptians were humiliated again, and without talks there would be no oil. So, Dayan complained, "the United States moved in and denied us the fruits of victory." Kissinger handed down "an ultimatum—nothing short of it." Of course, Kissinger's ultimatum was the threat to stop the flow of arms that had made the victory possible in the first place.

Simultaneously with Kissinger's pressure on Dayan, the Russians made a startling move. On October 24 Soviet Party Chairman Leonid Brezhnev proposed to Kissinger that they send a joint Soviet-American expeditionary force to Suez to save the Third Army from Dayan. If Kissinger was not interested, Brezhnev added, the Soviet Union would go in alone. The C.I.A. meanwhile reported that the Russians had seven airborne divisions on alert, ready to go.

Kissinger responded in the strongest terms possible, short

of actual war.* He persuaded Nixon to proclaim a world-wide alert of American armed forces, including nuclear strike forces. The Pentagon prepared plans to fly American troops to Suez to confront the Russian paratroopers, if necessary. Kissinger then informed Brezhnev, who now understood that Kissinger would go to the limit to keep Russian troops out of the area. The U.N. peacekeeping force must be drawn from the armies of nonnuclear powers, Kissinger insisted. Brezhnev agreed and the American alert, which had alarmed everybody, was called off. Dayan ended the pressure on the Third Army and the war was over.

Now Kissinger could step onto the center stage, previously occupied first by the contending armies, then by the American nuclear forces on alert. It was time for diplomacy, and never had the world seen a diplomat quite like the Secretary of State. It was true that the United States had previously acted as honest broker in the Middle East, bringing the Egyptians and Israelis together to arrange local cease-fires or border adjustments, but Kissinger added his own special touch to the process. Flying from Israeli to Arab capitals in his specially equipped jet airliner, surrounded by the world press corps, appearing on the evening news with a different monarch or head of state each night, dazzling reporters with his wit and statesmen with his charm, overwhelming everyone with his detailed knowledge (he knew the height, in meters, of every hill in Sinai), the Jewish refugee from Hitler's Germany became a genuine worldwide superstar.

His essential role was more modest—as he himself often declared, all he could do was explain to one side the constraints under which the other side operated. He did so with impressive patience, thoroughness, goodwill, and skill. To the Israelis he said: All the world is against you, and you cannot stand against the whole world. To the Arabs he said: Only the United States can persuade Israel to retreat from the conquered territory, but you cannot expect

* He later called the alert "our *deliberate* overreaction."

the United States to invest so much time and energy in an operation that is so clearly in the Arab interest as long as you withhold your oil. To both sides he said, over and over: You must compromise.

But he said it in the context of step-by-step diplomacy, which meant that instead of taking on the big questions, such as the status of Jerusalem or a homeland for the Palestinians, he began with the little problems, mainly disengaging the armies, which were badly intermixed on both sides of Suez and in the Golan Heights. The trouble with step-by-step, according to Kissinger's numerous critics, was that it was myopic, precisely because it ignored the real issues. How could you have peace in the Middle East if you ignored the P.L.O.? According to Kissinger's numerous defenders, it was obvious that if you began by discussing the P.L.O., the talks would end right there.

Kissinger also took advantage of his position as spokesman for the world's richest nation. Although the evidence is inconclusive, and no details are known, he evidently made vast promises about the American economic and technical help that would be available to both sides in the event of genuine peace in the region.*

Step one began on November 7, 1973, when Kissinger flew to Cairo to meet with Sadat. The United States and Egypt reestablished diplomatic relations, broken since 1967.

---

* He had done the same in Vietnam. Kissinger's willingness to make promises became the subject of a popular joke in Israel: Kissinger goes to see a poor man and says, "I want to arrange a marriage for your son." The poor man replies, "I never interfere in my son's life." Kissinger responds, "But the girl is Lord Rothschild's daughter." "Well, in that case . . ."

Next Kissinger approaches Lord Rothschild. "I have a husband for your daughter." "But my daughter is too young to marry." "But this young man is already a vice-president of the World Bank." "Ah, in that case . . ."

Finally Kissinger goes to see the President of the World Bank. "I have a young man to recommend to you as a vice-president." "But I already have more vice-presidents than I need." "But this young man is Lord Rothschild's son-in-law." "Ah, in that case . . ."

Next Kissinger arranged for an exchange of prisoners of war and the lifting of the Israeli sieges of the city of Suez and of the Third Army. He set up a Geneva conference that met in December and accomplished nothing; in private he arranged for an Egyptian-Israeli accord (signed January 18, 1974) that provided for a mutual disengagement and pullback of forces along Suez and the establishment of a U.N. Emergency Force buffer zone between them. The Russians, like everyone else, watched in amazement as Kissinger moved the pieces around the chessboard.

His great triumph, the reward for all his hard work, came on March 18, 1974, when the Arab states lifted the oil embargo. During May 1974 he shuttled back and forth between Syria and Israel, finally (May 31) achieving a cease-fire and complex troop disengagement agreement on the Golan Heights.

In the remaining two and a half years of the Nixon-Ford administrations, the United States provided Israel with more than $3 billion worth of weapons. These included precision-guided munitions, cluster-bomb units, tanks, armored personnel carriers, self-propelled artillery, cargo trucks, cargo aircraft, rifles, helicopters, antitank guided rockets, electronic counterradar boxes, Phantoms, and Skyhawks. One Pentagon official declared, "Israel wants one thousand percent security and she's getting it. She can decisively defeat any combination of Arab armies at least through 1980."

This extraordinarily important commitment to Israel's defense was not Kissinger's doing alone. By the mid-'70s Congress was beginning to exert itself in foreign affairs (see chapter twelve). It was usually an interference on the side of caution—pull out of Vietnam and Cambodia, stay out of Angola, and so on—but in the Middle East, where everything gets turned around, the Congress was determined to stand by Israel. Thus on May 21, 1975, more than three-quarters of the members of the Senate (seventy-six to be exact) wrote a collective letter to President Ford to endorse Israel's demand for "defensible" frontiers. The letter was spiced with such phrases as "the special relationship between our country and Israel," "withholding military equipment from Israel would be dangerous," and "the United States . . . stands firmly with Israel." As if this demonstration of the strength of the Jewish lobby in Washington were not enough, it was followed in the summer of 1975 by another humiliation of Kissinger, when the Senate blocked the sale of defensive Hawk missiles to King Hussein of Jordan.

Kissinger was also caught in his own trap by the Senate, when Senator Henry Jackson of Washington turned Kissinger's concept of linkage against him. Jackson linked Jewish emigration from Russia with American trade deals with the Kremlin. Kissinger, never one to see consistency as a virtue, was furious at this use of linkage, because it jeopardized the trade agreements that were to be the payoff for détente. He tried to patiently explain to Senator Jackson that emigration and trade were not and should not be linked, but he failed to convince the Senate.

As Kissinger left office in January 1977 he had little to show for shuttle diplomacy, except that the Arabs were selling oil—at a fourfold price increase—to the United States and Europe. The Senate's letter on the defense of Israel made the Israelis immune to his threats of the withdrawal of American support, enabling them to continue to take a tough line in the peace negotiations. The Israelis still occupied most of the Sinai, the Golan Heights, and the West Bank of the Jordan. The P.L.O. problem was worse than ever, punctuated by a confusing civil war in Lebanon between Christians and Muslims, with Syria deeply involved, the P.L.O. in the thick of it, and Israeli-manned, American-built modern weapons devastating Lebanese villages suspected of harboring the P.L.O.

Peace in the Middle East remained a goal, rather than a reality, of American foreign policy at the end of Kissinger's term of office. Permanent solutions still were completely out of reach. The Middle East overall remained, as it had been so often described by American Presidents, a tinderbox, ready to set the world afire from a single spark.

[14]

America and Africa Since 1942

Our interests in [southern Africa] are important but not vital.

National Security Study
Memorandum 39, 1969

South Africa has always been regarded by foreign investors as a gold mine, one of those rare and refreshing places where profits are great and problems small. Capital is not threatened by political instability or nationalization. Labor is cheap, the market booming, the currency hard and convertible.

Fortune magazine,
July 1972

Africa is the second-largest continent. In a general way it is dominated by Europe, the continent to its north, as South America is dominated by North America. Africa gets her manufactured goods, her education, and her political forms from Europe, and sends back raw materials in return. America has had no colonies, and with the sole exception of the period from 1942 to 1945, no military forces in Africa. Russia and China have also been involved only on a sporadic basis. The African "problem"—poverty, cultural crisis, illogical boundaries, racism—is a European creation that requires an African solution.

Africa has a population of nearly 250,000,000 people, who are as diverse and varied as the land itself. The tallest people in the world, the Watusi, live there, along with the smallest, the Pygmies. Every race, color, and religion is represented. Africa has sent hundreds of thousands of black immigrants to other parts of the world, most of all North

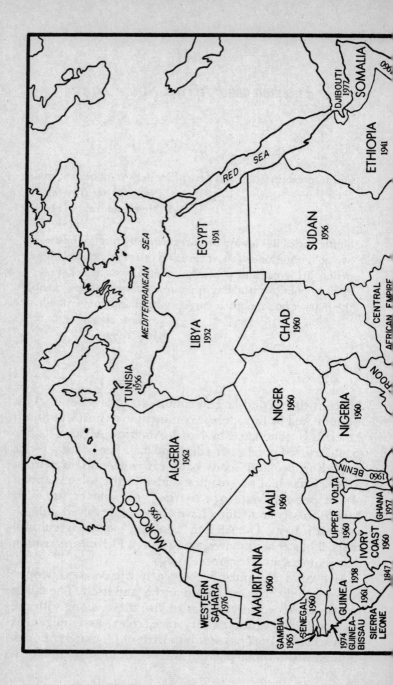

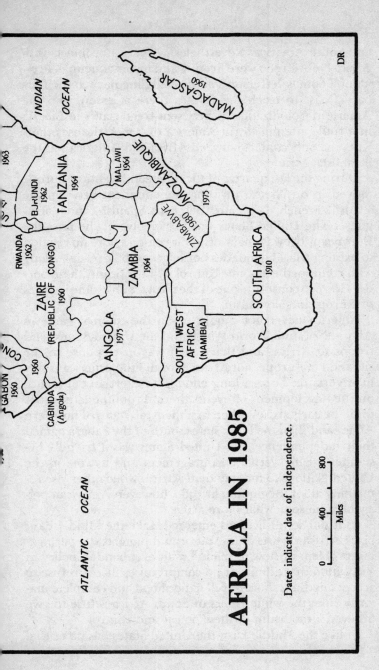

AFRICA IN 1985

Dates indicate date of independence.

0   400   800

Miles

and South America. Nevertheless, American contacts with
Africa before 1960 were fleeting and inconsequential. President Thomas Jefferson sent his fledgling navy to the Barbary Coast to teach the pirates there a lesson, and the
American Colonization Society sent freed slaves to Liberia
in a futile attempt to rid America of her Africans; otherwise, the only contact between Africa and America was the
illegal slave trade.

During the last quarter of the nineteenth century Europe
moved in on Africa, dividing the continent between the
British, French, Germans, Belgians, Spanish, and Portuguese. The United States was not involved. The lines the
Europeans drew to mark off their colonies bore no relation
to existing tribal boundaries nor to geographic reality: Along
with continued economic control by Europeans, these borders were to constitute one of the most troublesome legacies
of European colonialism.

America never got caught up in the colonial game in
Africa. Not until World War II did the United States send
troops to Africa, and that action was in response to the
situation in Europe, not Africa. Nor did the Americans stay
in Algeria or Tunisia long enough to exert any influence
on the development of events there. From the late forties
until the early sixties, when first the Arab states of northern
Africa and then the black states south of the Sahara gained
their independence, the United States was a friendly bystander, giving verbal encouragement and its vote in the
United Nations to independent Africa, while otherwise remaining aloof. Beginning in 1960, however, American policy became somewhat more active.

As it did so, difficulties emerged. Like the Middle East,
black Africa thrusts onto American diplomats the perplexing problem of how to maintain an evenhanded policy in
a situation that admits of no compromise. Blacks refuse to
accept anything short of full nationhood and complete majority rule; the white rulers of South Africa refuse to give
up even a modicum of their power and control.

Unlike the Middle East, the United States has no crucial

economic interest in Africa. There are mineral deposits, especially gold, that do (or could) play a major role in the world economy, and southern Africa is one of only two or three sources for a handful of exotic minerals, but in comparison to the role played by Middle Eastern oil, Africa is unimportant to the American economy. For American policymakers the other major difference between the Middle East and Africa is the nature of the American political body. There are almost no Arabs on the voting rolls in the United States, and only a relatively small number of Jews. But the American Jewish community is well organized, highly motivated, and more than ready to put considerable funds into political campaigns for Israel's benefit. It is only a question of time before the Arabs, now rich themselves, start throwing large sums of their money into the struggle for control of American foreign policy.

By way of contrast, there are millions upon millions of African descendants living in the United States—indeed, at 12 percent of the whole they constitute the single largest distinguishable voting bloc in the country—but they are generally unorganized, uninterested in African affairs, and altogether too poor to have the kind of impact on their country's foreign policy their numbers entitle them to. Their presence, nonetheless, makes any armed intervention into the black-versus-white struggle in southern Africa unthinkable to an American politician.

America has been unable (or unwilling) to help black Africa achieve its two main goals—majority rule throughout the continent, and the creation of a modern economy. American investors in Africa have stayed in or close to the white-ruled territories, making their heaviest investment in South Africa. For the most part, American investors have failed to see enough political stability or potential profit to invest in black Africa. And although the State Department has consistently denounced white minority rule in southern Africa, and at times has taken the lead in imposing sanctions on Rhodesia and South Africa, the United States has not taken any practical steps to topple the white rulers.

The first active American involvement in Africa came in the closing day's of the Eisenhower Administration. By 1960 enough central and northern African states had achieved independence to give the African bloc a major voice in the U.N. General Assembly. For a variety of reasons, one of which was the convenience of both superpowers, the United Nations played a large role in both the Middle East and African affairs. In December 1960 the General Assembly passed Resolution 1514, in effect an amendment to the U.N. Charter that proclaimed the rights of all people to self-determination and independence and called for a "speedy and unconditional end to colonialism in all its forms and manifestations." This Declaration on Colonialism passed 90–0, with eight abstentions: the United States, Australia, Belgium, the Dominican Republic, France, Portugal, South Africa, and Britain. The American abstention made African leaders furious.*

Events in the Congo, meanwhile, brought the Cold War to central Africa for the first time and in the process added greatly to African suspicions about Americans. In June 1960 the Congo had won its independence from Belgium. But the Belgians had done almost nothing to prepare the Congo for statehood; except for the Belgians, there was no officer corps for the army, no civil servants were available, no technical experts there to run the mines. Joseph Kasavubu was President, Patrice Lumumba the Prime Minister of the new country. Kasavubu was thought to be conservative, Lumumba radical. When the army mutinied against its Belgian officers, Belgian paratroopers entered the country to protect the white residents. Meanwhile fighting broke out among the various tribes, each anxious to repay old scores.

---

* President Kennedy's administration patched up some of the damage the next year, when U.N. Ambassador Adlai Stevenson endorsed steps in the Security Council calling for "full self-determination" in the Portuguese colony of Angola, and in November 1961 Stevenson declared that the United States wished to associate itself with the Declaration on Colonialism.

The Katanga Province,* rich in minerals and the key to the Congo's economy, governed by an alliance between the Belgian mining owners and a local politician named Moïse Tshombe, declared its independence from the Congo. Lumumba asked the Russians for arms and appealed to the United Nations for help to restore order and to subdue the secessionist Katanga Province.

These events took place at the same time as the Cuban revolution, catching American policymakers at a time when they were determined to prevent the rise of more Castros. Allen Dulles was then at the height of his career, the C.I.A. at the peak of its global interference. It was taken for granted that if Lumumba was a radical he must be an agent of the Soviet Union. In fact, Lumumba's "radicalism" consisted of nothing more than an uncompromising commitment to African independence. In July 1960 the U.N. Security Council voted to send a peacekeeping force into the Congo, but the United States still feared that the Congo might become another Cuba.

These fears were fed by the C.I.A. Station Chief in Leopoldville, the Congo's capital, who sent the following classic Cold War telegram to C.I.A. headquarters: BELIEVE CONGO EXPERIENCING COMMUNIST EFFORT TAKEOVER GOVERNMENT. MANY FORCES AT WORK HERE: SOVIETS . . . COMMUNIST PARTY, ETC. ALTHOUGH DIFFICULT DETERMINE MAJOR INFLUENCING FACTORS TO PREDICT OUTCOME STRUGGLE FOR POWER, DECISIVE PERIOD NOT FAR OFF. WHETHER OR NOT LUMUMBA ACTUALLY COMMIE OR JUST PLAYING COMMIE GAME TO ASSIST HIS SOLIDIFYING POWER, ANTI-WEST FORCES RAPIDLY INCREASING POWER CONGO AND THERE MAY BE LITTLE TIME LEFT IN WHICH TO TAKE ACTION TO AVOID ANOTHER CUBA.

Dulles and Eisenhower conferred with the National Security Council; the result of the meeting was an order from Dulles to his agents in the Congo: Kill Lumumba.† The C.I.A. bungled various attempts to commit the murder, but

* Now Shaba

† Whether or not President Eisenhower knew of the order, or approved it, is hotly disputed.

in January 1961 Lumumba was captured by Tshombe's Katanga forces and assassinated.

Over the next three years, until June of 1964, the United Nations, with troops from a number of countries, tried to restore order. In 1963 the U.N. forces captured the rebellious capital of Katanga and returned that province to the central government. Tshombe fled, only to return a year later to become Prime Minister of the Congo.* He had wide connections in Europe and was trusted by the Belgian business and mining interests. The United States responded willingly to his requests for military hardware. The United States also supplied airplanes and logistical support for Belgian paratroopers in December 1964, when they landed at Stanleyville to put down a rebellion that involved white hostages. The United States was roasted in the General Assembly for this action. It was accused of being the agent responsible for—among other things— wanton and premeditated aggression, deliberate massacre, a murderous operation, massive cannibalism, and genocide.

Such obviously exaggerated charges were encouraged by the Chinese, who since 1958 had intervened actively in African affairs, evidently attempting to develop a new revolutionary International among the poor peoples of Asia, Africa, and Latin America—the southern, or rural, half of the globe. Much of the Chinese invective in Africa, however, was directed not against the United States but at the Soviet Union, with whom the Chinese had to compete for power and influence. Africa's new priority in Chinese foreign policy reached a peak early in 1964, when Premier Chou En-lai and a staff of sixty made a seven-week visit to ten African countries.

The United States, meanwhile, had been so humiliated in the Congo, where to make a bad situation worse it had to pay the United Nations' expenses for the peacekeeping force, that it was ready to retreat from any active involve-

---

* In 1971 President Mobuto changed the name of the Congo to Zaire.

ment. At the same time the publication of *Neo-Colonialism: the Last Stage of Imperialism,* a stinging indictment of the West and especially America, written by Kwame Nkrumah, the leader of the Pan-African movement and President of Ghana, helped convince President Johnson that he had little to gain and something to lose in Africa, and that the best policy was therefore one of neglect. He was reinforced in this conclusion by the fact that the Vietnam War was demanding most of his attention.

For the United States, in the sixties and seventies, southern Africa became the "African problem." In Zambia, Rhodesia (Zimbabwe), Angola, Southwest Africa (Namibia), Mozambique, and South Africa, four million whites ruled thirty million blacks. These states were roughly united by their minority government status and by a shocking exploitation of black labor* by an elite of fabulously wealthy whites.

But just as the white-ruled states followed different traditions, so would they take different paths. By 1979 Zambia, Angola, and Mozambique had achieved majority rule, and Rhodesia was on the way toward the creation of a democratic state based on a one-man, one-vote principle. In Namibia, on the other hand, the situation worsened, as South Africa tightened her grip on her colony. And in South Africa itself, independent since the turn of the century, the most racist white-ruled state in the world grew even more racist. The white minority had a monopoly of force that it did not hesitate to use and of power that it would not yield or share.

All the states of southern Africa had some economic importance to the United States. Consequently American pol-

---

* In South Africa workers had to live in camps next to the mines for twelve to eighteen months and could not see their families during that time. Wages in the mines, which were seventy-two cents per day in 1910, had fallen to fifty-seven cents per day in 1975.

icy, as summed up by N.S.S.M. 39,* was "to try to balance our economic, scientific and strategic interests in the white states with the political interest of dissociating the U.S. from the white minority regimes and their repressive racial policies." The problem was that this was less a policy than a hope and has thus contributed to the relative paucity of American influence on developments in southern Africa.

A good example of this ineffectuality was to be found in Rhodesia. There, unlike the former British colonies in central Africa, white residents refused to accept the idea, much less the reality, of majority rule. The United Kingdom was willing (in fact, eager) to grant Rhodesia its independence, even before the regime of Ian Smith gave way to the blacks, but only if Smith guaranteed unimpeded movement toward majority rule. Instead, in November 1965 Rhodesia's whites issued a unilateral declaration of independence from Britain. The proposal of a declaration of independence had a stirring ring to it, but unfortunately only 4 percent of Rhodesia's people participated in the decision to issue it. Rhodesia was immediately branded as an outlaw state by the U.N. Security Council, which imposed comprehensive mandatory economic sanctions in an effort to topple Smith. The whites defied the world—on March 12, 1970, Smith proclaimed a new constitution and the establishment of a republic.

The Johnson Administration had supported the U.N. call for economic sanctions, but in 1971 Nixon changed the policy. The United States had only a small investment ($56 million) in Rhodesia, but before adopting sanctions America had bought about 30 percent of her chrome ore there. Since the other major source was the Soviet Union, the Southern bloc in Congress used this as an excuse to pass the Byrd Amendment (named after Senator Harry Byrd of Virginia and pushed by Senator Strom Thurmond of

---

* National Security Study Memorandum 39 was a comprehensive National Security Council review of American policy in Africa, and an analysis of American economic and political interests in Africa, done in 1969 at Henry Kissinger's request.

South Carolina), which authorized the purchase of chrome from Rhodesia in order to avoid dependence on Russia. Although the State Department was strongly and openly opposed to the Byrd Amendment, Nixon let it become law.

In 1972, bending to the pressure of events, Kissinger announced that the "United States is wholly committed to help bring about a rapid, just and African solution in Rhodesia" and would cooperate with the British in their efforts to achieve majority rule through negotiations. He specifically promised that he would "urge Congress this year to repeal the Byrd Amendment," but his efforts were to no avail.

Nevertheless, by the mid-seventies, due to British pressure, world opinion, and the effects of economic sanctions, plus rapidly escalating guerrilla warfare, the Smith regime was moving in the direction of a constitutionally based majority rule. Black leaders were suspicious at best, and when Smith visited the United States in late 1978 he was studiously ignored, even insulted, by the Carter Administration. But some Rhodesian blacks joined Smith's government, and in April 1979, an elected assembly of blacks and whites took power in the renamed Zimbabwe. In December of 1979 the British Foreign Minister, Lord Carrington, announced the completion of an agreement among Smith, the black leaders, and the British government on a formula for independence with majority rule. The Carter Administration then lifted the U.S. sanctions against Zimbabwe and, in April 1980, Zimbabwe became fully independent with constitutionally guaranteed majority (i.e., Black) rule.

In 1969 N.S.S.M. 39 predicted a continued stalemate in the Portuguese colony of Angola,* where black liberation forces waged a guerrilla war against the government. Angola differed from South Africa and Rhodesia in that all overt racial discrimination had been eliminated by the Portuguese, who in the sixties started a crash program to ed-

---

* Held by the Portuguese to be legally a part of Portugal, as the French once held Algeria to be part of France.

ucate blacks and integrate them into the economy. Many black leaders rejected this program as a none-too-subtle attempt to retain white control.

There were three major movements demanding full independence for Angola, namely, the Popular Movement, or M.P.L.A., the National Front, or F.N.L.A., and UNITA (National Union for Total Independence). All received some aid from Russia and/or China, but the M.P.L.A. leaders had Marxist, antiimperialist views and had once denounced the United States for its support of Portugal. American newspapers spoke of the "Soviet-backed" M.P.L.A. and the "moderate" F.N.L.A. The American intelligence community accepted that analysis, but in 1969 scarcely worried about the situation because it was certain the Portuguese had the situation well in hand.

The United States had attempted to remain an observer of the problems of Angola and Mozambique (also a Portuguese colony), while maintaining a posture of coolness toward Portugal itself, until 1971 when Nixon moved in a pro-Portuguese direction. Kissinger wanted a strong NATO and access to Portugal's strategic base in the Azores. In exchange for the latter, Nixon signed an executive agreement that gave Portugal a $436-million loan. The next year Nixon authorized the sale of military transports to Portugal, then lent more money, which the Portuguese used to buy helicopters for use against the guerrilla warriors in their colonies. The payoff for Kissinger came during the Yom Kippur War of 1973, when Portugal was the only NATO ally to allow American planes bound for Israel to refuel on its territory.

In April 1974 a military coup in Lisbon created a new situation. Tired of fighting unending and unsuccessful wars, the Portuguese military leaders decided to give the colonies their independence. In January 1975 a transitional government was established in Luanda, the capital of Angola, with each of the liberation movements sharing in the preparations for independence and each group campaigning throughout the country for the elections scheduled for October 1975. Independence day would be November 11, 1975.

The F.N.L.A., the M.P.L.A., and UNITA found it impossible to work together; according to the big powers, because of ideological splits over communism versus capitalism, but according to more knowledgeable African sources, because of major ethnic and tribal cleavages. In any event, the chaos in Luanda invited outside intervention.

The United States was the first to respond. Although later Kissinger and C.I.A. Director William Colby would contend that the United States entered the Angolan civil war only to counter a Russian threat there, in fact—as John Stockwell, the Chief of the C.I.A. Angola Task Force later revealed—the United States made the first actual move.* Given Angola's political options, the C.I.A.'s choice was the F.N.L.A. Also acceptable was UNITA. The M.P.L.A. was thought to be radical, Communist, and Russian-backed, so it had to be stopped. In fact, nothing more nor less than great-power rivalry was involved, for outsiders moved in on Angola almost before the Portuguese could get out of the way. It was not merely the great powers, either; at one time or another the F.N.L.A. and UNITA received support from not only the United States and China, but also Rumania, North Korea, France, Israel, West Germany, Senegal, Uganda, Zaire, Zambia, Tanzania, and South Africa. The M.P.L.A. was supported by the Soviet Union, Cuba, East Germany, Algeria, Guinea, and Poland, surely a record of some sort for politics making strange bedfellows.

American military aid, eventually totaling about $60 million, was sent secretly into Angola by the C.I.A. via Mobuto in Zaire. The Soviets then responded with an air lift of material to the M.P.L.A. that was, in the end, about ten times as large as the American aid program. Meanwhile, the F.N.L.A. needed instruction on the use of the weapons the United States was providing. The C.I.A. was on the

---

* China was a close second, sending 112 military advisers and some equipment to help the F.N.L.A.

defensive at this time, due to its disastrous handling of the final evacuation of Saigon a few months earlier. In addition, no one wanted "another Vietnam." So the "40 committee," an agency of the National Security Council that had been created to oversee C.I.A. covert operations, flatly forbade the use of American advisers in Africa. But as agent Stockwell calmly records, "We did it anyway."

In addition to sending in advisers, the C.I.A. made a de facto alliance with South Africa, which entered the conflict with regular army troops in September 1975. This was the first time South Africa had involved itself in a war in Black Africa. It brought about a situation in which Washington, Pretoria, and Peking were fighting side by side.

The South Africans hoped to gain sympathy by supporting the same side as Zaire and the United States. They convinced themselves that their troops, although white, would be more acceptable to Angola—because they were native Africans*—than Blacks coming from Cuba. They also thought they would win, which encouraged them to embark on such a dangerous course. Eventually South Africa sent an armored column of its regular troops to fight beside UNITA, which then came close to winning the war.

The South African offensive was finally stopped. The Soviets gave the M.P.L.A. massive arms support and the Cubans sent fifteen thousand highly trained and efficient regular troops of their own. The Cubans decisively tipped the balance and the M.P.L.A. quickly won the war. If a Soviet presence in Africa upset Kissinger, the Cuban presence made him livid. He stormed and thundered. "The United States will not accept further Communist military intervention in Africa," he declared in March 1976. Senate Majority Leader Mike Mansfield dismissed this as "useless

---

* South Africans think of themselves as Africans for the good reason that, in some cases, their ancestors came there three hundred years ago. Unlike the whites in Rhodesia, they do not have a "home" in Europe or Britain to which they can return—Africa is home. South Africans also claim that when their ancestors settled at the tip of the continent, no one else lived there.

rhetoric," and House Majority Leader Thomas P. O'Neill, Jr., demanded that President Ford "publicly repudiate" Kissinger. The Secretary of Defense, Donald Rumsfeld, then lamely explained that the Ford Administration was reviewing "only economic or political action against Cuba, not military."

It was another example of Congress taking charge of foreign policy in a way unthinkable in the Truman, Eisenhower, Kennedy, or Johnson years. Congress used the same power it had exercised to force Nixon to pull out of Vietnam, the power of the purse. On January 27, 1976, despite last minute appeals from Ford and Kissinger, the House voted 323 to 99 to ban covert military aid to Angola. A frustrated President accused the Congress of having "lost its guts."

Perhaps so, but to many Americans it seemed that Congress was finally living up to its responsibilities and in the process exerting a much needed restraining influence on the adventurers in the C.I.A. and the White House. That the M.P.L.A. won in Angola scarcely seemed a crucial development to a Congress that was less worried about American prestige in Africa, more concerned with costs, and less willing to charge at the sound of the trumpets than the C.I.A. In 1976, for example, when Ethiopia and Somalia were on the verge of war, the C.I.A. was ready to intervene on the Ethiopian side, on the grounds that the Soviets were arming Somalia with modern weapons and that Cuban advisers had joined the Somali forces. Kissinger agreed with the C.I.A., but Congress was suspicious, and with a new administration's coming to power in Washington, nothing was done. A year later, in the fall of 1977, the Russians were expelled from Somalia and began to arm Ethiopia. The C.I.A. then urged the Carter Administration to intervene on behalf of Somalia.

At the southernmost tip of Africa is the Republic of South Africa, almost in another world, a world that the ruling whites say they are determined to defend forever. Around the rest of the world, since 1945, the main political movement has been either in the direction of majority rule or toward socialist collectivism. Colonial rule has all but disappeared (outside the Soviet Union). It is true that one-party rule in the socialist states is a far cry from any real democracy, but it is also true that in the past forty years the world has managed to rid itself of many monarchies and one-man dictatorships. And the socialist states are committed, in theory at least, to such principles as equality of opportunity, education, and basic rights.

South Africa has moved in the other direction, away from democracy and away from the idea of equality of all citizens under the law. Since the war, South African racial policies have steadily hardened. As her economy boomed, she needed more black labor. As black participation in the economy increased, the level of repression to enforce apartheid was stepped up. Real wages were lowered, black political dissidents were arrested and murdered; absolute separation of the races vigorously enforced. South Africa came to be a police state that, if it does not rival Hitler's death camps or Stalin's labor camps, its bitter realities, like modern Russia's psychiatric wards, are still abhorred by the rest of the world.

South Africa, though an international pariah, was also a marvelous investment opportunity, because of cheap labor and the mineral wealth of the country. Profits were high, risks low. Some private American investment money has, inevitably, found its way into South Africa, but not to be compared with the levels of American investment in Europe, the Middle East, or Latin America. Total American investment in South Africa in 1973 was $1.2 billion, representing a 73 percent increase in the years of the Nixon Administration, which was not much greater than the rate of inflation. The $1.2 billion was about one-third of the total American investment in Africa, and about 15 percent of the total foreign investment in South Africa. The United States also sold South Africa roughly 17 percent of her imports. South Africa produced 60 percent of the Western world's gold, and was the third largest supplier of uranium.

In addition, the United States had a NASA satellite-tracking station and an Air Force tracking station in South Africa, and the Navy wanted port facilities (the best in Africa) on or near the Cape, one of the most strategic points in the world.

Taken altogether, that is not a large investment. The United States, in sum, has no vital interest in South Africa. Further, on the grounds of civil rights, it was obviously impossible for any American politician to take a pro-South African stance (the last to do so was Dean Acheson, who was notoriously pro-South Africa). It was nearly as difficult to propose policies that would force South Africa to move toward majority rule. Consequently, American policy toward South Africa was mixed and confused. On the one hand the United States did maintain diplomatic relations; on the other hand Ambassador Stevenson in the early sixties took the lead in the United Nations in denouncing apartheid. The United States government has never forbidden investment in South Africa, and Nixon came close to actually encouraging it, despite the fact that the United States had led the effort in 1963 to establish a U.N. arms embargo on South Africa.

To the south of Angola lies Namibia (Southwest Africa), a colony of South Africa. The United States has insisted that South Africa's continued domination of Namibia is illegal,* to the point that President Nixon, acting at Kissinger's insistence, informed potential American investors that the United States would henceforth discourage investment in Namibia. In any event, Namibia's major—almost only— export is manpower for the South African mines. Pretoria is not willing to give up this source of cheap, reliable, hardworking labor. As N.S.S.M. 39 summed up the problem in Namibia: "No solution in sight. South Africa is entrenching

---

* Namibia was mandated to South Africa by the League of Nations in 1920. It is the only mandated territory that did not become independent (or a U.N. trust territory) after World War II. South Africa has ignored all U.N. demands that it withdraw.

its rule and has extended its application of apartheid and repressive measures. South Africa considers the area vital to its security and an economic asset."

The United States is often denounced, by Black Americans as well as by African leaders, for failing to do more to stamp out apartheid. But the African states themselves are unwilling to do much, outside the U.N. The Organization of African Unity (O.A.U.) has taken a strong public position in favor of self-determination and majority rule in South Africa, but the financial appropriations from members of the O.A.U. for the African Liberation Committee have always been low, and are going lower. In many ways the O.A.U. campaign against South Africa is a campaign to bring pressure on outside powers, especially the United States, to achieve a result that Africa by itself is still too weak to achieve. But the United States scarcely knows how to solve the problem, which is a European creation.

Africa's cultural and economic ties are with Europe. The great bulk of African students are enrolled in Western European universities, not in American or Russian schools, and the level of Western European trade with and investment in Africa is much higher than that of either superpower. English and French are the "modern" and common languages of Africa, and African English is spoken with a British, not an American, accent.

Black Africa, in other words, was the one part of the world never included in America's rise to globalism, so that when the United States began its retreat to realism in its foreign policy, there were no embarrassing moments in Africa as there had been in Vietnam, or divisive ones as there had been in Panama and Taiwan. President Carter's appointment of a Black man, Andrew Young, as Ambassador to the United Nations, gave the United States a new prestige in Africa and a new opportunity to establish a coherent, progressive policy for the continent. When Young resigned in 1979, he was replaced by another Black man, Ambassador Donald McHenry, indicating America's continued concern for Africa.

[15]

Carter

Human rights is the soul of our foreign policy.
                                    JIMMY CARTER, 1977

Iran is an island of stability in one of the more troubled areas
of the world.
                                    JIMMY CARTER 1977

In November 1976 Jimmy Carter narrowly defeated Gerald
Ford for the Presidency. Carter had conducted a skillful
campaign that took full advantage of the public's response
to Nixon's Watergate debacle, widespread resentment of
big government in Washington, D.C., and the general perception of a need for a less-active, less-involved foreign
policy. In effect, Carter promised no more Watergates and
no more Vietnams.

What he was *for* was less certain. A Georgia businessman
and former Governor of the state, in terms of foreign affairs Carter was the least-experienced President of the post-
World War II era. In sharp contrast to the realpolitik of
the Kissinger years, Carter's chief characteristic was his idealism. Unlike his predecessors, he did not regard Communism as the chief enemy; he said repeatedly that
Americans had become too fearful of the Communists while
giving too little attention to the greater danger of the arms
race and too much support to repressive right-wing dictatorships around the world.

In his inaugural address, Carter said his ultimate goal
was the elimination of nuclear weapons from the earth. He
wanted to start immediately to limit arms and to decrease
America's arms sales overseas because he did not want the

United States to remain the arms merchant to the world. And he made a firm commitment to the defense of human rights everywhere, later calling human rights "the soul of our foreign policy" and making them the touchstone of American relations with the other nations of the world. All were noble goals, nobly stated. They raised hopes worldwide, especially the emphasis on human rights, which struck a responsive chord among the oppressed everywhere.

But all the goals were wildly impractical and none were achieved. Far from making progress toward eliminating nuclear weapons, the Carter Administration continued to increase the American nuclear arsenal at about the same rate as had the Nixon and Ford administrations. American arms sales abroad actually increased, rather than decreased, during the Carter years. Furthermore, Carter's emphasis on human rights badly damaged America's relationship with many of her oldest allies; it caused resentment in the Soviet Union and other Communist countries that contributed to the failure to achieve such major goals as arms control or genuine détente; and it contributed to the downfall of America's oldest and staunchest ally in the Middle East, the Shah of Iran, with consequences that were also disastrous for Carter himself. There was a huge gap between aim and achievement in the Carter Administration. The principal causes of the gap were an excess of idealism, a lack of experience, and an overreaction to Russian actions.

"We can never be indifferent to the fate of freedom elsewhere," Carter declared in his inaugural address. "Our commitment to human rights must be absolute."

The concept that every human being has certain inalienable rights is essentially Jeffersonian and American, but it had received worldwide backing in the U.N. Charter (1945) and again in the Helsinki Accords of 1975, when all the participants, including the Soviet Union, solemnly agreed to respect and protect the human rights of their own citizens. Unfortunately there was no enforcement machinery. Congress had endorsed the policy in the early 1970s, before

Carter's inauguration, when, in reaction to Kissinger's realpolitik and embarrassed by America's support of dictators around the world, it forbade American aid to countries that engaged "in a consistent pattern of gross violations of internationally recognized human rights." Thus Carter was not advancing an original idea, but no President before him had gone so far in the area of human rights.

Carter felt the issue deeply himself and, in addition, it provided an opportunity for him to distinguish his foreign policy from that of Nixon and Kissinger. Further, it offered something to both the Cold Warriors (who could and did use it to criticize the Soviet Union for its abominable record on human rights) and to idealists (who could and did use it to criticize Chile, Brazil, South Africa, and others for their abominable records on human rights). Carter established a Bureau on Human Rights in the State Department and gave or withheld economic aid, trade advantages, weapons, and other forms of aid on the basis of a nation's human rights record.

The campaign for human rights brightened Carter's image, but had little discernible positive effect and did considerable harm. He preached to the converted; the sinners deeply resented Carter's sermons on human rights and either ignored his pleas for improved treatment of their political prisoners or actually increased the repression. Still, the human rights advocates were convinced that the campaign was positive and helpful. As one of them put it, "The former reputation of the United States as a supporter of freedom was being restored, replacing its more recent image as a patron of tyranny."

A major difficulty, however, was that inevitably the campaign was directed against America's allies and friends rather than its enemies, if only because such allies as South Korea, Argentina, South Africa, Brazil, Taiwan, Nicaragua, and Iran were vulnerable to Carter's pressure, since they relied upon the United States for military sales and economic assistance. To critics, it made little sense to weaken America's allies because of objections to their morals while continuing to advance loan credits, sell grain, and ship advanced technology to the Soviet Union, which had one of the worst human rights records in the world and was clearly no friend of the United States.

In his relations with the Soviet Union, Carter's major goals were to free America from its "inordinate fear of Communism" and to complete a SALT II treaty that would reduce the chances of nuclear war. His Secretary of State, Cyrus Vance, a New York lawyer with long government experience, was a leading advocate of détente and consequently took a moderate and conciliatory approach toward the Russians. Carter and Vance believed that it was time to redefine the relationship between the United States and the Soviet Union. Vance stressed that the new approach to the Soviets had to be based upon "positive incentives" rather than a policy of containment. He rejected the notion that "the United States can dominate the Soviet Union" or otherwise "order the world just the way we want it to be." The United States had to accept a more limited role in world affairs.

The first "positive inducement" took place within twenty-four hours of Carter's inaugural, when he ordered the immediate withdrawal of American nuclear weapons from South Korea. This major step, with its tremendous potential, did not, however, elicit any Soviet response (and was in fact ultimately blocked by the Pentagon bureaucracy). This outcome was highly disappointing to Carter, who had, it must be noted, shown his inexperience by taking such a bold step without first discussing it with his own military leaders and without first informing the Kremlin and obtaining some promises for reciprocal action in advance. In general, during his first year in office, Carter was distressed by Soviet failure to respond to his signals. As America backed off from some of its more advanced positions around the world, the Soviets, far from responding in kind, became more adventuresome. They continued and even increased their arms buildup, became involved in both the Horn of Africa and in southern Africa, using Cuban troops as their advance agents. The Russians evidently saw Carter's "positive incentives" as signs of weakness and indecision and they responded by becoming more aggressive.

The Russian actions strengthened the position of Carter's Special Assistant for National Security Affairs, Zbigniew Brzezinski, a political scientist who immigrated to the United States from Poland in 1953. Brzezinski was in the Kissinger-realpolitik tradition, and he competed with Vance for influence over Carter. Brzezinski made powerful arguments for not trusting the Soviets, arguments that were strengthened by Russian actions. For example, in early 1979 the Russians began placing jet-fighter aircraft, a combat unit, and a submarine pen in Cuba. Carter was furious with Leonid Brezhnev for this violation of the 1962 Cuban missile crisis accord, and went on national television to denounce the Soviet Union for its actions. Brezhnev, predictably, replied that the airplanes and other equipment were not offensive weapons by their nature and thus did not violate the 1962 Kennedy-Khrushchev informal arrangement. Nor did Brezhnev remove the weapons. For Carter the experience was a stage on his journey from idealism to a hard line with regard to the Soviets.

The most important result of Carter's growing hostility toward and fear of the Soviets was the demise of SALT II. In the discussions, Carter was unwilling to go more than halfway in meeting the Russians; indeed, Carter eventually demanded more arms for the United States, and less for the Soviets, than Kissinger and Nixon had been willing to accept. Carter's demands, plus Soviet resentment at his public support for Russian dissidents and his linking of SALT talks to human rights, set back the negotiations for more than a year. Carter had said he wanted to complete the treaty in 1977, but not until June 1979 did Carter meet with Brezhnev in Vienna to sign the SALT II treaty. By then, Carter had already ordered the construction of cruise (Pershing II) missiles, which were not covered in the SALT I agreement, and an enhanced radiation (neutron) bomb. Brezhnev had responded by accelerating Soviet production of the Backfire Bomber and the new SS-20 missiles.

The SALT II treaty that the two leaders signed in Vienna was a strange accord. As had been the case with SALT I, it set upper limits toward which both sides could build rather than freezing nuclear weapons and delivery systems, and it failed altogether to even mention the Pershing II missiles or the Backfire Bomber or the MIRV problem (multiple warheads for individual I.C.B.M.s). SALT II, in short, was far behind the current technology. Specifically, the treaty limited each side to 2,400 launchers of all types. At that time, in mid-1979, the two sides were roughly equal: The United States had 1,054 I.C.B.M.s, of which 550 were MIRVed, while the Russians had 1,398 I.C.B.M.s, of which 576 were MIRVed. The United States had 656 submarine-launched ballistic missiles, of which 496 were MIRVed, while the Russians had 950, of which 128 were MIRVed. In addition, the United States had 574 heavy bombers carrying the largest nuclear weapons, while the Soviets had 156 such bombers. As both sides were free to build as many nuclear warheads as they wished, and to MIRV all their launchers, SALT II, for all practical purposes, put no limits at all on the arms race.

Nevertheless, the treaty was sharply criticized in the United States, especially in the Senate, where it was charged that it gave too much away and allowed Russia's supposed strategic superiority to continue and even to grow. Carter himself, as one part of his hardening attitude toward the Soviets, lost faith in the treaty. He did not press for ratification. Instead, in December 1979, the Carter Administration persuaded its NATO partners to agree to a program of installing Pershing II missiles with nuclear warheads in Western Europe as a response to the Soviet installation of hundreds of new medium-range SS-20 missiles in Eastern Europe. This was hardly a moved forced by the Americans on reluctant Europeans. The West Germans, British, Dutch, and other NATO members were greatly alarmed by the SS-20 threat and insisted upon an American response. NATO members made a "two-track" decision—to install American cruise missiles in Western Europe while simultaneously urging arms control talks on the Russians. The NATO states promised that if the Russians would remove SS-20s in Eastern Europe, the cruise missiles would not be installed. These steps were a major escalation in the arms race and had, as one immediate effect, the bringing to life of the moribund antinuclear movement in Europe, which soon spread to the United States. People throughout the world, from every walk of life and every political persuasion, found it increasingly difficult to understand how building more bombs enhanced their security. In an era in which each side had tens of thousands of nuclear warheads and overkill capacity was measured in factors of forty to fifty, it was equally difficult to see how adding to that capacity improved a nation's strategic position. Nevertheless, the arms race went on.

In December 1979 some 85,000 Soviet troops invaded Afghanistan. The event seriously jolted Carter. He said that "the implications of the Soviet invasion of Afghanistan could pose the most serious threat to world peace since the Second World War," and argued that "aggression unopposed becomes a contagious disease." The United States curtailed grain sales to Russia, suspended high-technology sales, and—at Carter's insistence—boycotted the 1980 Olympic Games in Moscow. In addition, Carter told the Senate to defer indefinitely consideration of the SALT II treaty. These were all most serious steps—except for the Olympic boycott, which was purely symbolic and for which the Russians got their revenge in 1984—and represented a reversal of long-standing policies that went back to the Kennedy years. Indeed, by 1980 Carter was taking a generally harder line toward the Soviets than any President since Eisenhower. He explained that Afghanistan was the reason, saying: "This action of the Soviets has made a more drastic change in my own opinion of what the Soviets' ultimate goals are than anything they've done in the previous time I've been in office." He called the invasion "a stepping-stone to their possible control over much of the world's oil supplies."

Carter's critics saw his response as an overreaction. They argued that the Soviets went into Afghanistan not for offensive purposes—the terrain was about the least suitable to offensive warfare of any in the world—but for defensive reasons. There already existed in Afghanistan a pro-Moscow government, put in power after a coup in April 1978; that government, however, was unable to suppress Muslim insurgency and the Russians—evidently fearful that the Muslim uprising that had already swept through Iran would spread to the millions of Muslims within the Soviet Union—reacted by invading.

But Carter insisted that the Red Army was on the march—and it was true that this was the first time the Soviets had sent their own troops into an area not conquered by the Red Army in 1945. Fearful for the West's oil supplies, Carter not only backed away from SALT II but also increased defense spending; he announced that restrictions on the activities of the C.I.A. would be lifted and proclaimed a Carter Doctrine for Southwest Asia. Defining the Persian Gulf area as within the zone of American vital interests, Carter declared that the United States would repel an assault in that region by the Russians "by any means necessary—including military force." Critics asked how the United States could defend, singlehandedly, an area thousands of miles from any American military base, except through the use of nuclear weapons, and expressed the wish that Carter had consulted with the Persian Gulf states and the NATO countries before promulgating the Carter Doctrine.

When Carter left office, relations with the Soviet Union were worse than they had been when he was inaugurated. Soviet dissenters were persecuted more actively and severely in 1980 than had been the case in 1976. The nuclear arsenals of the superpowers had increased. Soviet SS-20s threatened Western Europe as never before, while America was producing cruise missiles so as to equally threaten Eastern Europe and Russia. Trade between the United States and the Soviet Union had fallen off sharply.

Carter had begun with a firm policy, a policy that in many ways held hope for a new beginning—lowered expenditures for armaments, greater trust between the two sides, more trade and more cultural exchanges, in short, a genuine détente. But he had been unable to hold to that policy, in largest part because of the failure of the Soviets to respond to his "positive incentives," but also because of internal political pressure to "get tough," because his own inexperience led him to overreact to events, as in Cuba and Afghanistan, and because the momentum of the arms race could not be even slowed, much less halted, as each side reacted to its fears of technological or numerical breakthrough by the other. And because, too, Carter was not a strong enough captain to set a course and hold to it. By 1980, the word most often used to describe his foreign policy was "waffle." It was a stinging indictment.

Aside from the human rights campaign, Carter's idealism had its greatest impact on policy in relations with Africa, Latin America, and China. In Africa, Ambassador Andrew Young's outspoken support in the United Nations for the emerging nations of the continent, plus his insistence on majority rule in southern Africa, won many new friends for the United States. In Latin America, Carter withdrew support from the repressive military junta in Chile, thus reversing Kissinger's policy. In February 1978, Carter also cut all military and economic aid to one of America's oldest allies, Anastasio Somoza of Nicaragua, because of Somoza's odious record on human rights. In June 1979, the United States supported an O.A.S. resolution calling for Somoza's resignation, and without American assistance Somoza could not withstand the attacks of the Sandinista guerrilla movement. In July 1979, Somoza fled to Miami; a year later, he was assassinated in Paraguay. The United States immediately recognized the new Sandinista government and provided it with $16 million in economic aid. A year later, Carter signed a $75-million aid package for Nicaragua. Insofar as the Sandinistas were left-wing, with a strong Communist element in the government, Carter's response to the revolution represented a major shift in United States' relations with Central America.

In May 1980, left-wing guerrillas in El Salvador, encouraged and aided by the Sandinista victory in Nicaragua, and by Castro, began a civil war. The El Salvador government fought back with brutal, but inefficient, search-and-destroy missions. El Salvador's army sent out right-wing death squads to slaughter civilian opponents in the hundreds, indeed ultimately in the thousands. Following the murder of three American nuns and a lay worker by government troops, Carter suspended military and economic aid to El Salvador, although on January 14, 1981, in one of his last acts as President, he announced the resumption of limited aid.

One of Carter's great triumphs in foreign policy came in 1978, when he took a bold and courageous stand on the Panama Canal Treaty, which returned to Panama full sovereignty over the Canal Zone. By no means could Carter take full credit—negotiations had begun during the Johnson Administration and were brought to near-completion under the Republicans in the seventies. But when it came time for the crucial Senate vote, a highly charged, emotional opposition nearly blocked it. Ronald Reagan, campaigning for the Presidency, denounced the treaty. One Senator said irritably, "We stole it [Panama] fair and square." But both Ford and Kissinger gave the treaty their support, and Carter put the full weight of the Presidency behind ratification. The treaty narrowly passed.

Carter also followed the Republican lead with regard to China. Nixon's 1972 trip had opened the door to a new United States-Chinese relationship, but the problems of full recognition of Communist China and what to do about America's treaties with Nationalist China still had to be overcome. Carter announced in 1978 that as of January 1, 1979, the United States and China would extend full recognition to each other and exchange ambassadors. Further, the United States unilaterally ended its 1954 mutual defense treaty with Taiwan and withdrew diplomatic recognition of the Nationalist regime there, simultaneously recognizing Taiwan as part of China. Senator Barry Goldwater and Presidential candidate Reagan led Republican criticisms of this "betrayal" of one of America's staunchest allies, but Carter forced the new policy through anyway, primarily because it was a logical outgrowth of the Nixon-Kissinger initiative in China, a fact that strongly muted Republican criticism.

Carter also followed Kissinger's lead in the Middle East, where he played a central role in bringing about a peace treaty between Egypt and Israel, something almost no one—including Kissinger—had thought possible. In the process Carter raised his own prestige both in the United States and around the world. Carter's success was possible, primarily, because of Nasser's successor, Anwar el-Sadat. Sadat recognized that Egypt could afford no more war and was, in any case, incapable of driving the occupying Israeli army out of the Sinai. He decided to offer Israel peace and recognition in return for the occupied Egyptian territory. In December 1977, Sadat went to Israel to speak to the Israeli Parliament, an act of great courage and drama hat captured the imagination of the world. Sadat was risking not only denunciation by his fellow Arabs but assassination as well. He also risked being misunderstood by the Israelis. He was forthright in what he told the Parliament, insisting that any agreement between Israel and Egypt would have to include an Israeli retreat from the West Bank of the Jordan River and from the Golan Heights, a homeland for the Palestinians and a recognition of the P.L.O. as their government, and a relinquishment of Israel's unilateral hold on the city of Jerusalem. Such objectives seemed impossible, as the new Israeli Prime Minister, former terrorist and right-wing politician Menachem Begin, was unwilling to compromise on Jerusalem or the P.L.O. Nor would Begin make concessions on the Golan Heights or the West Bank. But Begin was willing to sign a separate peace with Egypt (it had long been an aim of Israeli foreign policy to divide the Arabs). Sadat could not abandon the other Arabs, especially the P.L.O., not even for the return of the Sinai, but he was willing to talk. This gave Carter his opportunity.

In the fall of 1978 Carter invited Begin and Sadat to meet with him at the Presidential retreat at Camp David, Maryland, with the United States acting as a "full partner" in the negotiations. For nearly two weeks the three men carried on intensive discussions. They could not reach a final agreement, however, because they could not settle the issues of Jerusalem, the West Bank, the Golan Heights, or the P.L.O. By December, they had reached an impasse. Carter called it "the most frustrating experience of my life."

Still, he persisted. In early 1979 he made a sudden, dramatic journey to the Middle East, where he met with Sadat in Egypt and Begin in Israel, and eventually persuaded them to sign a peace treaty. Essentially it was an agreement for Egyptian recognition of Israel, and peace between the two nations, in return for a staged Israeli withdrawal from the Sinai. The future of the P.L.O. was also mentioned, but in a vague way that allowed conflicting interpretations as to what was meant. The agreement did not mention the Golan Heights or Jerusalem (indeed, Begin incorporated the Golan Heights into the State of Israel in 1982, and Jewish settlers in large numbers moved into the West Bank). The treaty was therefore unacceptable to the other Arab states, who vigorously denounced Sadat. But the treaty did lead to an Israeli withdrawal from the Sinai, completed in April 1982, and the opening of diplomatic and economic relations between Egypt and Israel. Sadly, it also led to Sadat's assassination, by Egyptian soldiers, in October 1981.

Ironically, it was events in the Middle East, site of Carter's greatest triumph, that led to his downfall. In one of the most bizarre incidents of the twentieth century, the Iranian revolution almost brought the American government, in 1980, to a standstill. Events in Iran played a major role in the Presidential election that year and led to Carter's electoral defeat.

Since 1953, the year in which the C.I.A. participated in a coup that restored the Shah of Iran to his throne, American relations with the Shah had wavered. Eisenhower had been an enthusiastic supporter of the regime, but both Kennedy and Johnson had limited arms sales and economic assistance to Iran on the grounds that the Shah was a reactionary dictator who could not be trusted. Nixon and

Kissinger, however, returned to the Eisenhower policy, and indeed expanded it. In their view, Iran was America's best friend in the Middle East, a principal partner in the policy of containing the Soviets and the only reliable supplier of oil to the West. The Shah was a prime customer for America's military hardware during the early seventies, purchasing up to one-third of all arms sold by the United States abroad, and thus was a major factor in solving America's balance-of-payments problems. He was also a staunch foe of Communism, and Iran's geographical position on Russia's southern border made it a strategically crucial nation. The Shah was a voice of moderation in O.P.E.C. and the only dependable source of oil for Israel. In addition, the Shah allowed the C.I.A. to station sophisticated electronic listening devices along Iran's border with the Soviet Union. Iran was much more clearly an American vital interest than South Vietnam or South Korea had ever been. On his frequent trips to the United States, the Shah was given royal receptions. Tens of thousands of young Iranians came to the United States to study; Iranian military officers were trained at the various American war colleges; SAVAK, the notorious Iranian secret police force, received its training and equipment from the C.I.A.; American oil companies provided the Iranians with technicians, financing, and general guidance, while sharing in the huge profits; and thousands of American businessmen operated in Teheran. Relations between the United States and Iran, in short, could not have been closer or better.

Or so it seemed. But in fact, except among the ruling elite in Iran, anti-American feeling was strong and growing stronger. Iranians blamed the United States for putting the Shah back in power in 1953, and keeping him there afterward. They believed that the United States encouraged the Shah as he increasingly gathered all power in Iran into his own hands; they felt that the United States was responsible for the Shah's enormous expenditures on the armed forces, expenditures that were out of all proportion to Iran's security needs and were designed to protect the Shah's position rather than improve the condition of the Iranian people. Countless Iranians believed that the United States was responsible for the Shah's modernization programs, which in their view violated fundamental Islamic law and traditional Persian customs. But because the Americans got their information about Iran from the Shah, SAVAK, the Iranian military, and the oil companies, the seething unrest among the Iranian masses was either unknown, ignored, or dismissed.

Carter, despite his human rights policy, accepted the Nixon-Kissinger thesis that the Shah was a bulwark of American interests in the Middle East and he continued the practice of selling the Shah military equipment at a record pace. (American arms sales to Iran, which had totaled $1.2 billion over the twenty-two years since 1950, increased almost sixteen-fold to a total of $19.5 billion from 1972 to 1979.) At the end of 1977, his first year in office, Carter went to Iran, where he was the guest of honor at a glittering dinner on New Year's Eve. The President proposed a toast: "Iran, because of the great leadership of the Shah, is an island of stability in one of the more troubled areas of the world." Carter failed to mention the massive anti-Shah demonstrations that had occurred that day in Teheran and which had led to hundreds of arrests. The C.I.A. was equally myopic. In August 1978, by which time strikes and demonstrations had virtually paralyzed Iran, the C.I.A. issued a sixty-page analysis of "Iran in the 1980s," in which it concluded, "Iran is not in a revolutionary or even a 'prerevolutionary' situation."

But by this stage Iran in fact was full of revolutionary activity. The Shah was under attack from both the left (the Fedayeen, which was closely connected to the P.L.O.) and the right (the Mullahs, or Islamic clergy, who were demanding an Islamic republic and a retreat from modernization). The C.I.A. failed to see the seriousness of the challenge or understand the depth of Iranian hatred for the Shah, even though it had more agents in Iran, per capita, than anywhere else in the world. American intelligence also failed to uncover a crucial fact: The Shah had an incurable cancer and was being treated with massive doses of drugs by French doctors. His will was shattered; he was indecisive at critical moments; he had no stomach for turning his magnificently equipped army, or his secret police, against the rioters, who consequently grew increasingly bolder. But neither Carter nor the C.I.A. could believe that an absolute monarch, in command of a wealthy oil-producing nation, with huge armed forces and secret police giving him their enthusiastic support, could be overthrown by unarmed mobs led by bearded Mullahs. Indeed, so contemptuous was Carter of the Shah's political opponents that he made no attempt to open lines of communication with them. It was a momentous miscalculation.

By mid-1978, a single leader of the Iranian opposition had emerged. He was the Ayatollah Khomeini, an aged fanatic who was living in exile in Paris, from which place he sent instructions and exhortations to his followers in Iran. His message was to strike, disrupt, riot, and create chaos until the Shah was forced to abdicate. Hundreds of thousands of Iranians did as he instructed; soon Iran was not producing enough oil even for its own internal needs, and the country was indeed in chaos. The Iranian army, forbidden by the Shah to fire on the rioters (the Shah feared that a bloodbath would ruin his son's chances of succeeding him), was demoralized. Finally, on January 16, 1979, the Shah left the country for an extended "vacation." Two weeks later, the Ayatollah Khomeini returned to Iran, where crowds of supporters, numbering in the hundreds of thousands, greeted him with wild enthusiasm. Although Khomeini never took a formal position in the government, he immediately became the de facto ruler of Iran.

The Carter Administration hardly knew what to make of the Ayatollah. Accustomed, like its predecessors, to thinking exclusively in terms of the Cold War, it was unable to adjust to a fundamentalist religious revolution that denounced the United States and the Soviet Union equally. Discounting the Ayatollah's rabid hatred of Communism, Carter tended to hear only Khomeini's vicious assaults on the United States which he called "the great Satan." Thus Carter's fear was that Khomeini would allow a Soviet pen-

etration of Iran. This was seen as a possible first step in a
Soviet penetration of the entire Middle East, with incal-
culable consequences for the entire Western world. Once
again, in other words, Carter was seeing dangers that did
not exist, while ignoring those that did.

What the United States government never fully recognized was that the cement holding the otherwise incompatible Fedayeen and Mullahs together was anti-Americanism
and hatred of the Shah. The two sentiments merged into
one because the Shah had not abdicated (he went first to
Morocco, then to the Bahamas), because the United States
continued to maintain a large diplomatic corps and business
community in Iran, and because Iranians still blamed the
United States for the events of 1953. It was almost univer-
sally believed in Iran that the C.I.A. would attempt a repeat
performance. In fact, Carter had no intention of trying to
restore the Shah, as indicated by his recognition in February 1979 of the new Islamic government. Carter's hope
was instead to restore normal relations with Iran and make
it, once again, a pillar of stability in the Middle East. The
Iranians, however, could not believe that the United States
would abandon the Shah, and so long as he was alive they
anticipated another C.I.A. coup.

In July 1979, the Shah's sixty-day visa in the Bahamas
expired. The Carter Administration, after many aborted
talks with a number of countries, finally persuaded the
Mexican government to grant him a six-month tourist visa.
Meanwhile, however, Carter was under intense pressure
from David Rockefeller, Henry Kissinger, and other old
friends of the Shah to admit the Shah to the United States.
Kissinger said it was disgraceful that the United States had
turned its back on one of her oldest and closest friends.
Carter resisted this pressure, but he was moved ultimately
by humanitarian motives, the most important being the
argument that the Shah could receive proper medical treatment for his cancer only in a New York hospital. Carter
agreed to allow the Shah to come to the United States for
treatment. The Shah entered the United States in late October 1979; the Carter Administration had taken the pre-

caution of obtaining assurances from the Iranian government beforehand that it could protect the American embassy in Teheran. How Carter could have believed these assurances is somewhat of a mystery; it seemed obvious to most observers that allowing the Shah into the United States would have the effect of waving a red flag in front of an already fever-pitched bull.

On November 4, 1979, enraged Iranian "students" overran the United States embassy in Teheran and took some 100 hostages. The Ayatollah Khomeini condoned the takeover, saying that "if they do not give up the criminal then we shall do whatever is necessary." It was an outrageous action, the worst violation of the basic principle of diplomatic immunity in modern history. Prime Minister Mehdi Bazargan, head of a "government" that existed only at the sufferance of Khomeini, tried to secure the release of the hostages, failed, and resigned. Carter ordered the Pentagon to prepare a contingency plan for military action to rescue the hostages. He also told Attorney General Benjamin Civiletti to inform the 50,000 Iranian students in the United States to report to the nearest immigration office. Any student found to be in violation of the terms of his or her visa was to be deported. (Little came of this threat, as American courts consistently upheld the rights of the students.) Carter also suspended arms sales to Iran, froze Iranian assets in American banks, and announced an embargo on Iranian oil. As Iran no longer wanted American arms anyway, and was not even producing enough oil for her own needs, these actions had no immediate effect.

More important than his actions were Carter's public statements, which had the effect of enormously enhancing the value of the hostages to the Iranians. By word and deed, the President made it clear to the Iranians and the world that the lives of the hostages were his first priority. He met repeatedly with the families of the hostages and prayed publicly with them at the National Cathedral; he confessed to reporters that virtually his every waking moment was spent worrying about the fate of the captives; to the great frustration of Senator Edward Kennedy, Carter refused to

participate in the preconvention political campaigning for
the Democratic nomination on the grounds that he needed
to devote his full time to the hostage crisis, which helped
Carter in his contest with Kennedy but later hurt him badly
in the general election; he allowed the hostage crisis to
dominate American foreign policy for the next fourteen
and a half months. At the time, few questioned his priorities, although probably no other nation in the world would
have put the fate of the fifty-three hostages (Khomeini had
ordered the release of most black and female hostages)
ahead of all other considerations. The media, by giving the
crisis an extremely high level of coverage, including nightly
TV "specials" on the situation, added to the emotional response of the American people, and Carter's popularity
soared every time television showed huge mobs of crazed
Iranians in Teheran crying "Death to Carter." Carter's
choices—to allow the Shah to remain in an American hospital, to continue recognition of the Iranian "government,"
to put mild economic pressure on Iran, and to attempt to
negotiate a solution—originally won wide support.

Negotiations, however, required a stable government in
Iran, one that was really in power, and such a government
did not exist. The Iranians were in a revolutionary situation, attempting to draw up a new, basic Islamic constitution; meanwhile there were a series of prime ministers,
none of whom could stay in office a day without Khomeini's
blessing. As a consequence, not until February 1980 did
the United States have a list of Iranian demands to consider. As announced by the newly elected President of Iran,
Abol-Hassan Bani-Sadr, the conditions were the return of
the Shah to Iran for trial, the return of the Shah's wealth
to the Iranian people, an admission of guilt by the United
States for its past actions in Iran, plus an apology, and a
promise not to interfere in Iran's affairs in the future.
These were clearly unacceptable demands, especially the
first one, as the Shah had already (in December 1979) left
the United States to take up residence in Panama. In response to Bani-Sadr's demands, Carter threatened harsh
new sanctions against Iran and against Iranian citizens in

the United States unless some progress was forthcoming. In March 1980, the Shah left Panama, one day before Iran was to present formal extradition papers, and accepted a long-standing offer of safe haven from President Sadat of Egypt. With the Shah now in an Islamic country and with Bani-Sadr promising an early release of the hostages, Carter's spirits soared.

But Carter's elation was short-lived. Bani-Sadr stalled, then ruefully admitted that he did not have the power to effect the release of the hostages, and Khomeini's demands were unchanged. Carter was furious at this double-cross. On April 7 he announced the severing of diplomatic relations with Iran, the implementation of a complete economic embargo against Iran, an inventory of financial claims against Iran to be paid from Iranian assets in the United States, and told Iran's diplomats to be out of the country within twenty-four hours.

Carter also gave a go-ahead for a military attempt to rescue the hostages. The military operation, on April 25, 1980, was poorly planned and badly executed. Long before any of the American helicopters got anywhere near the hostages, Carter had to cancel the operation because of equipment failure. The botched operation made the United States appear to be a "pitiful helpless giant" and Carter more of a waffler than ever. Hard-liners condemned him for not having mounted a rescue operation sooner, not putting enough military force into it when he decided to go, and then backing down at the first sign of difficulty. From the wait-and-negotiate camp, Secretary of State Vance resigned his post in protest. Vance believed the attempted rescue, even if successful, would inevitably lead to the shooting of many of the hostages, would deepen the chasm between the United States and Iran, and might lead the Soviets to intervene, with dangerous consequences for American policy in the Middle East. In short, whether seen from the left or the right, Carter's abortive rescue mission was a disaster.

The President was widely perceived, by this time, as having gone from blunder to blunder. In an admittedly difficult situation, his decisions had been consistently wrong—his failure to support the Shah when the revolution began, his failure to open lines of communication with Khomeini, his recognition of a government in Iran that could not govern, his decision to allow the Shah into the United States, his highly emotional response to the taking of the hostages, his long-delayed and then botched use of the military rescue option. Carter's standing in the polls declined sharply.

An impasse in the hostage crisis had been reached, to continue through the summer of 1980. On July 27, the 60-year-old Shah died of cancer, but any hope that his death would improve the hostage situation was soon dashed. In September, Khomeini stated four conditions for the release of the hostages: The United States must 1) return the Shah's wealth; 2) cancel all financial claims against Iran; 3) free Iranian assets frozen in the United States; and 4) promise never to interfere in Iranian affairs. Since the Iranian demand for an apology from the United States for its past behavior was not mentioned, there was now at least a basis for talk. Chances for a settlement also improved after September 22, when Iraq invaded Iran's Khuzistan province and full-scale war began between the two countries.

The possibility of the dismemberment of Iran was highly disturbing to the United States, because the Soviets would be sure to take advantage of it, so in October Carter announced that he would release Iran's assets, end economic sanctions, and normalize relations if Iran would release the hostages. On November 4, Ronald Reagan defeated Carter in the Presidential election, thereby putting additional pressure on Khomeini, who could hardly expect the incoming Reagan Administration to offer as favorable a deal as the outgoing Carter Administration. (Reagan was denouncing the Iranians as "barbarians" and "common criminals" and hinting that he would take strong and direct military action against them.) Therefore, Iran, on December 21, demanded a specific ransom for the captives—$24 billion—deposited in Algeria. The new Secretary of State, Edmund Muskie, said the demand was "unreasonable" but indicated that it formed a basis for negotiations. On January 6, Iran reduced the demand to $20 billion, and a week later made another reduction, to $8 billion. Complex negotiations followed, in an atmosphere of haste, as Reagan would take office on January 20. Finally, on Carter's last morning in office, the Iranians agreed to a deal that gave them $8 billion worth of Iranian assets that had been frozen (but $5 billion was set aside to pay off Iran's debts to American and European banks) in return for the release of the hostages, who flew out of Teheran that day. The crisis was finally over.

Except for the return of its assets, Iran got nothing from the episode—no apology, no international tribunal to hear Teheran's grievances against the United States, no promises about the future, no return of the Shah's wealth. The outcome was nevertheless hardly a triumph for the United States, which had been humiliated for more than fourteen months and shown to be impotent even in defending its vital interests. Khomeini was left with a bankrupt and divided country that was involved in a dangerous and expensive war with Iraq. Carter suffered the worst electoral defeat of any incumbent President ever, including Herbert Hoover in 1932. The only real winner was Reagan, whose huge margin of victory was due in no small part to Carter's inept handling of the crisis. Indeed, most observers felt that had Carter secured the release of the hostages before the election, he might well have won; nearly everyone agreed that had the military rescue worked, Carter would have been triumphantly returned for a second term.

Reagan

The Soviet Union is the focus of evil in the modern world.
RONALD REAGAN, March 1983

With the advent of the Reagan Administration, American foreign policy underwent another of its periodic swings. The new team of President Ronald Reagan, former Governor of California and movie actor, and Secretary of State Alexander Haig, former general, NATO commander, and assistant to Kissinger, was far tougher in its public statements than the Carter-Vance team had ever been. The Republicans said they were determined to restore the shattered American prestige and position around the world. They set about accomplishing this goal by talking tough to the Russians, by taking a firm anti-Communist line in Central America, and by dramatically escalating the arms race. Reagan charged that Carter (and by implication Nixon and Kissinger before Carter) had allowed the Soviets to achieve strategic superiority, and insisted that the SALT II agreements would have to be revised before they could be considered for ratification. Reagan ordered the B-1 bomber, cancelled by Carter, put into production; he stepped up the preparations for basing Pershing II missiles in Western Europe; he sharply increased defense expenditures for both conventional and nuclear forces within the United States; he scrapped the human rights policy; and he allowed American arms manufacturers to sell arms at a record level. As a consequence the arms industry became the leading growth industry in the United States—and around the world, as the level of armaments reached unprecedented proportions. By the early 1980s, worldwide military spending was nearly $550 billion annually, or $150 for every person on earth. The Russians were actually exporting more arms than the United States, while France, Britain, Germany, and other industrialized countries were paying for their oil and other imports with arms sold to the Third World exporters of raw materials.

But just as Carter had discovered in the Iranian crisis that being the Commander in Chief of the greatest armed forces ever assembled on this earth (or the second greatest, depending on which statistics about the Soviet armed forces one believed) did not give him sufficient power to enforce his will, so did Reagan discover in the Polish crisis in late 1981 that for all America's missiles and bombers and submarines and NATO partners, he was no more able to influence events in Eastern Europe than Truman and Eisenhower had in the first years of the Cold War. When the Soviet Union forced the Polish army to impose martial law in order to crush Solidarity, a trade union that had nearly half the Polish population in its ranks, and which was moving Poland toward a genuine form of socialist democracy, Reagan was outraged. But he was also disconcerted to discover that he was helpless. He dared not risk war with the Soviets over Poland; he could not persuade his NATO allies to join in an economic blockade of either Poland or Russia; he was, in the end, reduced to verbal denunciation and the most limited and ineffective economic sanctions. As had happened so many times during the Cold War, the Russians had once again demonstrated that they would do whatever they felt they had to do to retain their hold on their satellites, no matter what world public opinion thought about their actions and no matter how much the United States blustered and threatened. Thus did Reagan, early on in his administration, feel the same frustrations over Poland and Eastern Europe that Truman, Eisenhower, Kennedy, Johnson, Nixon, Ford, and Carter had felt. The Cold War continued unabated, but it was more frightening than ever, because the level of armaments in the world was thousands of times greater in the early 1980s than it had been in the late 1940s.

In addition, there were more wars going on, in more places. By 1984 Europe, which had seen so many wars over so many centuries, and which had twice in the twentieth century dragged the rest of the world into war, was the only continent where no active fighting was going on. Everywhere else wars were raging. Many of them had no connection with the Cold War, or with political or religious ideology. In Southeast Asia, communists were at war with communists (China vs. Vietnam; Vietnam vs. Cambodia). In the Middle East, Muslims fought Muslims (Iran vs. Iraq) as Jews fought Arabs and Lebanese Christians fought Lebanese Muslims. The United States was involved in these conflicts, sometimes as a mediator, always as a supplier of arms. So were the Russians.

Virtually all Third World countries were spending enormous sums on war or preparation for war, despite staggering debts and dreadful poverty. In the Western economic boom of the second half of the 1970s, excess capital had piled up in American and European banks, and so large sums were loaned to the Third World. The money was used to purchase either arms or consumer goods, rather than as investment capital to increase production facilities. As a consequence, when the worldwide economic recession set in during the early 1980s, bringing with it a drop in the price of Third World exports (oil, minerals, commodities) and a rise in interest rates (caused in part by the previously unimaginable level of American deficits, as Reagan simultaneously cut taxes while increasing defense spending dramatically), many Third World nations faced literal bankruptcy. Billions of dollars in potential defaults were involved, putting the entire Western banking structure at risk. The world faced an economic crisis that was potentially worse than the Great Depression of the 1930s.

There was no easy solution, perhaps not even a hard one. A temporary respite—loaning more money so that the Third World countries could at least meet the interest payments—only made the long-term problem worse. By 1984, the American economy was again expanding, at near-record rates, but because of Reagan's success in holding down inflation (4% in 1984), prices of commodities, oil, and other Third World products were not rising. The dollar was strong, stronger than it had ever been. Thus interest rates remained high (over 10%), exacerbating the Third World's problems. Everyone agreed that a day of reckoning would have to come; no one could agree on what to do about it.

Another threat to worldwide stability was the Iran-Iraq war. The two sides began, in 1984, to attack with modern missiles oil tankers in the Persian Gulf. In 1979, the United States had proclaimed, in the Carter Doctrine, that it would use military force to prevent the Russians from controlling the region or disrupting the flow of oil. But in 1984, the United States watched helplessly as Iraq and Iran disrupted the oil flow.

In the other major war in the Middle East, in Lebanon, the United States had no economic interest of any consequence, but nevertheless it became deeply involved. The war was exceedingly complex (it pitted Lebanese Muslims against Lebanese Christians, Syria against Lebanon, the P.L.O. against everyone, and Jew against Arab) but the reason for American involvement was simple—to contain the Soviet Union. Reagan saw Syria as a client state of the Russians, and Israel as a potential Cold War ally in the Middle East. Secretary Haig and Defense Secretary Caspar Weinberger wanted close military ties with Israel, because they regarded Israel as the strongest and most reliable power in the region. The difficulty was that the Israelis, although eager to accept American arms and willing to cooperate with the Americans on military intelligence, viewed Arab nationalism and the P.L.O., not the Russians, as the chief threat.

Alliances are almost impossible to make when the potential partners do not agree on a common enemy. Haig and Weinberger realized that before they could persuade Israel to concentrate on an anti-Russian alliance, Israel had to be assured of peaceful, stable borders. Thanks to Carter's Camp David agreements, such borders had been achieved on Israel's Egyptian front. But on the West Bank of Jordan, on the Golan Heights, where Israel faced Syria, and on the

northern front, where Lebanon provided a base for the
P.L.O. fighting forces, Israel had major problems, which
Israeli leaders believed had to be solved before they could
turn their energies and power to an anti-Soviet alliance
with the United States.

American policy aimed to provide Israel with security,
primarily by eliminating the P.L.O. base in Lebanon, partly
through military action, partly by giving the Palestinians a
homeland on the West Bank. Such a two-track policy was
necessary, Reagan believed, because the moderate Arabs
could not simply stand aside as Israel eliminated the P.L.O.
Until the Palestinians had a homeland, they would be a
permanent source of turmoil, terrorism, and war in the
Middle East. The West Bank provided the best opportunity
for such a homeland, if only the P.L.O., Jordan, Syria, and
Israel would agree.

None would, however. The P.L.O. could not accept the
American formula of a Palestinian state tied to Jordan and
thus unable to follow its own foreign and military policy.
Jordan had no desire to take responsibility for the P.L.O.
Syria aimed at a regional predominance that had no room
for an independent P.L.O. And Israel would not agree to
a Palestinian nation, no matter how tightly controlled by
Jordan, on the West Bank. On the contrary, Prime Minister
Begin and his government continued to believe that Israeli
security depended on seizing and holding territory, and on
military might, rather than on political compromise. Thus
in direct defiance of strongly stated American wishes, Begin
continued to encourage Jewish settlement on the West Bank,
turning it from a potential homeland for the Palestinians
into a perhaps permanent part of greater Israel.

Reagan and Haig believed that if the P.L.O. could be
eliminated as a fighting force, Israel would be willing to be
reasonable about a Palestinian homeland on the West Bank.
The military base of the P.L.O. was in southern Lebanon.
Because Lebanon was torn by an endemic civil war, the
government in Beirut was incapable of asserting its authority over the P.L.O. As a first step in getting the Israelis
to be reasonable about the Palestinian question and to turn

Israel's attention to the Soviet threat, Haig decided to encourage Israel to solve the P.L.O. problem with a massive military stroke. On May 26, 1982, in Chicago, Secretary Haig delivered a major foreign policy address. Israel had just completed on April 25 her withdrawal from the Sinai, in accordance with the Camp David agreement. With a peaceful and stable southern border, Begin felt free to concentrate on his northern front. In his Chicago speech, Haig called for "international action" to end the Lebanese civil war. This was, most observers agreed, a signal to Israel to invade Lebanon.

On June 6, 1982, Israel did invade. Israeli troops drove northward and then beseiged West Beirut, where refugee camps held tens of thousands of Palestinians and provided a base for P.L.O. soldiers. Officially, the United States did not welcome the invasion, but neither would it condemn it. The immediate aim of the invasion was to crush the P.L.O., but the immediate result was a de facto Israeli occupation of southern Lebanon, thus adding to Israel's conquered territory. Haig stated publicly that the invasion created "new and hopeful opportunities" for a political settlement in Lebanon, which presumably meant the elimination of the P.L.O., but by this time the confused situation had the Reagan Administration working at cross-purposes. American Ambassador Philip Habib was laboring, with impressive energy, skill, and patience, to find a diplomatic solution. The Israelis were apprehensive that Habib would put together a compromise that would give the P.L.O. a permanent place in Lebanon (a solution supported by Saudi Arabia, Jordan, and Syria, as well as by Defense Secretary Weinberger). Israel began in August 1982 the systematic and heavy shelling of the P.L.O. camps in West Beirut. This action led to a general public demand that Reagan dissociate the United States from Israeli action and contributed to the resignation of Secretary of State Haig, who was replaced by George Shultz, a California businessman and former professor with long experience in government. By September, Ambassador Habib produced a political compromise. Israel agreed to lift the siege while a trilateral

force of French, Italian, and American troops supervised
the withdrawal of the P.L.O. army from Beirut to Jordan
and Tunisia, countries Habib had persuaded to give refuge
to the P.L.O. soldiers.

Reagan then tried to seize the opportunity to get the
Camp David process in motion once again. He delivered a
major foreign policy speech that committed the United
States to the general principles agreed to by Begin, Carter,
and Sadat in 1979—a homeland and self-determination for
the Palestinians on the West Bank and in Gaza in return
for a guarantee from the Arab states of the inviolability of
Israel's borders and its right to exist. But immediately upon
the removal of the P.L.O. troops from Beirut and the withdrawal of the trilateral force, the Israeli army moved into
Beirut again—just as P.L.O. leader Yasser Arafat had warned
that it would—and took control of the city. The Christian
militia of Lebanon, working closely with the Israelis, sought
revenge for the assassination of the Christian leader, President Gemayel. They entered the Palestinian refugee camps
and slaughtered hundreds of women and children. The
bloodbath horrified the world and forced Reagan once again
to send in the U.S. Marines (along with the returning French
and Italian troops), in an attempt to restore some semblance
of peace in Beirut.

The peacekeepers, however, found themselves virtually
beseiged in Beirut and completely unable to influence events.
There were not enough Marines, French and Italian forces
to enforce their will on any of the various warring factions,
but the mere presence of Western troops, especially American Marines, in Beirut was infuriating to the Muslims.
Every political party in Lebanon now had its own militia;
Syria occupied eastern Lebanon, Israel occupied southern
Lebanon, what remained of the P.L.O. (by 1983 itself divided into warring factions) occupied northern Lebanon,
while U.S. Marines, with neither a clear objective nor the
necessary force (there were only 1,500 of them) to accomplish anything, were isolated at the Beirut airport.

Far from solving anything, much less leading to a U.S.-
Israeli alliance directed against the Soviets, the Israeli in-

vasion of Lebanon had made a bad situation worse for everyone involved—most of all for Israel itself. The war was costing the Israelis billions of dollars and heavy casualties; the occupation of southern Lebanon brought worldwide denunciation; Israel's inflation rate was 400% annually; and Israel's body politic was badly split between hawks and doves. Still, Israel would not retire from Lebanon.

In February 1983, Reagan attempted to induce Israel to pull back by promising "this administration is prepared to take all necessary measures to guarantee Israel's northern borders in the aftermath of the complete withdrawal of the Israeli Army." It was an historic pledge—never before had an American President made an offer to guarantee any of Israel's borders—but the Israelis would not respond, primarily because the following day Reagan, in an attempt to maintain an evenhanded policy, called for "something in the nature of a homeland for the Palestinians." Meanwhile American Marines began taking casualties from sniper fire. Reagan told the Israeli Foreign Minister of the "necessity and urgency" of an Israeli withdrawal, again to no avail. Reagan also refused to release some 75 F-16 fighters to Israel, again without results.

In May 1983, with Secretary of State Shultz himself acting as mediator, an Israeli-Lebanese agreement was finally reached. But it was a paper accord, without substance. The new Lebanese President, Amil Gemayel, controlled only one small faction in his country and was not in a position to make good on any agreement, much less one that allowed the Israeli Army de facto control of southern Lebanon. The Shultz formula called for the simultaneous withdrawal of all Israeli, Syrian, and P.L.O. forces from Lebanon, but it allowed the Israelis to remain in southernmost Lebanon until the others had withdrawn. Worse, neither the Syrians nor the P.L.O. had agreed to either this or any other of Shultz' propositions, and indeed denounced the agreement immediately. Nevertheless, Reagan, grateful for Israeli "cooperation," lifted the embargo on the F-16 fighter planes, and in June, 1983, Defense Secretary Weinberger an-

nounced that the U.S.-Israeli alliance against the Soviet
Union could now be revived. The Israelis, meanwhile,
shortened their lines in Lebanon, but insisted they would
not completely withdraw until Syria and the P.L.O. also
withdrew.

By August, 1983, six distinct armies were fighting
throughout Lebanon—Syrians, Israelis, Christian Phalan-
gists, Muslim militia factions, the Lebanese army, and the
P.L.O. (also divided into factions). Beirut was under constant shelling; the Marines at the airport were taking more
casualties. It was increasingly difficult to see what point
there was to keeping the Marines in Lebanon, and Congress
was threatening to invoke the War Powers Act, which would
force Reagan to withdraw them within 90 days. Secretary
Shultz, in response, restated the Administration's position,
that although the Marines in Lebanon "are involved in a
situation where there is violence," they were not "in combat" and thus the War Powers Act did not apply. His statement confused more than it elucidated and satisfied almost
no one.

In truth, the Reagan Administration had blundered in
Lebanon as badly as Carter had blundered in Iran. Encouraging the Israeli invasion had turned out to be a dreadful mistake, made worse by sending in the Marines in
such insufficient force that they became hostages rather
than peacekeepers. The attempts at evenhandedness—
denouncing Israeli settlement on the West Bank, placing
an embargo on the sale of airplanes to Israel, speaking out
for a "sort of" homeland for the Palestinians that frightened
Israel while still leaving the P.L.O. far short of its aspira-
tions, demanding a Syrian and P.L.O. withdrawal while
allowing the Israelis to maintain their position in southernmost Lebanon, putting the Marines into a hostage situation at the airport—made all the participants angry at
and suspicious of the United States. It was difficult to see
how American diplomacy could have done worse.

Reagan tried to retrieve the situation by sending in more
force, in the form of U.S. warships stationed off the Lebanese coast. In September 1983, as fighting in Beirut es-

calated and the Marines took still more casualties, the Navy
began shelling Druse militia positions. This only exacer-
bated the problem and led many people to wonder who
on earth was in charge of American foreign policy, and
especially of the use of the military to support that policy.
Firing 16-inch naval guns into the Lebanese countryside
hardly seemed a proper application of force in a civil war
in which the United States professed to be neutral and a
seeker of peace.

The violence increased with every salvo from the huge
battleships, reaching a culmination on October 23, 1983,
when a suicide truck loaded with TNT drove into Marine
Headquarters and killed 230 Marines. Vice President George
Bush, visiting the site three days later, declared that such
terrorist acts would not be allowed to shape American foreign policy. Reagan denounced the "despicable" act, promised to find and punish those responsible, and forthrightly
declared that it was "central to our credibility on a global
scale" to keep the Marines in Lebanon. Naval shelling of
Muslim positions increased, supported by air strikes.

But for all the brave words and deeds, the situation had
in fact become intolerable. Reagan had no choice but to
withdraw the Marines, and in effect admit a terrible mistake. In January 1984, just as the campaign for his reelection was getting under way, he began the preparations
for the withdrawal. On a minor scale, it was like Nixon's
withdrawal from Vietnam—slow, painful, full of threat and
bluster, punctuated by random bombing and shelling,
and marked by misleading statements and downright lies.
Reagan insisted, in December 1983, that U.S. Marines and
Navy vessels (by then 40 in number, including three aircraft
carriers) would stay in Lebanon until the Lebanese government was in full control of the situation. The battleship
New Jersey and the Naval aircraft openly took the side of
Gemayel's government in the raging civil war—a strange
action for a "peacekeeping" force—but even as he was thereby
stepping up American involvement, Reagan announced on
February 7, 1984, that he was "redeploying" the Marines
to ships off Beirut.

That same day, the White House announced that the bombardment of Muslim militia positions was done for the purposes of "protecting" the Gemayel government; two days later it declared that the shelling was for "the safety of American and other multinational force personnel in Lebanon." Such contradictory pronouncements were a fitting way to end the American involvement in Lebanon, where no one, most of all Reagan himself, ever seemed to be clear on the purpose of that involvement.

By February 26, 1984, the Marines were gone. The Navy soon followed. The war went on. Completing the debacle, in March, Lebanon canceled its agreement with Israel. The Israelis still held southern Lebanon, but at a high cost; Syria still held eastern Lebanon; civil war still raged; there was no U.S.-Israeli alliance (although American officials were still hopeful); there was, in brief, nothing good to say about the Reagan Administration's policies in Lebanon, and much to denounce. But as had been the case in Vietnam after American withdrawal in 1973, no one wanted to learn the lessons of failure. Lebanon was not even an issue in the 1984 Presidential campaign.

Far more satisfactory to the Reagan Administration, and to the public, was a successful piece of gunboat diplomacy on the tiny Caribbean island of Grenada. In October 1983, a military coup in Grenada (a British Commonwealth nation) deposed and then killed Prime Minister Maurice Bishop, himself a leftist who had already greatly alarmed the Reagan Administration because he was allowing Cuban construction workers to build an airfield on the island, and had signed military agreements with Communist bloc countries. The military council that took power, headed by General Hudson Austin, was thought to be even more Communist than Bishop. When Austin murdered Bishop, the United States decided to intervene. On October 25, Reagan announced that he had ordered 1,900 Marines to invade Grenada and depose General Austin. The Cuban workers and troops, some 800 altogether, fought back, but had no chance of successful resistance and were quickly overwhelmed. A new government was formed, under Governor General Sir Paul Scoon. The Cubans were ordered off the island, the Soviet embassy was closed and all members expelled. Land redistribution policies carried out under the Bishop regime were cancelled.

Reagan called the invasion a "rescue mission," an interpretation that got vivid visual support when American medical students, returning to the United States from Grenada, kissed the ground upon arrival at the airport. Latin Americans, fearful as always of the Colossus of the North, condemned the invasion as Teddy Roosevelt Big Stick tactics. The United Nations General Assembly approved a resolution that "deeply deplored" the American action. Much of the American press was outraged, not so much by the invasion as by the fact that the Pentagon did not permit newsmen to cover it. Reagan personally saw it as a major triumph. It showed he could be tough and decisive; it enhanced American credibility in the Caribbean; it prevented the Russians from gaining a strategic airfield; it added to the President's popularity; it served as a warning to revolutionaries in Central America.

Like the press, the British were upset about the invasion, not because they disapproved, but because they were not consulted, and Grenada *was*, after all, a Commonwealth member nation. Reagan and the State Department simply ignored the British, a particularly gratuitous insult because if they had been asked, the British almost certainly would have given reluctant consent. This slighting gesture by the Reagan Administration caused a set back in Anglo-American relations, which had reached a high point only a year and a half earlier, during the Falklands War.

In March, 1982, the Argentine junta seized the Falkland Islands, a barren and sparsely inhabited British possession off the tip of South America. Those islands were of no significance to the world, with neither strategic nor economic importance or potential. But they did have tremendous political significance, enough to cause a war and once again illustrate the power of nationalism as the strongest of all political forces. What made the Falklands War the dramatic and incredible event that it became was that it was fought with the most modern weapons, which fascinated everybody, over the oldest issue of all: Whose territory is this? Whose flag flies here? It had absolutely nothing to do with any of the real issues now dividing mankind and causing wars, the modern issues such as Communism vs. capitalism, or the colored world vs. the white world, or the Muslims vs. the Jews. Such issues were irrelevant to the British-Argentine War of 1982.

The Falkland Islands had long been claimed by Argentina, but the British had always refused to negotiate seriously on the issue, which gave the military junta a reason for action. Patriotism was thus stirred up, diverting the public's attention from the botch the generals had made of the economy, not to mention their horrific record on human rights. The generals who twitched the British lion's tail became heroes. What the generals had not anticipated was the tough British reaction, because they ignored the obvious fact that British nationalism was at least every bit as strong as Argentinian, and the fact that the serving prime minister herself could use a boost in the public opinion polls.

When the Argentines took the islands, Margaret Thatcher's response was tough and immediate. She ordered a large naval task force to the Falklands, including using the ocean liner *Queen Elizabeth II* as a troop carrier—the largest fighting task force since the end of World War II. The public was overwhelmingly enthusiastic. The British were also delighted at the American reaction. Reagan told his military to give the British task force covert support, especially invaluable intelligence. Reagan also had his United Nations Ambassador, Mrs. Jeane Kirkpatrick, support the British in heated debates in the United Nations. British gratitude was widespread; when Britain won the short war, not without taking heavy losses, there was an outpouring of pro-American sentiment in the United Kingdom, where many public figures remarked that the strain on U.S.-U.K. relations created by Eisenhower's actions during the 1956 Suez crisis was now eliminated.

As noted, Reagan sacrificed much of this goodwill in 1983, when he invaded one of the Queen's possessions without informing, much less consulting, British Prime Minister Thatcher (it must be noted that she was in a secure position, having recently won a quickly called election that took full advantage of her victory in the Falklands War). To Reagan, however, the positive results of invading Grenada far outweighed the negative repercussions. The reason was that the Caribbean and, even more, Central America, were central to Reagan's thinking.

Central America was almost an obsession with Reagan. Unlike previous Presidents, who have looked east and west for the dangers and challenges, towards Europe and the Soviet bloc, and towards Japan and China, Reagan has looked south for his challenges. He has not been very persuasive in getting others to join him in regarding Central America as *the* critical area. This stems, in part, from a lack of experience; when he took office, Reagan was as inexperienced in foreign affairs as Carter had been. As a consequence, Reagan knew only what he was against. In Central America, he was very much against any expansion of the Sandinista movement. What he was for was less clear.

What Carter had been "for" was extending a helping hand to the Sandinista regime, in the hope that this really would bring about a viable social democratic government in Nicaragua, with political and economic justice. What Reagan was for was a 1980s version of Churchill's cry in 1919, "We must strangle Bolshevism in the cradle."

In Reagan's view, the threat from the Sandinistas and their partners, the rebels in El Salvador, was twofold. First, that Nicaragua would become another Cuba, providing the Russians with a base in Central America that they would use both to export revolution to their neighbors, north and south, and as a naval and military base. The second threat Reagan saw was that either continued chaos, or even worse a Communist victory throughout Central America, would lead to a massive flight of refugees from Central America into the United States itself. America already had serious problems with illegal immigrants from Mexico; the prospect of countless Central American refugees crossing the Rio Grande caused Reagan to view the situation with the greatest alarm. Far better, Reagan reasoned, to support the existing governments in El Salvador, Guatemala, and Honduras, however distasteful, than to abandon the region to the Communists.

Reagan moved immediately. Within days of taking office, he froze the last $15 million of Carter's aid package to Nicaragua because, he said, Nicaragua was "aiding and abetting violence" in El Salvador. Reagan also extended extensive military aid to a government in El Salvador that was, many charged, as objectionable as Somoza's in Nicaragua had been. According to his critics, Reagan grossly exaggerated both the extent of Communist infiltration and Cuban-Russian support for the guerrillas in El Salvador. In March 1981, Reagan nevertheless increased military aid to the military government in El Salvador by $25 million and soon sent in American military advisers. Reagan dismissed any analogy with Vietnam in the early sixties and pointed to the free election held in El Salvador in March, 1982.

Still, Reagan could not rally support sufficient to get the Congress behind the effort. Too many politicians, and too large a segment of the public, believed that Reagan was seeing the wrong threats and applying the wrong solutions, for Reagan to get a consensus behind him. His critics thought that it was precisely the governments themeselves, the ones Reagan was supporting with military aid, that were the danger and the problem. Narrowly based military regimes that perpetuated right-wing violence and a grossly unfair economic *status quo* based on a colonial relationship with the United States such as the governments of El Salvador, Honduras, and Guatemala could never bring stability to an area that cried out for change. Reagan's critics further charged that Reagan exaggerated the number and quality of arms supplied by the Communists to the rebels in El Salvador, the size of the Cuban contingent in Nicaragua, and even the degree of influence of Communists in the

Sandinista movement. The critics thought that the United States should be working with the Sandinistas, not against them, in order to promote the kind of social and economic democracy that is a prerequisite for stability. Economic aid to the forces of the left, rather than military aid to the forces of the right, was the proper policy. As to the "wave of refugees" Reagan so feared, the critics responded that an improvement in the political and economic situation in Central America, not more military rule, was what was needed to meet that threat.

Certainly the threat of deepening military involvement was there, and hanging over it, always, was the memory of Vietnam. In Congress and among the public there were widespread fears that Central America would become "another Vietnam." No matter how often Reagan explained that there was no comparison between the situations in Vietnam and Central America (a judgment that was more right than wrong), he could not dispel the fear. Congress proved extremely reluctant to meet Reagan's demands for military aid for the army of El Salvador, even after the State Department asserted that El Salvador had curbed its right-wing death squads and "made progress" in human rights. In March 1983, a year after the elections in El Salvador, fears of "another Vietnam" were markedly increased when counter-revolutionaries ("Contras") from Nicaragua, based in Guatemala and supported and trained by the CIA, crossed the border and began an insurgency operation against the Sandinista government. Reagan asked for more money to support the operation, but Congress remained hesitant.

Reagan tried to raise the level of alarm. He justified CIA support for the Contras in his press conferences as necessary to overthrow the Sandinistas, calling the Contras "freedom fighters." Secretary Shultz asserted that support for the El Salvador government was "moral" because the United States was preventing a "brutal military takeover by a totalitarian minority." In April 1983, Reagan went before a joint session of Congress to ask support for his Central American policy, asserting that the "national security of all the Americas is at stake in Central America." But to his dismay, the only sustained applause he received, from Republicans as well as Democrats, was when he promised to send no American combat units to the scene.

In the fall of 1983, Reagan nevertheless increased the pressure. The CIA-sponsored Contras expanded their activities, to the bombing of oil storage and other facilities in Nicaragua. The U.S. Army held major maneuvers in Honduras and began construction of a permanent military base near the Nicaragua border. Undersecretary of Defense Fred Ilké delivered a speech that struck the hardest line yet in expounding the Administration's policies and goals. Ilké declared that "the blocking of votes in Congress had denied the President the means to succeed" and charged that the public was being deceived by "a great deal of misinformation" about the death squads by the media, in what he characterized as a "well-organized and well-orchestrated" effort. Ilké said the the Sandinistas were "more dangerous than Castro's Cuba" because of their ability to export revolutions to their neighbors. Nicaragua had become "an arsenal of insurgency" and was forcing the United States to respond by becoming, once again, the arsenal of democracy. Failure to support Reagan's policies, Ilké warned, would force the United States to "man a new military front line right here on our continent." Rollback, not containment, of the Sandinistas, was the only proper policy. But Congress remained unconvinced.

Unconvinced not only because of painful memories of Vietnam, but also because Congress represented the split in the country as a whole over Central America. No other issue in the world—not even arms control, the Middle East, or relations with Russia—caused such a deep and broad split in American opinion. The result was Congressional stalemate. Reagan could not get the funds that were necessary to prosecute the war against the Central American revolutionaries successfully, but Reagan's critics could not force him to withdraw from the area, much less support the forces of change. This stalemate made it difficult for the United States to influence events in Central America, even though, as always, Uncle Sam was blamed by both the left and the right in Latin America for everything that went wrong. Adding to the frustration for both Reagan and his critics, the American public generally remained relatively indifferent.

In March 1984, Presidential elections in El Salvador gave the Reagan Administration some cause for optimism. The leader of the death squads, or so it was charged, Roberto d'Aubuisson, was the candidate of the right wing. He was defeated by the somewhat more moderate candidate, the man the United States supported, José Napoleon Duarte, who quickly set about trying—with some success—to improve El Salvador's image in the world.

Simultaneously, however, the Contras—using CIA-supplied equipment—began mining Nicaragua's harbors, and some Russian ships were damaged. That neither Reagan nor Ilké had been able to convince their critics was underscored in July, when Democratic Presidential nominee Walter Mondale promised—to great applause—in his acceptance speech that within 100 days of taking office he would end the "illegal" war against the Sandinistas. Reagan immediately denounced Mondale's position, but at the same time he was forced to announce that he was withdrawing his requests for additional military aid to El Salvador until after the elections. In other words, the hopelessly divided American perceptions of the nature of the threat in Central America continued to make it difficult for the United States to set, and hold to, clear policy goals. Violence and turmoil in Central America continued.

In his relations with the Soviet Union, Reagan had much clearer goals than he did in Lebanon and the Middle East, and a much broader and deeper consensus supporting his goals than he did in Central America. Reagan's goals were peace, limitations on the arms race, an actual reduction in the size of the nuclear arsenals, good trade relations with Russia, cooperation in solving such problems as acid rain and water and air pollution, and generally a mutually beneficial détente. Almost all Americans wanted the same general goals achieved. Where the consensus broke down was over the means used to achieve the goals.

Reagan's tactics for achieving peace and controlling the arms race included hurling insults at the Soviet Union. In March, 1983, he characterized the Soviet Union as an "evil empire" and "the focus of evil in the modern world." Outside of Japan and Western Europe, few people around the world accepted Reagan's analysis. In the southern half of the globe, the general perception was that poverty, imperialism, and racism were the true focus of evil. In the Middle East, the Israelis saw the radical Arabs as the focus of evil. The Arabs saw the Israelis as the source, while in Iran the perception was that the United States was equally a focus of evil with the Soviet Union.

Fewer Americans disagreed with Reagan, but many wondered how such accusations could further the cause of peace or détente. The argument was that there was no point to hurling gratuitous insults against the other superpower, because the United States had to live with the Soviet Union, like it or not.

With regard to arms control, by far the most important real issue challenging the superpowers, because it is by far the most dangerous and most expensive, Reagan rejected Carter's policy of offering the Soviets restraint and even accommodation, because, as he pointed out, Carter's policy had not worked. The Russians simply did not respond; indeed they took advantage of Carter. Reagan reverted to Nixon's policy of buildup, the old Cold War tactic of never bargaining with the Russians except from a position of strength (i.e., superiority). In his first three years in office, Reagan increased defense spending, in real terms, by 40%. This massive buildup did indeed alarm the Russians, but to Reagan's dismay it did not cause them to negotiate seriously. Instead, as they had always done in the past, they matched (and in some areas exceeded) the American increases.

Europe remained the area of greatest concern and danger. The most serious destabilizing factor in Europe was the Soviet emplacement, in the late seventies, of more than

345 SS-20 missiles (modern, intermediate-range weapons with three nuclear warheads each). NATO decided, in December 1979, to match this threat with some 500 American cruise missiles based in Western Europe. Carter, at the urging of the NATO allies, had made the cruise decision; Reagan heartily endorsed it, despite intense opposition in the NATO countries, an opposition that was well financed (from Russian sources, it was charged by opponents), well-organized, and highly motivated.

To many Europeans, the most frightening aspect of the situation was that it appeared that the United States and the Soviet Union had agreed that if war ever came between them, Europe was the battleground on which it would be fought. If that happened, then there surely would be no more Europe. This realization put a great strain on NATO and the individual countries involved. But all the governments remained steadfast behind the original decision, despite massive demonstrations.

On November 23, 1983, deployment of the cruise missiles began in Great Britain and West Germany. The Russians immediately discontinued the arms control talks in Geneva. Russian-American relations were at one of their lowest points since the Cold War began. There was widespread alarm, and there was good cause for it. The arsenals of both sides had reached huge, indeed unbelievable proportions (except that they were all too real). In strategic weapons, the United States had more than 9,000 nuclear warheads on bombers and missiles, the Soviet Union more than 7,000. These were aimed at targets inside the other superpower's homeland. In theater nuclear weapons, the Soviet Union had 3,580 of all types (land- and sea-based) directed at targets in Western Europe, while NATO had 4,445 aimed at Eastern Europe and the western sections of the Soviet Union (including 98 French and 64 British theater nuclear missiles). Aside from the dangers to human existence, the cost of these arsenals, and of the conventional forces in the Warsaw Pact and NATO, was horrendous. By 1985 the United States was spending $300 billion per year on defense, the West Europeans nearly $150 billion. (Ac-

curate figures for the Warsaw Pact nations are impossible
to come by, but were somewhat less than the total for Western Europe).

"This is not a way of life at all," President Eisenhower
had declared in 1953, when the costs and the dangers of
the arms race were one-tenth or less of what they had
become 32 years later, but no one could find a way out of
the arms race. Both sides made proposals—the Russians
offered to reduce their SS-20 deployment to the size of the
French and British missile forces if NATO agreed to deploy
no cruise missiles; Reagan offered a "zero-zero" option, in
which NATO would forgo the deployment of cruise missiles if the Soviets dismantled all the SS-20s—but in each
case the offer was seen by the other side, correctly, as propaganda, not to be taken seriously.

A principal Soviet aim, Western leaders agreed, was to
divide and weaken NATO, and certainly the huge costs
were putting a great strain on the alliance. Europeans protested against the prospect of Europe becoming the battleground in a superpower nuclear war; Americans protested
against paying so much for what was widely regarded as
the defense of Europe. By 1985, one-half or more of the
American defense budget went for NATO defense. It was,
therefore, galling to hear West Germans refer to the American troops in their country as an occupying force, rather
than West Germany's defenders; it was irritating that the
Europeans would not spend more on their own defense.*

In Congress, there was growing sentiment for the United
States to reduce its NATO commitment and costs, unless
the Europeans did more for their own defense. In 1984,

---

* With regard to Japan, which paid practically nothing for its
defense, but rather relied completely on American arms, the situation was maddening. The Japanese were free to put their scientists and technicians to work on consumer goods and to use
their funds for research and investment, thus gaining a clear
advantage over the United States in the competition for world
markets, while the United States had to put its scientists and
technicians, and tax dollars, to work on programs partly for Japan's defense.

Senator Sam Nunn, Democrat of Georgia, proposed that 90,000 of the 360,000 U.S. troops stationed in Europe be withdrawn within five years if the Europeans declined to increase their share of the burden. The Reagan Administration opposed Nunn's proposal, and it lost in the Senate, but only by a vote of 55 to 41. Obviously Nunn had struck a responsive chord. In 1953, Eisenhower had said that American troops could not remain in Europe indefinitely, because America could not afford to maintain a "Roman wall" forever. By 1985, it appeared that the Senate, and millions among the public, agreed with Eisenhower's assessment. The consensus on both sides of the Atlantic as to what NATO was, what it should do, and how it should do it, was under severe strain.

Reagan's economic policies toward the Soviet Union contributed to the difficulties. Originally, Reagan had supported Carter's decision to put an economic blockade against the Soviets into effect in response to the invasion of Afghanistan. Indeed, Reagan went beyond refusing to sell grain to the Russians, as he attempted to prevent America's European allies from trading with the Eastern bloc. In the late seventies, the Western Europeans had concluded an agreement with the Soviet Union that allowed them to purchase Soviet-produced natural gas in return for building a pipeline from Siberia. But the pipeline was dependent upon American technology, which was to be supplied by European-based multinational corporations. Reagan, outraged by this, attempted to block the construction of the pipeline by imposing economic sanctions on those corporations that sold American-produced equipment to the Soviets. But the sanctions were insufficient to deter the Europeans.

Furthermore, Reagan himself was eager to trade. For all his "evil empire" talk, Reagan had a huge grain surplus and a major balance of payments problem. By 1985, although the Soviets were still very much involved in attempting to subdue Afghanistan (where they had taken nearly 50,000 casualties, roughly equal to American losses in Vietnam, and where they were widely believed to have used poison gas and chemical weapons), Reagan had abandoned nearly all the restrictions and embargos Carter had instituted against the Soviets. In September 1983, the Reagan Administration concluded the biggest grain deal in history with the Soviets. To Europeans, Reagan's actions seemed contradictory, as he was simultaneously selling more wheat and corn to the Soviets while insisting that they *not* sell pipeline technology. Reagan responded that the pipeline was a strategic issue (presumably food sales were not). More to the point, Reagan argued that the Soviets could buy grain elsewhere, but they could only get the technology for the pipeline from the United States. His arguments, however, convinced few if any Europeans, and the pipeline, like the grain sales, went forward. Indeed, by 1984 Reagan was actually encouraging pipeline and other high-tech sales to the Soviets, completing the reversal of Carter's policies. Amazingly, most of the public continued to regard Jimmy Carter as "soft on Communism," Ronald Reagan as "hard."

In October 1981, when the military rulers of Poland outlawed the Solidarity union, Reagan again tried to use economic sanctions to force the Poles to liberalize their regime. The only effects, however, were to make life even more difficult for Polish citizens while strengthening the resolve of the Polish generals. In August 1984, after the Polish military released some of its hundreds of political prisoners, the Reagan Administration lifted most of the sanctions.

Reagan's actions confused many Americans. They wondered why, if the U.S.S.R. was their enemy, the United States was selling it badly needed commodities and goods. And if the U.S.S.R. was not America's enemy, then why was the United States spending such enormous sums on missiles directed against Russia?

Such questions, simple enough in themselves, could not be answered in a simplistic way. The situation was exceedingly complex as well as dangerous. As Professor Paul Marantz has written in *Current History*, "Looking at the many vital interests shared by the United States and the Soviet Union, it is a tragedy for both sides that they have not been able to forge a more stable and harmonious relationship.

However, considering the explosive issues dividing them, it is remarkable that they have not done even worse in managing their differences."

The worst fear is obvious—that the differences will some-day escalate to a crisis that will lead to the use of the nuclear arsenals and thus to the extinction of human life. The best hope is that the world can learn to not only live with but even profit from diversity. Although the vision of the good life is different in Washington and Moscow, there are nevertheless essential goals binding the two sides together.

First and foremost, of course, there is life itself. Second, both superpowers want and need worldwide political sta-bility and predictability. Third, both sides profit from ex-tensive trade relations. Fourth, they have a mutual interest in holding down the costs of the arms race. Fifth, both the United States and the Soviet Union have severe environ-mental problems that can only be solved through cooper-ative activity. Most of all, the best that can be hoped for is the least that must be insisted upon—that the leaders on both sides continue to recognize the truth of John Ken-nedy's insight: "In the final analysis, our most basic com-mon link is the fact that we all inhabit this planet. We all breathe the same air. We all cherish our children's future. And we are all mortal."

Suggestions for Further Reading

A good overview of American policy in the past forty years is the sprightly and informative *American Foreign Policy: A History* (1977), by Thomas Paterson, J. Garry Clifford, and Kenneth Hagan. It is thorough, judicious, and up to date in its interpretations. There are a number of good general histories of the Cold War although unfortunately most tend to begin in 1945. An exception is D. F. Fleming's *The Cold War and Its Origins, 1917–1960* (1961), a comprehensive two-volume study that, although poorly organized, is vigorous in its criticism of American policy. A better-balanced treatment is Walter LaFeber's *America, Russia, and the Cold War* (1975). Louis Halle's *The Cold War as History* (1967) attempts with some success to view with detachment, and has been described as the confessions of a former Cold Warrior. For a traditional interpretation of the Cold War, see John Spanier's *American Foreign Policy Since World War II* (1977). One of the first, and still the most important, critical accounts of America's Cold War policies is *The Tragedy of American Diplomacy* (1962), by William A. Williams. Herbert S. Dinerstein looks at events from the Russian point of view in *Fifty Years of Soviet Foreign Policy* (1968). Walt W. Rostow explains his view of the world in *The United States in the World Arena: An Essay in Recent History* (1960). A good general survey of the personalities involved is Lloyd C. Gardner's *Architects of Illusion: Men and Ideas in American Foreign Policy* (1970). On the C.I.A., see Ray S. Cline's *Secrets, Spies and Scholars* (1976), the best book on the subject. For this section, as well as for those that follow, the interested student should consult LaFeber's excellent bibliography.

World War II

The literature on American policy in World War II is staggering in scope. One happy result is that there are a number of excellent, short, interpretative works, such as Robert A. Divine's *Roosevelt and World War II* (1969), Kent Roberts Greenfield's *American Strategy in World War II: A Reconsideration* (1963), which is stronger on military than foreign policy, John L. Snell's *Illusion and Necessity: The Diplomacy of Global War* (1963), and Gaddis Smith's *American Diplomacy During the Second World War* (1965). *The Supreme Commander: The War Years of Dwight D. Eisenhower* (1970), by Stephen E. Ambrose, is a detailed account of American policy in Europe. *Atomic Diplomacy* (1965), by Gar Alperovitz, examines the motives behind the use of the atomic bomb. Although long, detailed, and somewhat dated, Robert E. Sherwood's *Roosevelt and Hopkins: An Intimate History* (1950) is still very much worth reading. The standard work for wartime diplomacy is Herbert Feis, *Churchill, Roosevelt, Stalin: The War They Waged and the Peace They Sought* (1957), which is almost an official history. For a forthright revisionist account, highly critical of American policy, see Gabriel Kolko, *The Politics of War: The World and United States Foreign Policy, 1943–1945* (1968). Volume three of Forrest C. Pogue's biography of George C. Marshall, *Organizer of Victory: 1943–1945* (1973), is a magnificent book about the man who was at the center of the whirlwind for the last two years of the war. B. H. Liddell Hart's *History of the Second World War* (1971) is the best of the one-volume histories of the conflict. A book that cannot be put down, once begun, and that as a bonus has many insights into the politics of the use of the atomic bomb, is *Enola Gay* (1977), by Gordon Thomas and Max Witts, the story of the bomb from its inception to the first shock wave over Hiroshima.

The Truman Years

A comprehensive view of the early Cold War is Herbert Feis, *From Trust to Terror: The Onset of the Cold War, 1945–*

1950 (1970). Truman's own two-volume *Memoirs* (1955) and those of Dean Acheson, *Present at the Creation* (1969), provide a comprehensive official view, and George Kennan's *Memoirs 1925–1950* (1967) is a joy to read, not only because of Kennan's matchless style but also because he is somewhat detached, admits to mistakes, and examines the assumptions on which policy was based. All these virtues are lacking in Truman's and Acheson's works. *The Forrestal Diaries* (1951), edited by Walter Millis, and Arthur H. Vandenberg's *Private Papers* (1952) are important sources. Joseph M. Jones's *The Fifteen Weeks* (1955) examines in detail, but uncritically, the events leading to the Truman Doctrine and the Marshall Plan. David Rees's *Korea: The Limited War* (1964) is a good general treatment that should be supplemented with I. F. Stone's *The Hidden History of the Korean War* (1952), which raises crucial questions about American policies in Korea. *N.A.T.O.: The Entangling Alliance* (1962), by Robert E. Osgood, is a model study. A scathing denunciation of American policy, from a Marxist perspective, is Joyce and Gabriel Kolko's *The Limits of Power* (1972). Robert James Maddox has blasted the revisionists' work, especially that of William A. Williams and Gabriel Kolko, in his controversial *The New Left and the Origins of the Cold War* (1973).

The Eisenhower Years

Eisenhower's memoirs, *The White House Years: A Personal Account* (two volumes, 1963 and 1965), are primarily concerned with foreign policy. For a comprehensive and critical view, see Stephen E. Ambrose, *Eisenhower: The President* (1984). Samuel P. Huntington, *The Common Defense: Strategic Programs in National Politics* (1961), a truly outstanding work, is essential to any study of Eisenhower's (and Truman's) military policy. There was a multitude of critics of the New Look; perhaps the most important was Maxwell Taylor, *The Uncertain Trumpet* (1959). Herman Finer's *Dulles Over Suez* (1964) is a critical account of the Secretary of State's role in the 1956 crisis. Edmund Stillman and William Pfaff, *Power and Impotence: The Failure of America's Foreign*

Policy (1966), while covering far more than the Eisenhower
years, is a brilliant examination of the assumptions about
the world of the Eisenhower Administration. The most
searching attack on Eisenhower's policy toward Castro is
William A. Williams, *The United States, Cuba and Castro* (1962).
Theodore Draper's *Castro's Revolution* (1962), expressed the
view that Castro betrayed the revolution. A good biography
of Ike is Peter Lyon, *Eisenhower: Portrait of the Hero* (1974).
Herbert Parmet's *Eisenhower and the American Crusades* (1972)
is a solid account of Ike's years in office. The politics of oil
is explored by Burton Kaufman in *The Oil Cartel Case* (1978).
Blanche Cook's *Eisenhower: Anti-Militarist in the White House*
(1975), is a path-breaking study of Ike's New Look and
foreign policy.

Kennedy and Johnson

For a blistering view of Kennedy, see Henry Fairlie's *The
Kennedy Promise: The Politics of Expectation* (1974). Arthur M.
Schlesinger, Jr., *A Thousand Days: John F. Kennedy in the
White House* (1965), and Theodore Sorensen, *Kennedy* (1965),
are accounts by insiders who are fully devoted to the memory of the late President. Schlesinger has more on foreign
affairs than Sorensen does. Philip Geyelin, *Lyndon B. Johnson and the World* (1966), and Rowland Evans and Robert
Novak, *Lyndon B. Johnson: The Exercise of Power* (1966), are
good. Elie Abel's *The Missile Crisis* (1966) is a first-rate account by a professional journalist; a part of the inside story
is told by Robert F. Kennedy in his *Thirteen Days: A Memoir
of The Cuban Missile Crisis* (1969). The literature on Vietnam
is overwhelming and growing; the best short scholarly account is probably George Kahin and John W. Lewis, *The
United States in Vietnam* (1967). David Halberstam's *The Best
and the Brightest* (1972) is sprightly reading. All of Bernard
Fall's books are good; students should begin with the collection of his articles, *Vietnam Witness, 1953–1966* (1966).
Townsend Hoopes, *The Limits of Intervention* (1969), is
an exceptionally good memoir by a key participant in the
crucial decision to halt the bombing of North Vietnam.

Robert W. Tucker's *Nation or Empire?* (1968) is an excellent
essay. David Kraslow and Stuart Loory, in *The Secret Search
for Peace in Vietnam* (1968), give the details of Hanoi's peace
moves and Washington's reactions. Johnson's own memoirs, *From the Vantage Point* (1971), are rather dull and un-
informative. Philip Caputo's *A Rumor of War* (1978) is the
exact opposite, an autobiography that skillfully captures
the mood of the time and the war as it was. Peter Brae-
strup's *Big Story* (1977) is a detailed, excellent analysis of
press coverage of the 1968 Tet offensive.

The Nixon Years

There is no up-to-date biography of Nixon, although there
are many works on various stages of his career, as well as
his own memoirs *RN* (2 volumes, 1981). The most thoughtful and thoroughly researched of the current biographies
is Garry Wills's *Nixon Agonistes* (1970); Wills does an outstanding job on Nixon's personality, his career, and his
culture. Highly critical of Nixon, Jonathan Schell, *The Time
of Illusion* (1976) is good reading. Dan Rather and Gary
Paul Gates, *The Palace Guard* (1974), is full of wonderfully
interesting gossip and some insights, but is weak on foreign
policy. The best single work to appear so far on the foreign
policy of the Nixon Administration is Marvin Kalb and
Bernard Kalb, *Kissinger* (1974). The Kalbs are reporters,
and their work is full of insider information based on extensive interviews. They are sympathetic toward Kissinger
and their work suffers from an absence of analysis, but it
does have a great deal of detailed information. Kissinger's
White House Years (1979) and *Years of Upheaval* (1982) are
massive in size and ego. Monumental in scope, they are
witty, detailed, frequently self-serving, highly quotable, often
informative, never dull, sometimes brilliant—in short, rather
like the amazing Dr. Kissinger himself. Much the best work
I have seen on Vietnam is Frances Fitzgerald, *Fire in the
Lake: The Vietnamese and the Americans in Vietnam* (1972),
which is must reading for anyone who wishes to understand
the Vietnam War. Michael Herr, *Dispatches* (1977), is also

on the list of must-read for Vietnam; it is an impressionistic look at Vietnam in the late sixties, with the emphasis on how the war was fought. Frank Snepp's *Decent Interval* (1978) is well described by its subtitle: *An Insider's Account on Saigon's Indecent End Told by the CIA's Chief Strategy Analyst in Vietnam.*

The Middle East and Africa

General histories that cover both areas well include James Nathan and James Oliver, *United States Foreign Policy and World Order* (1978), which is especially strong on the relationship between foreign policy and domestic politics, and Stewart C. Easton, *World History Since 1954* (1968), a comprehensive review. Books on Kissinger abound; he is a fascinating subject, irresistible to many authors, including Matti Golan, *The Secret Conversations of Henry Kissinger: Step-by-Step Diplomacy in the Middle East* (1976), a book that caused a sensation when it appeared and remains invaluable. G. Warren Nutter's *Kissinger's Grand Design* (1975) is a thoughtful denunciation of détente and Kissinger's Middle East policy. Gil Carl Alroy's *The Kissinger Experience: American Policy in the Middle East* (1975) is a bitter criticism of Kissinger for his supposed abandonment of his own people, the Jews. Much more balanced and trustworthy is Edward Sheehan, *The Arabs, Israelis, and Kissinger* (1976), a detailed account of Kissinger and the Yom Kippur War. The best overview of America in the Middle East is Robert W. Stookey, *America and the Arab States: An Uneasy Encounter* (1975), by a former foreign-service officer who has a good grasp of the Arab world view.

A good background for Africa is Jerah Johnson's *Africa and the West* (1974); another excellent concise account is Roland Oliver and J. D. Fage, *A Short History of Africa* (1969). Vernon McKay's *African Diplomacy* (1966) is a collection of essays on emerging Africa by various African scholars; so is Yassin El-Ayouty and Hugh Brooks, *Africa and International Organization* (1974). Kwame Nkrumah's *Neo-Colonialism: The Last Stage of Imperialism* (1965), the book that made Lyndon Johnson furious, is an African account of how economics works in Africa. John Stockwell's *In Search of Enemies: A CIA Story* (1978) is the memoir of the C.I.A. Chief of the Angola Task Force; Stockwell had second thoughts about what he was doing, resigned from the C.I.A., and published a book about his experiences, in what had become a relatively common practice for disgruntled ex-C.I.A. agents in the seventies.

The best raw source on the C.I.A. and its impact on foreign policy is in government publications, especially hearings, and most especially the various volumes of the Church Committee Hearings (the "Senate Select Committee to Study Governmental Operations With Respect to Intelligence Activities"). Published in 1976, the volumes contain a history of the C.I.A. and testimony from dozens of ex- and current agents and their bosses about various operations dating back to 1948. One entire volume is devoted to "Alleged Assassination Plots Involving Foreign Leaders." Another government document that is most helpful in understanding American policy in Africa is N.S.S.M. 39, published as *The Kissinger Study of Southern Africa,* edited and with an excellent introduction by Mohamed A. El-Khawas and Barry Cohen (1976). Seymour M. Hersh, *The Price of Power: Kissinger in the Nixon White House* (1983) is a scathing attack on both Kissinger and Nixon.

Carter and Reagan

Zbigniew Brzezinski's memoirs, portions of which appeared in 1982, are the first insider's account of the Carter Administration to appear. They reveal his frequent policy differences with Secretary of State Vance and probably overstate his own influence with the President. No scholarly biography of Carter has yet appeared. The event of the Carter years that has attracted the most attention is, of course, the Iranian revolution and the hostage crisis, which has produced a number of excellent books. First among them is Barry Rubin, *Paved with Good Intentions: The American Ex-*

perience and Iran (1981), a masterful study that is indispensable. Nearly as good is John Stempel, *Inside the Iranian Revolution* (1981), by the former Deputy Chief of the Political Section of the American Embassy in Teheran. A *New York Times* team of reporters led by Robert McFadden published *No Hiding Place: Inside Report of the Hostage Crisis* (1981), which provides extensive, excellent coverage. Michael Ledeen and William Lewis, *Debacle: The American Failure in Iran* (1981), is a useful short summary. William H. Sullivan, *Mission to Iran* (1981), is a candid report by the last American Ambassador to Iran. Strobe Talbot, *Endgame: The Inside Story of Salt II* (1979), is a fascinating account of the intricate nature of arms talks.

Index